ALEX MASKEY
Man and Mayor

Barry McCaffrey was born in Belfast in 1970. After a period working on building sites, he returned to adult education at the University of Ulster where he was awarded a degree in Irish History and Politics.

He became a journalist in 1997 and has worked for the *Down Democrat*, *North Belfast News* and *Ireland on Sunday*. He is currently an investigative reporter with the *Irish News* and has covered all the major stories during his time there.

Outside working hours, he claims to "live a sad and lonely existence" in South Belfast with his Irish setter, Cuan.

ALEX MASKEY
Man and Mayor

Barry McCaffrey

Foreword by Ken Livingstone

THE BREHON PRESS
BELFAST

First published 2003 by The Brehon Press Ltd
111 Brooke Drive, Belfast BT11 9NJ,
County Antrim, Northern Ireland

ISBN: 0 9544867 1 4

Front cover photograph: Ann McManus
Back cover photograph: Mal McCann, *Andersonstown News*
Cover and photographic section design: The Valkyrie
Printed by The Woodprintcraft Group Ltd

CONTENTS

Dedicated to Kate and Gab

FOREWORD

I was delighted to welcome Alex Maskey to London earlier this year in his capacity as Lord Mayor of Belfast. Amazingly, it had taken the elevation of Alex to this position for our two cities to address, in a very practical way, how both could benefit from ties of friendship and co-operation. It quickly became clear to the officials of the Greater London Authority and Belfast City Council that we had many common problems and much to learn from each other in fields as varied as economic development, planning, transport and equalities. To take just one example, London faces almost as big a challenge as Belfast in working out how to achieve a police service truly representative of the communities it serves.

Chatting before the official reception to welcome Alex, we wondered whether we should remind the assembled guests of the circumstances of our first meeting nearly 20 years ago in Belfast. On that occasion, as Alex showed me round his city, I had my first experience of being stopped by young British soldiers – and they were clearly more than a little surprised to find themselves questioning a Member of Parliament from London.

Before Margaret Thatcher abolished the Greater London Council, it had welcomed leaders of Sinn Féin to explore the ways forward towards peace in Ireland. We were roundly denounced for this by a government, which at that time, was already conducting its own secret negotiations. I said then and have continued to say that these were people trying to address the same issues as us in the far more difficult and tragic circumstances of Belfast.

Who could deny that now, having seen the way in which Alex used the post of Lord Mayor to represent all of the people of Belfast, irrespective of their political or religious affiliations?

The efforts of people like Alex, Gerry Adams, John Hume and so many others of all political persuasions to make the Good Friday Agreement work have also brought enormous benefits for London. In the context of peace and reconciliation, all things Irish are flourishing. For the first time, the enormous contribution of generations of Irish men and women to our city is officially celebrated in the annual St Patrick's Day Parade.

And I can certainly say that, when I met Alex in Belfast – in what seems now like a different era – I never would have believed that 20 years later he would be guest of honour, marching as Lord Mayor of Belfast with the first elected Mayor of London, at the head of that very parade.

KEN LIVINGSTONE
Mayor of London
July 2003

INTRODUCTION

First they ignore you, then they laugh at you, then they fight
you, then you win.

—Mahatma Gandhi
1869 - 1948

ALEX Maskey has been many things to many people since he
became Sinn Féin's first councillor to enter Belfast City Hall politics
twenty years ago. For the unionist community he became one of
the most hated men in Northern Ireland. For republicans he came
to personify the political struggle inside City Hall.

Ironically there is little mention of Alex Maskey in the abundance
of authoritative books written about the conflict over the last three
decades. While various political figures have justifiably been given
a footnote in history for their efforts in building peace in the North,
the unassuming Maskey has more often than not been content to
let others take the political limelight. However, the Belfast
grandfather's life has, arguably more than any other, embodied
the development of republicanism throughout the Troubles.

Growing up in North Belfast in the 1960s, Maskey's neighbours
and friends were both Catholic and Protestant. As a teenager he
vividly remembers the July 'Twelfth' bonfires in Upper Meadow
Street where he lived. By 1969 the 18 year-old Maskey had found
himself caught up in a conflict which erupted throughout the
Northern state and changed the lives of so many people.

By 1971, he found himself imprisoned without trial in Long Kesh
internment camp along with hundreds of other nationalists. From
behind the barbed wire of Long Kesh, Maskey watched as the North
tore itself apart. Released in 1975, Maskey remained committed to
republicanism and lived the life that went along with outright
opposition to the Northern state. He does not question, or make
any excuses for the fact that he was wedded to militant
republicanism. He does not attempt to distance himself from the

IRA's "armed struggle" but insists that it was a product of a state policy that saw nationalists disenfranchised and denied basic human rights.

The former docker remained so implacably opposed to republicans entering into constitutional politics, Northern Ireland style, that he refused to play any part in the 1981 Fermanagh-South Tyrone by-election contested by IRA hunger striker Bobby Sands.

The key role which Maskey held within the republican movement and, more importantly, the role which he would play in the "Armalite and Ballot Box" strategy is witnessed in the two short years in which he overcame his opposition to republican involvement in electoral politics to become the first Sinn Féin councillor to enter Belfast City Hall.

As the first Sinn Féin figure to enter the unionist-dominated council, Maskey became the focus for more Protestant hatred than almost anyone else in the North. For unionists he was the hard-liner who, throughout the 1980s and 1990s, appeared on television screens to defend the latest IRA attack on members of the RUC or British army.

Some unionists were content to verbally confront the "Provo Pariah" in the council chamber, but there were others within loyalism and the British security services who were determined to eliminate Maskey from the equation. There have been more loyalist and British security service attempts on his life in the past 30 years than on any other republican politician. His close friend Alan Lundy was killed by UDA gunmen as he helped build a security porch at the Sinn Féin councillor's West Belfast home. Even more sinister was the fact that members of the security agencies were involved in a number of plots to kill him. In 1992, Brian Nelson of the British Army's shadowy undercover Force Research Unit (FRU) pleaded guilty to conspiring to murder him.

Twenty years after Maskey first took his seat on the opposition benches as a lone republican councillor, Sinn Féin is now the largest party in City Hall. When he was elected as the city's first republican Mayor, observers predicted that his year in office would be filled with controversy. It was, but Maskey managed to surprise even his harshest critics, and even some grassroots republicans, by his determination to reach out to unionists.

When Maskey and other leading republicans sat alongside senior members of the British army in St Anne's Cathedral to take part in a civic service to remember the war dead, many believed that the "hard-liner" had gone soft. But Maskey's decision to attend, and a series of other initiatives which he would carry out during his year in office, were part of a much larger Sinn Féin initiative aimed at convincing unionists that republicans could be trusted with civic leadership.

This book does not attempt to excuse the responsibility republicans have to accept for the people killed and injured during the Troubles, or indeed the pain caused to the unionist community. Nor does it claim to be a critique of the Troubles.

It simply attempts to tell the remarkable story of an Irish republican and his involvement in the turbulent political cauldron which has existed throughout the last 30 chaotic years.

CHAPTER ONE

TROUBLED TIMES

TERESA Maskey gave birth to the second of her seven children on January 8, 1952. As tradition would have it, the first son in the family would take the name of his father, Alex.

Like many Catholics who worked in Belfast's deep sea docks in the late 1940s, Alex Maskey Sr set up home for his young family in Lancaster Street in the nationalist North Queen Street area. By the time his first son was born, the Northern state had been in existence for three decades.

Apart from sporadic rumblings throughout the previous 30 years, the Irish Republican Army (IRA), formed at the turn of the century to oppose British rule in Ireland, now appeared to be in a semi-permanent slumber. But in the streets of tiny terraced houses where the growing number of nationalist families in North Belfast lived, the memory of the sectarian bloodshed witnessed with the formation of the state continued to bubble just beneath the surface.

Between 1920 and 1922, some 439 people died and another 1,780 were injured in the sectarian violence that followed partition. It was to be one of the bloodiest periods of violence that Ireland, north or south, would ever endure.

Established in 1921, Northern Ireland was an unequal mix of Protestant unionism and Catholic nationalism. For the Protestant majority its Britishness but, more crucially, its perceived anti-Catholic doctrine, was to become the very backbone of the new state. Some 430,000 Catholics made up around a third of the population but, from the beginning, the unionists were determined to ensure that political power rested solely in their hands.

Catholics believed that they could be Northern Irish citizens but only on the terms set by the Protestant ascendancy. They also believed that the position offered to them in the social structure meant that they were destined to become *de facto* second-class citizens.

As a consequence, a large number of the North's nationalists, while having little alternative but to live there, steadfastly refused to give their allegiance to the state. For their part the unionists left the British government in no doubt that they should be allowed to run things as they saw fit. The architects of the state were determined to create a "Protestant parliament for a Protestant people".

As a result, successive London governments, having just endured two decades of Irish revolt, were happy to allow the unionist population to plough its own furrow. It came as little surprise then, when in the late 1920s and 1930s, a series of draconian laws, including internment without trial, were introduced in an attempt to shore up unionist rule and suppress militant Irish republicanism.

Even more significant was a widespread paranoia among unionists who were convinced that the minority were intent on undermining the new status quo. This led to a series of government policies which Catholics regarded as nothing short of blatant discrimination. An example of this was seen in March 1934 when Agriculture Minister Basil Brooke addressed a Unionist Association meeting in Derry, urging Protestant factory owners not to employ Catholics.

He told them: "I recommend those people who are loyalists not to employ Roman Catholics, 99 percent of whom are disloyal. I want you to remember one point in regard to the employment of people who are disloyal … You are disenfranchising yourselves in that way. You people who are employers have the ball at your feet. If you don't act properly now, before we know where we are, we shall find ourselves in the minority instead of the majority."

Dispelling any lingering doubts as to whether this was government policy or not, he continued: "I want you to realise that, having done your bit, you have got your Prime Minister behind you."

These comments caused widespread public anger among nationalists and demands were made on the North's Prime Minister, Sir James Craig, to disassociate himself from the remarks and to censure Brooke. But far from distancing himself, Craig actually chose to go further.

"There is not one of my colleagues who does not entirely agree with him," he told the Stormont Parliament. "And I would not ask him to withdraw one word he said."

The message appeared to be clear: while Catholics would be tolerated, many unionists would regard them as a threat to the very state itself. As a result, when Alex Maskey was born in 1950s Belfast, Catholics still found themselves living an uneasy cheek-by-jowl existence with the larger Protestant community.

Although the IRA re-emerged in the mid-1950s for an ill-fated campaign along the border, the violence did not reach Belfast and, by 1962, had petered out due to what republicans claimed was a "lack of public interest". It appeared, to all intents and purposes, that the minority had finally chosen to accept its lot.

By 1960, the sectarian tensions that had dogged the previous decades were not a concern for Teresa Maskey's eldest son. It was the lure of the overseas vessels that regularly docked in Belfast harbour and the exotic cargo that lay hidden beneath their decks that would excite the interest of eight-year-old Alex.

On Sunday mornings, after his wife had brought her children home from Mass, Alex Sr would gather up his sons and daughters and bring them to the deep sea docks to take them onboard the boats moored along the quayside. For the Maskey children, the huge ships and foreign sailors were a world apart from the dreary grey existence of Belfast's working-class neighbourhoods. They would be given coins from far-off countries, many of which they had never heard of. On the walk home, they would pester their father to bring them to an ice-cream parlour on nearby York Street.

Maskey and his brothers and sisters were typical youngsters and loved to get to the local picture houses like the Lyceum or the Duncairn to see the latest cowboy and Indian films. While there might not always have been a lot of spare money in the household, he remembers his childhood as happy and carefree.

The numbers in the Maskey household had, by this stage, grown to six and the family moved the short distance from Lancaster Street to a more spacious home at 51 Upper Meadow Street. They had stepped up the social ladder in that their new home had the luxury of a front room parlour.

"I can remember moving house that day," says Maskey, "walking along North Queen Street carrying cardboard boxes with what little possessions we had. As a youngster we thought we were the bee's knees moving to a bigger house."

Maskey attended St Patrick's Christian Brothers Primary School in Donegall Street near his home. He remembers that one of his most embarrassing moments as a child was getting his head stuck between the railings of the schoolyard and having to wait until the bars were bent open before he could escape red-faced.

While his early school days were taken up in a battle of wits with the formidable Christian Brothers teaching staff, in the evenings he spent long hours honing the bobbing and weaving skills of the boxer. Much of his later adult life would be caught up in "the Troubles" and the rise of Sinn Féin but, in the 1960s, the diminutive Maskey's early confrontations were in the ten-foot by ten-foot confines of the Holy Family Club's boxing ring. When he stepped into the ring to face his first challenge he was just ten years of age. At four stone and seven pounds, Maskey weighed little more than the medicine balls the older boxers trained with. However, under the tutelage of coaches Gerry Storey and Jim Hall, and his own ever-watchful father, he became an Ulster Champion with 75 fights under his belt.

"My mother made all my boxing costumes, shorts and dressing gowns and even decorated my boxing vests," he now recalls. "Her whole family was steeped in the boxing tradition and still is. It was good being a boxer because at home I was given the most meat at dinnertime. My mother would tell the rest of my brothers and sisters that I needed more than them because I had to keep my energy up for my next fight. If you asked my brothers and sisters now, they might tell you that I was a little bit spoilt by my mother. When I wasn't training in the gym I would pound the streets of North Belfast, running mile after mile to the Cave Hill and back every weekend."

Although Maskey had a small and wiry frame when he first started with the Holy Family Club he soon realised that he was a gifted pugilist. Throughout his boxing career he lost only four fights and managed to overturn the decision on two of these victors later. One of those defeated by the two-fisted Maskey was the talented Irish boxer Mickey Tohill who later went on to win the coveted Golden Gloves title in the United States. On a number of occasions, the young fighter found himself on the same bill as future Hollywood superstar Liam Neeson. Neeson, born and reared in Ballymena, County Antrim, fought for All Saints ABC.

The reality of living in a society which had been deeply divided from its very inception was soon to be brought home. Being only the third Catholic family to move to Upper Meadow Street, the Maskey children found themselves coming into regular contact with Protestants for the first time.

Elderly Protestant neighbours would bring the children into their homes, playing the piano for them while the young Catholic audience feasted on the inevitable cakes and sweets that had been laid out. Even when the loyalist celebrations of July 12 came round, these neighbours would ensure that the Maskeys got the same share of treats as their own children. However, for others, the fact that the Maskeys were Catholics was an issue that could not be ignored. Even now Alex Maskey is reluctant to name his Protestant childhood friends for fear that the relationship might cause them problems in their own community.

"My older sister Marion and myself were the same age as a young Protestant brother and sister who lived up the street from us. They were our best friends. We did everything together but, once it came to the start of July, they weren't allowed to play with us.

"Their father was a leading member of the Orange Order and worked in the shipyard. This man was very good to us for eleven months of the year but, once it came to July, he wouldn't allow his children to speak to us. As an adult it's hard to fully understand someone when they do that to you but when it happens to you as a child it's impossible to fathom. It was one of those lessons that you learned in life but it never made it right."

In 1963, Maskey did well in the Eleven Plus secondary school selection process and later passed junior examinations in French,

English, Geography and History. He became the first in his family to attend St Malachy's College, a prestigious grammar school on the nearby Antrim Road. He did not know it then but he was rubbing shoulders with some of those who would become political opponents in later life.

"I had a great opportunity at St Malachy's to further my education, but unfortunately I passed it up," he says.

After rushing from school to do his homework, the schoolboy became an entrepreneur and set about making a little pocket money. His first job as a teenager was chopping sticks and tying them into bundles to sell to neighbours as firewood. Maskey used this money plus his earnings from a newspaper round to collect foreign stamps and coins, a hobby which instilled in him a passion for travel.

"Myself and my uncle John, who was only a few years older than me, had an allotment behind the Waterworks Park where we grew vegetables which we sold around the doors and to local fruit and vegetable shops.

"Lancaster Street was surrounded by local industry and there were always ways in which we could make money as children, collecting unwanted things from the street. There was a season for collecting rags, which we would sell to a woman called Mrs Dankers; there was a season for collecting scrap metal, which we brought to a scrap yard in Great George's Street; and there was another season for collecting waste paper, which we would bring to Cooke's paper store. We may not have been well-off, but we were a happy family and I enjoyed my teenage years."

Maskey recalls being summoned from class at St Malachy's by the school bursar, Fr McAllister, one day to be told that his father had been sent to Crumlin Road Prison. Somewhat ironically, the jail shared a common wall with the college.

"My dad had gotten into a dispute with his employers and was sent to jail for assault. I remember the school bursar telling me that everything would be alright because my father was just over the other side of the school wall."

As the young Maskey stood gazing at the imposing wall that

separated father from son, he did not realise that, less than a decade later, he would find himself inside the prison.

The teenager's life seemed carefree but, towards the mid-1960s, the fragile truce that had existed between the two communities began to give way to an unspoken form of sectarian hatred. The first signs of serious trouble came during the Westminster elections of October 1964. Sinn Féin, running on an abstentionist ticket, had chosen to stand veteran republican Liam McMillen as a candidate for the West Belfast seat. An Irish tricolour took pride of place in the window of McMillen's election campaign headquarters, an empty shop in Divis Street in the lower Falls Road area.

While the police force, the Royal Ulster Constabulary (RUC), had little love for Sinn Féin, displaying a tricolour in a strongly nationalist district was not seen as an issue serious enough to warrant taking action. However, weeks before the election, a new firebrand Protestant cleric named Ian Paisley threatened to lead a march to the Sinn Féin offices and remove the flag himself unless the RUC addressed the situation within 48 hours.

The day after Paisley's threat the RUC smashed down the door of the offices and removed the offending tricolour from the window. Maskey recalls leaving school with some of his friends to go to the Falls Road protests that followed the incident. The protesting pupils were given a dressing-down in the school assembly hall next morning.

The removal of the flag was a feather in Paisley's cap and he called for a victory rally to be held at Belfast City Hall the following day. Protestants were celebrating but outraged nationalists on the Falls Road were in no mood for such amusements. Two nights of rioting followed with serious clashes between nationalists and the police. On the third day, the RUC again broke down the door of the Sinn Féin offices and removed a second tricolour which had replaced the earlier confiscated flag. This led to the worst night of violence Belfast had witnessed since the 1930s with the RUC using water cannons on rioters who responded with petrol bombs. The following night 350 RUC men battled with nationalists on the Falls, resulting in more than 50 civilians needing hospital treatment.

With the situation getting dangerously out of control, nationalist and republican leaders in Belfast appealed for calm. By the end of the week, an uneasy truce was being observed and the RUC made no attempt to intervene when a tricolour was carried during a republican march along the Falls.

While disaster seemed to have been averted, the Divis Street flag riots would prove to be a foretaste of what was to come. By the late 1960s, nationalists began to demand basic civil rights such as equality in the allocation of public housing, fair employment opportunities and "one-man, one-vote" – a not very politically correct slogan directed at gerrymandered local councils. The age-old unionist fear that Catholics were hell-bent on bringing about a united Ireland appeared to be re-emerging with more vigour than ever.

Around this period the teenaged Maskey became involved in local residents' groups as they campaigned for decent housing standards. At the request of well-known nationalist politician, Paddy Devlin, he agreed to work for Labour candidate, Martin McBirney, in the local government elections of 1964.

In 1965, a meeting between Stormont Prime Minister, Captain Terence O'Neill, and southern Taoiseach, Sean Lemass, led to Ian Paisley making a series of controversial speeches. The Protestant community's fear of being "led down the road to Dublin and a united Ireland" fanned the flames of loyalist extremism.

Paisley's apparent distaste for Catholicism – coupled with criticism of moderate unionists' attempts to establish a relationship with their southern neighbours – was attracting a growing audience. For the older generation of northern nationalists who had witnessed the bloody pogroms of the 1920s and 1930s, the future appeared anything but hopeful. For the growing Maskey household too, these were worrying times.

"As a Catholic family, you knew you were different," Maskey recalls. "By the end of the 1960s, the level of intimidation and harassment was becoming a near constant."

Maskey remembers regular occasions when his mother and father had decorated the front of their home but, by next morning, loyalists had daubed the house in paint.

"That sort of intimidation was happening more and more," he says.

Sectarian murder returned to stalk the streets of Belfast in May 1966 with a fatal gun attack on Catholic storeman, John Scullion. Initial statements from police and hospital authorities claimed that the 28-year-old had died after being stabbed. However, after a public outcry, Scullion's body was exhumed in June and it was confirmed that he had been shot.

Catholic barman Peter Ward was shot dead by loyalists on June 26. The following day, 77-year-old Protestant pensioner Matilda Gould died from burns received seven weeks earlier when loyalists had mistakenly set fire to her Shankill Road home while attempting to firebomb the Catholic-owned bar next door. Gusty Spence, later to become a loyalist icon, was charged with murdering the two Catholics. Subsequently, the charges against Spence regarding Scullion's death were dropped but he was sentenced to life imprisonment for Ward's murder.

The growing tensions erupting in his native city engaged Maskey's mind, in particular the killing of the young Catholic barman.

"I remember Peter Ward being shot dead and the rise of Paisleyism at that time. I gathered every political bulletin or leaflet that I could get my hands on. There used to be a stall at the bottom of Bank Street and Royal Avenue where the *Protestant Telegraph* was sold and I went and bought that."

By 1968, Maskey had left school with a handful of qualifications and started his first job in an electrical shop in Gresham Street. At night he worked part-time as a barman in the Christian Brothers Past Pupils' Union and then in the Civil Service Club in Lower Garfield Street. But any hope of a normal life-style was lost forever as the North plummeted towards open conflict. Living in an interface area – a sectarian flashpoint between Protestant and Catholic neighbourhoods – he soon found his world turned upside down.

Maskey explains that his parents' thinking at that time reflected the concerns of many within the nationalist community.

"I remember my father regularly having to find lorries and vans to help rescue families from places like the Rathcoole estate, previously mixed communities which had been quickly taken over by the loyalists. He and other men had to help the Catholic families to move when they were intimidated from their homes while the mothers cared for the refugees. I remember being on the back of coal lorries in places like Tiger's Bay and the Crumlin Road, moving out Catholics whose homes had been attacked and who had been left with nothing."

Some 30 years later, Maskey would be doing the same thing at the height of the Drumcree protests.

With tensions rising on a daily basis and violence becoming increasingly prevalent, Teresa and Alex Sr were anxious that their sons and daughters were not drawn into the emerging conflict even though they themselves were in the thick of things. Many Catholic parents, says Maskey, were concerned about their children becoming involved in the Civil Rights campaign. While they supported the calls for one-man, one-vote and the demands for decent housing and jobs, being seen to openly challenge the authority of the state was not the "done thing" for Catholics at that time.

"The rule of thumb in those days, if you were a Catholic family in a predominantly Protestant or even mixed area, was to keep your head down," he says.

By 1969, Upper Meadow Street had become a full-blown interface between nationalists and loyalists and sectarian attacks were taking place right on the Maskeys' own doorstep. In a peculiar twist, Maskey found himself in the unusual position of standing shoulder to shoulder with Protestant neighbours as they defended their homes against attack.

"Our street was like every other in that part of Belfast in that we had vigilantes and I was one of them. All of the men were expected to take part in protecting our houses. Bear in mind, at that point in time, where we lived was a mixed area between the nationalist New Lodge Road and the loyalist Tiger's Bay. There had been a number of attacks on our street by the loyalists from Tiger's Bay with windows broken and paint thrown at houses.

"The vigilantes were both Catholic and Protestant. The street was mixed and the houses were coming under attack so it was commonsense that the Catholics and Protestants stood together to protect them. But then, after a period of time, the Protestants started to leave and soon disappeared altogether. At the end of the day, they were coming into confrontation with their own community and that was very dangerous for them. If they were seen to be staying in a street with nationalists, they would have been shunned by their own community or perhaps worse. A few stayed but the majority opted to leave."

Maskey's story was verified in 1993 when he found himself on the opposite side of the Belfast council chamber from a Protestant boyhood neighbour. Sandy Blair was a member of the hard-line Democratic Unionist Party (DUP) and an ardent opponent of all things republican.

"I grew up in the same street as Alex Maskey," Blair says. "I didn't know Alex well, but you can't not know a lad who lives in the same street."

Blair confirms that Protestant families were not forced from their homes in Upper Meadow Street but left for personal reasons, adding: "They weren't moved out as some people have claimed. They left of their own free will."

Ironically, had it not been for the secret intervention of his parents, Alex Maskey could easily have escaped what was to become known as "the Troubles". In early 1969, he and childhood friend Eoghan O'Neill applied to be included in the Big Brother project, an emigration scheme which offered cut-price fares to Australia. Since the pair were still only 17 years of age, they needed their parents' permission to go.

"We went down to Australia House, filled in the applications and were accepted on to the scheme. We had passed the medicals and were waiting for the flight details and were all ready to go."

As the weeks passed by and the teenagers had still not heard anything from the Australian authorities, they became concerned that their adventure to the outback had hit a snag. Assuming that bureaucracy was putting an unnecessary delay on their planned emigration, the would-be explorers began to inquire what was holding up their departure. Unknown to them, their parents had been in consultation and had hatched their own plan to keep the arrival of the forms a closely guarded secret.

"Our parents decided that, if we were really serious, we would have pursued it further and they decided not to tell us they had received the forms. There were serious rows in both our houses when we found out. Eoghan decided he was leaving anyway and went off to the Channel Islands for the summer, where he has been ever since, and I went to work on the docks."

In 1987, when Maskey was shot and seriously wounded by an Ulster Freedom Fighters (UFF) gunman, it was to his childhood friend in Guernsey that he went to recuperate.

"Eoghan went and I stayed and I have no regrets. It was just one of those things."

It was not long after the departure of his friend that Maskey developed a new interest. Alex Sr decided it was time for his son to learn a practical skill.

"My father taught me to drive," he says, "and I passed the driving test first time round in October 1969. I remember one of my proudest moments was when I bought my first car, a Ford Anglia, for £25. That was a lot of money at the time but I thought I was on top of the world."

If a youthful Maskey was in search of stimulation, the bloody years that followed would more than occupy his mind. On October 11, 1969 the Hunt Report – commissioned by the British government to investigate recent disturbances – was published. Two of its recommendations were that the RUC should be disarmed and the controversial police reserve, the 'B' Specials, disbanded. The report provoked immediate anger within the unionist community and street violence intensified. That night, Constable Victor Arbuckle became the first RUC fatality of the Troubles when he was shot dead during a confrontation with loyalists on the Shankill Road. Alex Maskey remembers the date well. It was the evening of his older sister Marion's wedding day.

"I remember an aunt coming rushing into Marion's wedding celebrations to say that the loyalists were attacking our street. The men left the wedding and went to defend the houses and when that threat was dealt with, we went back to the celebrations."

As loyalist areas of the city erupted, a decision was taken to end the wedding reception early. Leaving the Clifton Hotel on Glenravel Street that night, Maskey saw hundreds of British soldiers lined up outside the RUC barracks opposite waiting to be moved to the Shankill where the worst rioting was taking place.

"These soldiers were just kids themselves and they looked terrified. There was the constant sound of gunfire coming from the Shankill. That was the first real gunfire I had heard up to that time."

Around this time Maskey, aged 18, appeared in court for an incident which he now describes as one of the most embarrassing moments of his life. He had gone to the Northern Bank in Waring Street to withdraw money from his account as he was going to a wedding the next day. While standing in line to be served, a large bundle of notes was placed on the counter in front of him.

"The next thing I remember, I had reached over and grabbed a handful of notes and ran out the door. It was a stupid thing to do and I was quickly grabbed by one of the customers in the bank," he remembers.

Maskey pleaded guilty to stealing £563 and apologised to the court, explaining that he had acted on impulse and had been unable to resist the sight of so much money. Resident magistrate John Adams described the young docker as "naïve".

"It was a very foolish action and I am accepting that it was an impulsive act," said the judge as he imposed a conditional discharge.

Now a grandfather, Maskey admits that he had caused major embarrassment to his family.

"It was a moment which I have always regretted but it taught me a valuable lesson – that in life you have to work for things. It is not something of which I am very proud."

Maskey's first brush with the law was soon to pale into insignificance against the backdrop of events unfolding across the North. By 1970,

Belfast was in turmoil and hundreds of people were forced to flee their homes because of intimidation. It was to be the single biggest population shift in western Europe since the end of the Second World War.

For Maskey, the die was cast and he found himself embroiled in the Troubles. The Belfast republican says that, like hundreds of other young men and women of his generation, he "played an active part in the defence of his community". In September 1971, he was arrested in Andersonstown and taken to the British army base at Palace Barracks near Hollywood where he was questioned for two days. From there he was transferred to Crumlin Road Prison where he joined the ranks of the internees imprisoned without trial.

Internment had been introduced in the early hours of August 9 when thousands of British troops and RUC men swamped nationalist communities across the North. By the end of the day, 342 men had been taken from their homes under the emergency legislation. The arrests caused panic with Catholic families not knowing where the detained men had been taken. Many internees later reported that they had been badly beaten and tortured. While 116 were released within two days, the remainder were held in cells in Crumlin Road jail or aboard the Maidstone prison ship in Belfast Lough.

The policy of internment, demanded by Stormont Prime Minister Brian Faulkner, seemed designed to create maximum anger among nationalists whose representatives highlighted the fact that, while widespread violence emanated from the unionist community, the RUC had failed to arrest any loyalists. Two Protestants were arrested during the first waves of internment; one was a republican sympathiser, while the other belonged to the left wing group, People's Democracy.

Alex Maskey vividly remembers his arrival at Crumlin Road Prison.

"C Wing, where the internees were held, was an education in itself. The wing held men of all nationalist persuasions and none. I was shocked at the age of some of the internees. Many had endured similar experiences in previous decades. It was as if an old black and white war movie had come to life with prisoners-of-war negotiating with the governor and running their own affairs."

His tenure here lasted only a matter of weeks. One grey, dreary Sunday afternoon, he was flown by helicopter to the newly-erected Long Kesh compounds. For many, Long Kesh at first sight appeared remarkably like the POW camps depicted in numerous films. At the height of internment in March 1972, a total of 924 people were imprisoned behind miles of barbed wire, perimeter fencing and watchtowers.

While the majority of the IRA volunteers escaped arrest on the morning of August 9, 1971, a lot of veterans from the republican campaigns of the 1940s and 1950s had been lifted in the swoops. The majority of these men had long since become inactive and practically all were middle-aged or older. Therefore, when Maskey entered the caged enclosures of Long Kesh a month after internment began, he was faced with a strange mixture. A substantial number of his fellow internees were not even republicans. Some had been interned because of their involvement in the Civil Rights campaign; others found themselves behind the barbed wire because of their left-wing tendencies. Some were in Long Kesh for no reason other than they were unfortunate enough to have been at home when the British army and RUC raided. While many internees were in their late teens, there was also an older generation of men in their late thirties and forties.

Some of those interned were Provisionals and Officials, the names given to the two groups which grew out of a split in the IRA in late 1960s and early 1970s. Maskey soon fell under the influence of veterans such as John O'Rawe, Jimmy Drumm, Seamus Loughran, Leitrim's John Joe McGirl, Willie John McCorry and Gerry Maguire, who had all been previously interned during the 1940s and 1950s.

"The older generation was a very steadying influence on the younger lads like myself," Maskey now recalls, "because they had the jail history behind them and they instilled a political discipline in us, organising education classes and getting people to make handicrafts."

Many internees believed they would be released within days or weeks and allowed to return home. Some pinned their hopes on the belief that the international community would react.

"People were saying that the United Nations would intervene," says Maskey, "and that the world wouldn't allow this to happen. But as far as the British government was concerned they could do what they wanted and we would be kept there for as long as they wanted."

If internment was designed to stop the violence, it proved to be a catastrophic failure. A total of 34 people had been killed in the first nine months of 1971. In the remaining three months of the year following internment, 139 died.

On December 4, 1971, Maskey was faced with the frustration of being locked in jail when fifteen of his North Belfast friends and neighbours were killed by a loyalist bomb. The Ulster Volunteer Force (UVF) no-warning bomb planted in the entrance of McGurk's Bar caused the single biggest loss of life of the Troubles at that time.

Among the dead were mother and daughter, Philomena and Maria McGurk; 13-year-old schoolboy James Cromie; Edward Keenan (69); Sarah Keenan (58); John Colton (49); Thomas Loughlin (55); David Milligan (52); James Smyth (55); Francis Bradley (61); Thomas Kane (45); Philip Garry (73); Kathleen Irvine (45); Edward Kane (25) and Robert Spotswood (38).

Maskey vividly remembers his feelings about being behind bars when word of the bombing began to filter into the cages.

"I was born in the top house in Lancaster Street just yards from McGurk's Bar and passed it every day when I was growing up. I knew some of the McGurk family and a lot of the people who died. I remember seeing the pictures of the scene on the television and recognising my uncle Jim, who was using his bare hands to dig through the rubble, trying to find the bodies buried underneath.

"My father regularly drank in McGurk's and, in the beginning, I didn't know if he was alive or dead. I knew Ned Keenan and his wife Sarah who were killed."

Less than two months later, it was Maskey's turn to console other internees from the Northwest when, on January 31, 1972, British paratroopers shot dead 13 unarmed people in Derry. One of the most seriously wounded casualties died weeks later. To this day, Maskey feels that the inaction of some of those in the Catholic hierarchy and the Irish government after the killings on Bloody Sunday "was unforgivable".

"I just think the biggest problem was that there was not the political leadership on this island to make Britain accountable for what they did that day. I personally think that the response of the church leaders and the Irish government was absolutely shameful. It meant that young men and women in places like Ballymurphy and the Creggan had to stand up and fight a war on their own. If the people in power had chosen to stand up and be counted after events like Bloody Sunday and internment, then maybe those young people would not have had to fight."

Maskey was released in the summer of 1972 when the IRA announced a truce to facilitate negotiations with the British government. But within weeks, the truce broke down after a confrontation between the British army and nationalists – intimidated out of their homes in other parts of Belfast – who were blocked by soldiers from moving into vacant houses on the Lenadoon estate in the west of the city. Maskey was soon back behind the barbed wire of Long Kesh. This time he found himself in the same cage as leading Belfast republicans Dickie Glenholmes, Ivor Bell and Gerry Adams. The 20-year-old was by now a veteran of the Cages.

"We had a routine in the Cages in that everyone would have their turn on the rota to clean the floors of the hut and fill the water boiler and so on. It was a good discipline and helped to pass the day. Of course some of us took better to cleaning than others and it's hard to keep a hut clean with 30 grown men walking in and out every minute of the day."

The internees held their own political education and history classes. Some also turned their skills to handicrafts, making Celtic harps and painted handkerchiefs to send out to loved ones.

"Some of us became so good at it that we developed a sort of production line. Someone would carve out the harp, another would be making the little strings to go with it, while someone else would varnish it and put Celtic designs on. At one stage we were even cutting the middle out of two-shilling coins to make Claddagh rings. These

29

rings were a big hit on the outside – until people realised that they were left with a semi-permanent green mark on their finger if they wore it for more than a day. It got to the stage that only true republican die-hards on the outside would ask for a Claddagh ring from the men in the Cages."

While some of those in Long Kesh dreamed of escape, for others the possibility that they could be released at any time meant that they were prepared to sit and wait. By late 1972, there was an acceptance among republicans in the jail that wholesale releases were a long way off. Realising that he was likely to remain inside Long Kesh until internment ended, Maskey concentrated his mind on escaping.

Along with Billy Kelly and George Burt, Maskey approached the IRA leadership in the jail with a plan. Republican internees dreamt up a range of ideas to get to the outside, including swapping clothes with visitors, digging tunnels and trying to get out in bin lorries. Maskey and his two accomplices became the first to attempt to escape from Long Kesh by cutting through the wire.

The would-be escapers began to elaborate on their plan. They managed to get their hands on wire cutters knowing they would have to crawl through a series of coils of razor wire. Although they initially made arrangements for a car to pick them up on the outside, in the end they simply decided to escape on the first winter's evening with suitable weather conditions.

While they believed their biggest obstacle would be climbing over the huge fences which framed the camp, they discovered when they set off on a rainy night in March 1973 that the timber posts used to keep the fences in place made climbing relatively easy. The escapers were in luck when they observed that some of the lookout posts towering over the compounds were not manned. They quickly managed to get across the fence and onto open ground where they started to make their way through hundreds of yards of tripwire.

"We had to step over the wire and at the same time keep low because of the risk of being spotted," says Maskey. "We couldn't make any noise at all. It was a terrible night, foggy and cold and every time we cut through the razor wire I was convinced that the noise of it could be heard all over the camp. I was expecting that the spotlights were going to come down on us at any minute or that the guards patrolling with the dogs would find us but, luckily, no one did."

The three had successfully negotiated the tripwire and were left with the last few strands of wire to cut through when their luck ran out and they were confronted by soldiers with guard dogs who had been patrolling the camp perimeter.

"I think the dogs must have picked up our scent because one of them came straight over to us. We decided that one of us still had a chance to get away so myself and George told Billy Kelly to go on and we would hold off the soldiers."

Not expecting to be faced down by the remaining two escapers, the guard patrol initially appeared shocked but quickly recovered their composure and held them at gunpoint while radioing through a report that they had detected "two intruders".

"They seemed to think we were breaking into the camp rather than out of it," Maskey recalls with a smile. "They seemed really shocked that we were actually there at all."

Refusing to answer the soldiers' questions, Maskey and Burt were taken to the punishment cells to be identified. The pair reported that they were severely beaten during this period. Maskey had a bone in his leg broken and was unable to leave his bed in Crumlin Road Prison's hospital wing for three weeks. He was later awarded £1,100 compensation for injuries received after his recapture.

While the authorities were attempting to identify their two "intruders", Kelly had managed to make it out of the prison and had started walking towards what he thought was Belfast. He quickly changed direction when he ended up outside a local police station.

His escape could easily have been short-lived when he managed to hitch a lift with what turned out to be a courier for the Ulster Defence Regiment (UDR), the locally recruited and mainly Protestant part-time army reserve. Realising the precariousness of his position, Kelly told the driver that his van had broken down and he was trying to get back to Belfast to fetch a friend to fix it.

The unsuspecting soldier was happy to drop the IRA escaper into

Belfast city centre where Kelly waved goodbye to the Good Samaritan. When news of what had happened filtered back to republicans in the jail, Kelly's escape was used to chide their captors that, while the British had placed them in Long Kesh, the UDR were helping them to get out.

For their part, Maskey and Burt were taken to Lisburn RUC station where they refused to answer questions about their attempted escape. Remanded to Crumlin Road, they were eventually brought to court and convicted of attempted escape. Both were sentenced to nine months imprisonment. As was the practice, once Maskey and Burt had completed their sentence in Crumlin Road Prison and were about to be released, they were served with another internment order. The pair were then taken back to Long Kesh. Maskey was eventually released in the spring of 1975, just before the policy of internment was ended.

Although he was born on Elvis Presley's birthday, he does not offer this as the reason for his intense interest in the Belfast entertainment scene when he was released.

"I loved music before going to prison and often went to the Astor Dance Club and spent Saturday mornings at the Plaza Dance Hall, listening to Brian Rossi who was a big name singer at the time. When I was released from jail in 1975, I bought myself a Transit van and worked as a roadie for Tara Folk, a well-known band around Belfast at the time.

"I was still working part-time as a docker and I also delivered furniture for shops in Belfast's Smithfield Market but decided to give it up when I found myself going into Protestant estates. It wasn't particularly safe for someone who had been a republican internee to be going into those places at the time."

Though he could not have known it then, Liz McKee, the woman Maskey was to marry, had been carrying out her own escape attempt from Armagh Women's Prison while he was making his bid for freedom. McKee and her friend Tish Holland, who would later join Maskey on Belfast City Council, were among five republican prisoners who made the escape bid in March 1973.

As Maskey, Burt and Kelly were preparing to cut their way out of Long Kesh, McKee and Holland were using smuggled hacksaw blades to saw through the window bars in their own cell.

Using home-made ropes, they lowered themselves down the outside wall of their cell block and ran to an elevated army observation post on the jail's perimeter wall. There, joined by three other prisoners, they could see their transport waiting on the street below. But as Holland tried to climb down the outside wall she and the others became caught in razor wire and could not free themselves. After an hour trapped on the wall, the five's escape bid was finally discovered.

Like her future husband, Liz McKee was sentenced to nine months imprisonment for her attempted escape.

Alex Maskey and Liz McKee had been acquainted briefly before their respective terms in jail but only got to know each other properly after finding themselves seated together at a welcome home party for a mutual friend who had been recently released from Long Kesh.

"In those days you didn't know if you were going to be alive the next week so you lived every day as your last and, if you met someone you liked, you weren't going to let them out of your sight," Maskey explains. "I don't know if I captured Liz or she captured me, but we joke now that it's been a life sentence for us both. I have to say that throughout this last 30 years, Liz has always been at my side through thick and thin."

On September 4, 1976 the pair married and moved into the McKee family home. However, any dream of an extended honeymoon period was short-lived. As former republican prisoners, their house was raided on a regular basis with one or both of them often being taken off for questioning at the RUC's infamous Castlereagh holding centre or one of the numerous British army bases.

"I would leave home some mornings to go to work and almost immediately be stopped by a foot patrol and beaten black and blue. That was practically routine in those days. You considered yourself lucky if you managed to get to work at all," says Maskey.

Meanwhile, his potential leadership skills must have been noticed by some within the republican movement. During the IRA ceasefire of 1975, he was chosen as one of two representatives to attend round-table talks with loyalist paramilitaries in Holland.

"I suppose the trip could be described as the very early stages of conflict resolution discussions," Maskey explains. "Myself and another republican were sent out along with people from the Ulster Volunteer Force (UVF), Ulster Defence Association (UDA), officials and various church and community leaders.

"The first week was taken up with discussions and workshops. People from the Dutch government and church and business leaders were brought in to speak to us.

"We were then sent out to various parts of Holland where we worked with community groups. I stayed with the Mayor of Dernice and worked in a community centre for a week. Then we went back to the group and took part in another week of discussions. We might not have called it conflict resolution in those days, but that's what it was."

While these attempts at addressing the situation in the North may have worked in Holland, back home none of those involved in the conflict were ready for a resolution. In 1976, a new British government policy aimed at ending the image of republican and loyalists as prisoners-of-war was to have a hugely significant impact on the life of Alex Maskey and on the North as a whole.

Special Category or Political Status for inmates had been introduced in 1972 after a 35-day hunger strike in Crumlin Road jail by IRA prisoners fighting for the right to run their own wings. By 1976, the British government realised that its war against the IRA should be two-pronged: fighting on the physical front while wooing the world's media. As a result, the then Secretary of State Merlyn Rees announced that, from March 1, 1976, political status would be abolished. From that date, all prisoners would be deemed to be criminals.

A new prison had been built on the Long Kesh site specifically to accommodate the new strategy of criminalisation. But if the British government believed that republicans would meekly accept the status of criminals they were mistaken. Even the name of the new jail could not be agreed on. The Northern Ireland Office called it the Maze, republicans continued to call it Long Kesh and loyalists used both names.

In time, the shape of the jail's eight cell blocks themselves would provide a solution to this problem. The prison consisted of self-contained blocks built in the shape of the letter 'H'. Each of the H-Blocks had been designed as a prison within a prison with a 16-foot high steel fence topped with rolls of barbed wire and, later, razor wire. Outside each H-Block, the prison was in turn divided into more sections surrounded by a 2,000 metre-long concrete wall enveloped in even more barbed wire fencing. Armed sentries in watch towers which had been erected every 200 yards surveyed everything that moved within the jail. The look-out posts were manned around the clock.

The British government's decision to withdraw political status signalled the start of a five-year battle within the jail. Republicans had indicated from the beginning that they would not accept this new policy and, in particular, would refuse to wear prison uniform. The battle lines were drawn but no one could have foreseen what was to follow.

On September 15, 1976, Kieran Nugent, the first IRA man sent to the H-Blocks after the removal of special category status, was ordered to strip naked and put on the prison uniform. He refused, insisting that as an IRA prisoner he was entitled to political status and the right to wear his own clothes. When again ordered to don the uniform, Nugent told warders that if they wanted him to wear prison garb they would have to "nail it" to his back. With neither side prepared to back down, Nugent was brought to a cell where he used a blanket to cover his nakedness.

It is doubtful whether Nugent or prison chiefs realised it but, in those first few moments, the five-year "blanket protest", as it became known, had begun. In little over a year there were 300 other republicans refusing to wear prison uniform and they too wrapped themselves in blankets. As more and more republicans joined the protest there were daily confrontations with warders. The situation was spiralling dangerously out of control.

"Families visiting their loved ones in the H-Blocks were coming out and telling how the screws (prison officers) were engaged in systematically beating the men at every opportunity," Maskey recalls.

By March 1978, the situation had deteriorated to such an extent that the prisoners started a "no wash" protest. Republicans refused to leave their cells, claiming they were being attacked by the prison staff when they went to the toilet or to wash.

Left with a situation where they no longer felt safe outside their cells, the prisoners stopped going to the toilets and used chamber pots instead. The pots were then emptied into a bin brought around the wings by warders. Soon, this too sparked confrontation with prisoners claiming that warders were deliberately spilling the contents of the chamber pots in the cells. When the warders refused to enter the cells to lift the pots, the prisoners began to dispose of the urine by pouring it under the cell door where it ran out onto the passage ways.

The "blanket men" were then faced with the problem of what to do with their excreta. After much discussion, it was decided that it should be spread onto the walls of the cells. In August, Catholic Primate of Ireland, Tomás Ó Fiaich, visited the protesting prisoners and later said he could only compare the conditions in the H-Blocks to those experienced by the homeless people living beside the open sewers on the streets of Calcutta.

By 1980, the protest was into its fourth year and newly-elected British Prime Minister, Margaret Thatcher, showed not only no sign of compromise but also a determination to break the blanket men's resolve and deal a severe blow to the IRA.

The prisoners decided that the issue had to be brought to a head. On October 27, 1980, IRA jail leader Brendan Hughes led seven republicans in a hunger strike protest for the restoration of political status. The protest spread to Armagh jail where three women prisoners, Mairéad Farrell, Mary Doyle and Mairéad Nugent also embarked on a hunger strike. The protest was called off after 53 days, on 18 December, with hunger striker Sean McKenna close to death and prisoners believing that a deal had been agreed with the British government. Convinced that compromise had been reached, Bobby Sands, Hughes' replacement as the prisoners' leader, met with prison governor, Stanley Hilditch. They agreed that 21 republicans would move into clean cells with furniture and be issued with both civilian and prison clothing.

The move was to be an experiment to test the willingness of both sides to co-operate. But within days, the prisoners accused government representatives at the Northern Ireland Office of reneging on the deal after inmates were refused the clothes which their families had sent into the jail.

At the end of January, convinced they had been double-crossed by the British, the prisoners took a decision to break the furniture in their cells and, by the next morning, the agreement had collapsed. With the blanket men deeply angered at what they perceived to be betrayal, a statement was issued on February 7 announcing that a second hunger strike was to be undertaken.

This time there was little sign that either side was in a mood to compromise.

CHAPTER TWO

ENTERING THE LION'S DEN

B OBBY Sands refused food for the first time on the morning of March 1, 1981, exactly five years to the day that the British government announced that it was withdrawing political status from loyalist and republican prisoners.

The 27-year-old blanket man had consistently counselled that the government would allow a second hunger strike to end in the death of at least one prisoner. He decided, therefore, that he would be the first to risk his life.

While the protestors were determined to bring the battle in the jail to a head, there were those outside who saw that the move would have far reaching implications way beyond the walls of the H-Blocks.

The republican leadership and Margaret Thatcher's government both knew the huge risks which hung on the outcome of the new hunger strike. The IRA's Army Council was concerned about the impact that a second fast in a matter of months would have on its ability to carry on its armed campaign effectively. While the leadership technically had the power to order the prisoners not to embark on the second strike, it was well aware that such an order could be ignored.

If the prisoners chose to disregard such an order it would have created a dangerous division which would inevitably have been exploited by the British government. So while stating its serious reservations the republican leadership reluctantly agreed to the prisoners embarking upon a second fast. The Army Council, however, made known their opposition to a suggestion from republican prisoners in Armagh Women's jail that they too be allowed to join the hunger strike.

Maskey says he had only known Bobby Sands briefly on the outside.

"I met Bobby a few times during the 1970s and only knew him a little bit but, even then, I was impressed by his energy and commitment. He was a mild-mannered young guy, but you sensed there was a steely determination beneath the surface."

On the last Sunday in February, days before Bobby Sands was due to start refusing food, 3,500 people took part in a march along the Falls Road in support of the prisoners. The previous October, 10,000 marchers had turned out to show support for the first hunger-strikers.

With the earlier protest ending in confusion and bitter recrimination, there was a large degree of public scepticism about a renewed hunger strike with many believing it too would be called off at the last moment. Behind the scenes, the Catholic Church was also divided over the issue. Edward Daly, then Bishop of Derry, criticised the prisoners' decision to launch another fast.

So it was that two determined forces – Margaret Thatcher and the hunger-strikers – found themselves on a collision course. While the prisoners were determined that their protest would end only when political status was restored, the British government was resolute that they would be defeated.

Indeed, sensing an opportunity to deal a crushing blow to republicans, Thatcher publicly proclaimed that the IRA had now played its last card. But as the two sides prepared for the inevitable round of brinkmanship the second protest would bring, it was an intervention of fate that was to swing nationalist support behind the prisoners.

Frank Maguire, the Independent Nationalist MP for Fermanagh-South Tyrone, died suddenly five days after Bobby Sands began to refuse food. His death had an enormous impact, not only on the prison protest, but also on the future course of the battleground on which republicans and the British government would meet. It was from this point that Maskey and other republicans trace the beginning of a shift that was to develop into a coherent political strategy.

Maguire had been interned during the 1950s and had visited the blanket men in the H-Blocks in the late 1970s. He had held discussions with Bobby Sands and another prisoners' leader, Brendan Hughes, in their cell and even managed to pass them some much-prized tobacco which he had smuggled into the jail. Although the 52-year-old Maguire had been MP for Fermanagh-South Tyrone since 1974, he had rarely attended Westminster and had not seen value in making a maiden speech by the time of his death on March 5, 1981.

Brendan McFarlane, who became the IRA leader in the H-Blocks when Bobby Sands began his hunger strike, later recalled that even in death Frank Maguire had managed to come to the aid of the prisoners.

Maguire's death immediately sparked debate within the nationalist community about the possibility of an agreed candidate being selected to succeed him. Initially, the dead MP's brother Noel, the Social Democratic and Labour Party's (SDLP) Austin Currie and the socialist republican, Bernadette McAliskey, all publicly expressed interest in fighting the election. McAliskey subsequently stated that she would be willing to withdraw if a prisoner chose to stand. After serious discussion within the republican movement, it was announced on March 26 that Bobby Sands would be put forward to fight the by-election. Under severe pressure, both private and public, the other nationalist candidates eventually announced they would also withdraw in favour of Sands.

Only two names appeared on the ballot papers, those of Bobby Sands and Ulster Unionist Party (UUP) candidate Harry West. Jim Gibney was the man who first suggested that the hunger-striker should contest Maguire's seat. But even with an inbuilt nationalist majority in Fermanagh-South Tyrone and the worldwide exposure that running a hunger-striker as a candidate would gain for the prisoners, the IRA was still faced with a major dilemma. At the very heart of the republican psyche was the strongly-held belief that any involvement in constitutional politics was not only self-defeating, but was a threat to the "armed struggle" itself.

Unlike many of his IRA contemporaries, Bobby Sands had been an active member of Sinn Féin in the 1970s and could see the political capital which an election victory could capture for the prisoners. But the very suggestion that republicans should allow themselves to become involved in state politics, no matter how small the part, was enough to cause anger. Jim Gibney recalls two Tyrone republicans at a Sinn Féin Ard Fheis in the mid-1970s arguing that the party should enter into constitutional politics.

"Ruairí Ó Brádaigh, who was Sinn Féin president at that time, stood up and told them that if they ever suggested such a thing again, he would personally drive them out of the party," Gibney remembers. "This was the type of deep suspicion which existed among republicans about anyone who even suggested that we take part in politics. Republicans believed that once you got involved with constitutional politics, you were on a slippery slope. Don't get me wrong – people bought into the suggestion that Bobby should run as a candidate in Fermanagh-South Tyrone as a means of highlighting the hunger strike but anything further than that, to actually get involved in electoral politics, was firmly rejected."

It was not that republicans were opposed to politics; rather they were only prepared to enter the political arena when the circumstances suited them. Gerry Adams had argued from the mid-1970s the need to establish political structures to run alongside armed struggle and eventually beyond it. Crucially, while he argued the need for the "politicisation" of republicanism, it was on the understanding that this did not include active participation in any "British institutions".

In a throwback to IRA strategy after the 1916 Easter Rising, the republican tactic was to establish its own community forums outside of, and in direct opposition to, state politics. While politicisation would be allowed to run alongside the armed struggle, it was on the understanding that it would always take second place to militant republicanism.

"There was always an argument that the struggle needed to be widened out, to appeal to as many people as possible," Gibney explains. "But republicans felt alienated from the constitutional politics of the state. Pre-1981 Sinn Féin was about protest and reacting against everything that the state stood for. After 1981, we were still opposed to the state. It was just that another front had been opened up where the struggle could also be fought and won."

Government institutions such as local councils, Stormont and

Westminster were an irrelevance as far as republicans were concerned. Those opposed to electoral politics used the example of the Official IRA's demise after it had entered the constitutional system to argue that Provisionals had nothing to gain from taking the same road. The one guaranteed result from engaging in state politics, these opponents claimed, was that the British government would use it to pacify republicanism. That was not a risk the IRA leadership was prepared to take.

While Bobby Sands would contest the Fermanagh-South Tyrone seat, the clear understanding was that the sole objective was to put the hunger strike issue on a world stage. Republicans told the people of Fermanagh-South Tyrone that they only wanted to "borrow" the seat to save Sands' life; once the hunger strike had been won, the people could have it back.

The Adams leadership won the argument to put Sands up for election although there were still many within the republican movement, including Alex Maskey, who supported the hunger-strikers but had serious objections to the electoral strategy, believing that it would weaken the armed struggle.

Maskey had been heavily involved in the political agitation campaign throughout the 1980-81 period and had been charged with a string of public order offences arising out of anti-H-Block protests. Many, if not all, of the protests ended in violent confrontation with the RUC and British army and Maskey was often bloodied and bruised as a consequence. Even though he knew Bobby Sands and was close friends with Kieran Doherty and Joe McDonnell, the other two Belfast men who were also to die on hunger strike, he could not bring himself to support the new electoral plan.

"Political agitation and protests which people could understand was okay as far as they went," says Maskey. "But I couldn't bring myself to take part in an election campaign because, as a republican, I just didn't believe that it was the legitimate thing to do. That was in no way taking away from the lads on hunger strike. It was simply that I was opposed to going into, or taking part in, any British institutions. I just wasn't comfortable with the movement taking part in elections and I wasn't alone in thinking this way. It would have been the standard feeling within republicanism at that time. It was firmly fixed in my mind that constitutional politics was the wrong way to go."

Ironically, Maskey was one of just a handful of republicans with any first hand experience of fighting an election. At the behest of prominent Belfast nationalist, Paddy Devlin, a teenaged Maskey had worked on the campaign for the Northern Ireland Labour Party candidate Martin McBirney in 1964 in the Docks ward. Devlin did not know it then but the teenager handing out ballot papers to nationalist voters would later become one of his fiercest opponents in Belfast City Hall.

While not prepared to take part in the electoral strategy, Maskey was still heavily involved in the overall drive to rally support for the hunger-strikers. On April 9, the day of the Fermanagh-South Tyrone election result, he was below decks on a cargo ship in Galway Harbour trying to convince dockworkers to support the prisoners by taking part in a national strike. Late that night, as he was driving back from the west of Ireland to Belfast, he had a chance encounter that was to have a dramatic impact on his future.

Unknown to Maskey, 30,492 nationalists had voted for Bobby Sands giving him a 1,446 majority over Harry West. Republicans saw Sands' victory as an overwhelming public vindication of the prisoners' protest. Many came to the conclusion that Margaret Thatcher could not allow a fellow MP to die and would be forced to negotiate with the prisoners.

Jim Gibney recalls sitting in a house on the Falls Road with a senior republican on the night of Sands' election victory.

"When news that we had won came in, I remember this person saying that Bobby's victory was worth ten bombs in London."

Maskey says the memory of the night of Sands' win remains vivid in his mind.

"I can still remember trying to concentrate as I drove this tiny Allegro car along those narrow country roads. I had no radio and was trying to get home before dark when I unexpectedly ran into this victory cavalcade. It was only when I saw the tricolours hanging out of the cars that I realised that Bobby had done it. The people of

43

Fermanagh-South Tyrone had elected him as their MP and he had beaten the might of the British establishment.

"Any remaining doubts I had in my head about the rights and wrongs of the electoral strategy disappeared that night. Instead I felt guilty for not being involved in Bobby's campaign. His victory was a seminal moment for me. It proved to me that the electoral politics was another tool which could be used to expand the movement and to disprove the British propaganda that republicans had no support within the nationalist community. The 30,000 people who came out and voted for Bobby couldn't be wrong."

Maskey did not know it then but Sands' success was to lead to a dramatic change in his own personal circumstances. However, those who believed that Margaret Thatcher would be swayed by Bobby Sands' victory seriously miscalculated the British prime minister's personal determination not to bow to either republican or international pressure. Some later came to the conclusion that at least part of Thatcher's resolve was steeled by the fact that her closest aide and shadow Northern Ireland spokesman, Airey Neave, had been blown up by the Irish National Liberation Army (INLA) in March 1979. For Thatcher the battle with the hunger-strikers was personal.

While secret talks did take place between republicans and the British government, Thatcher refused to allow herself to be seen as publicly negotiating with the prisoners. As the protest grew to a climax, the hunger-strikers let it be known through secret channels that they were willing to compromise if the British were prepared to be reasonable. But for Thatcher it was all or nothing.

After 66 days on hunger strike, Bobby Sands died in his sleep on May 5 at just 27 years of age. Maskey remembers receiving the news of Sands' death.

"We were sitting in my house in West Belfast, just waiting for the news that we knew was going to come. I remember the phone call and everyone in the room just went numb. You felt like you were boiling up inside. You were so frustrated and angry that you just wanted to bang your head against the wall. You just couldn't believe that the British government had let Bobby die."

Margaret Thatcher and her administration came in for widespread condemnation around the globe. Days later, more than 100,000 people took part in the IRA man's funeral as it wound its way through West Belfast. It was, and remains, the largest show of nationalist strength in the history of the state.

Despite the huge groundswell of public sympathy, the IRA leadership continued their attempts to persuade the prisoners to call off the fast. Prior to Sands' death, the Army Council had informed inmates that no one should join the fast in the event that any of the hunger-strikers died. The prisoners were furious, arguing that if no one took the dead man's place, Thatcher would claim to have won.

A week after Bobby Sands' death, Francis Hughes from Bellaghy in South Derry became the second hunger-striker to die. Hughes had achieved almost mythical status within the IRA and, as in Sands' case, widespread rioting followed the announcement of his death.

Eventually, the prisoners and the IRA leadership came to an agreement and a fortnight later Maskey's friend Kieran Doherty joined the hunger strike.

"I knew Kieran and Joe McDonnell very well from the outside and the fact that they had joined the hunger strike was very personal for me. They were two great lads but so different. Kieran was a very sensible guy who, for me, epitomised traditional republicanism. Joe on the other hand loved nothing better than a laugh. He was a real character and revelled in devilment. Looking back now, Joe and Kieran were like chalk and cheese but they were two of the best republicans you could hope to meet.

"The one thing that showed me that the blanket men would not be defeated was the fact that Joe would not even take visits to see his wife Goretti and his kids because it would have meant putting on the criminal's uniform. Joe loved his family dearly but to put on that uniform was just too much. That was the level of sacrifice they were prepared to endure."

On May 21, in the midst of the turmoil taking place both inside and outside the H-Blocks, local council elections were held throughout the North. While republican strategists were well aware that they could have scored more electoral victories by standing candidates, it was decided that Sinn Féin would not contest any seats. Jim Gibney admits that the elections, held within weeks of the deaths of Bobby Sands and Frank Hughes, were "just too soon for republicans".

"We were still in the middle of a hunger strike. Bobby and Frank had just died and the belief was that, while Fermanagh-South Tyrone was a morale booster, to take the decision to go into state politics was a step too far. If the elections had been a year later we would have had time to look at the bigger picture but it was just too soon."

Other republicans, however, did fight the elections on an anti-H-Block ticket. Five republican candidates were elected to Belfast City Council. The left-wing People's Democracy picked up two seats in Belfast with one candidate, Fergus O'Hare, taking a seat from Gerry Fitt in his North Belfast heartland. Fitt, formerly one of the most popular politicians in the North, had been vocal in his opposition to the hunger-strikers, a significant factor in his vote being slashed to just 500.

The Irish Republican Socialist Party (IRSP), the political wing of the INLA, also took two seats in West Belfast. Independent community candidate, Larry Kennedy, picked up a fifth seat in the staunchly republican Ardoyne area in the north of the city. While the five were the first advocates of republicanism elected to Belfast's City Hall since 1921, they refused to take their seats as a gesture of support for the hunger-strikers.

The day after the election result, 24 year-old Raymond McCreesh (IRA) and 23 year-old Patsy O'Hara (INLA) died after 61 days without food. A sign of support shifting towards the prisoners was seen when Cardinal Tomás Ó Fiaich openly criticised the British government's attitude to the protest.

In June, hunger-strikers Paddy Agnew and Kieran Doherty contested elections to the Dublin parliament and won seats in the Cavan-Monaghan and Louth constituencies. Again it was on the understanding that the victory was aimed at highlighting the prison protest. On August 20, Owen Carron succeeded Bobby Sands as MP for Fermanagh-South Tyrone defeating Ulster Unionist Ken Maginnis. Carron, a Sinn Féin activist who had been Sands' election agent in the April by-election, increased the anti-H-Block votes by 786.

As the summer months wore on six more men, Joe McDonnell (30), Martin Hurson (27), Kieran Doherty (25), Kevin Lynch (25) Tom McElwee (23) and Mickey Devine (27) were to die. Maskey remembers the sense of pain and anger as he carried the tricolour-draped coffins of his friends.

"We were literally numb with anger at what the British government had done to the prisoners. I think Thatcher seriously miscalculated the effect that letting the ten lads die on hunger strike would have on the nationalist community. A generation later and still nationalists have not forgotten what was done to those men."

Eventually, the fast was ended on October 3 after prisoners' families gave permission for the authorities to intervene and provide medical attention once the hunger-strikers slipped into comas. It was a bitter irony that the prisoners' battle with the British was ended as a result of the compassion of their families.

Three days later, Secretary of State Jim Prior announced a series of changes to the way in which the H-Blocks were to be run. Prisoners would wear their own clothes at all times and there would be a 50 percent cut in remission lost by republicans during the protests. They would be given more visits and be allowed access to adjacent wings of the H-Blocks. The issue of work was also to be reviewed so that prisoners who took part in education classes were regarded as being "at work".

With ten hunger-strikers dead and a total of 43 people killed on the streets during the protest, neither side was claiming victory. What was clear to everyone, however, was that Bobby Sands and the prison protest had opened up a new front in the "war" where battles would be fought from then on.

Just days after the hunger strike ended, one of the five candidates elected to Belfast City Council on the anti-H-Block ticket was murdered. Like the other protesting candidates, Larry Kennedy had intended taking his seat in the City Hall once the fast had finished.

The 35-year-old community worker was shot dead by UFF gunmen as he left the Shamrock Social Club in Ardoyne on October 8, 1981. Kennedy had gone to the club to buy cigarettes and was the victim of a random loyalist gun attack. He had been a councillor for just five months and had not yet had the opportunity to see the inside of the council chamber.

It was traditional when a councillor died to co-opt a nominee as their replacement, thereby avoiding the expense of a by-election. Unionists, however, objected to the co-option of Jim Weir, a friend of the murdered councillor. Alliance councillor, Will Glendenning, who was no friend to republicans, castigated unionists for their behaviour.

"This refusal by the DUP, backed by the leader of the Official Unionist grouping, not to allow Mr Weir to be co-opted means that gunmen have succeeded in altering the make up of Belfast City Council by murdering Councillor Kennedy," Glendenning said.

While the Adams camp had argued the need for republicans to establish an alternative to state politics, Sands' victory had shown they could deal a more devastating blow to their political foes at the ballot box. The armed struggle would take primacy for the next 15 years but the seed of electoralism had been sown.

Sinn Féin's annual Ard Fheis took place in Dublin's Mansion House on October 31, just weeks after the hunger strike was ended. Jim Gibney remembers the occasion with mixed emotions.

"We had lost comrades and friends, but out of the tragedies had come a new weapon which the state parties feared most – a republican mandate. Because of these two things it was a difficult Ard Fheis for everyone."

But it was a speech by Adams' close aide Danny Morrison – who was attempting to reassure the grassroots that a turn towards electoral politics was not selling out the armed struggle – which was to crystallise the next generation for republicans.

"Who here really believes that we can win the war through the ballot box?" Morrison asked a rapt audience. "But will anyone here object if, with a ballot paper in this hand and an Armalite in this hand, we take power in Ireland?"

While Morrison admits creating the phrase on the spur of the moment, the thinking behind it had been hammered out during the previous weeks and months in the back kitchens of Belfast and Derry, where the majority of republican policy was devised.

By the end of 1981, the republican leadership had come to the conclusion that, despite mass support for the prisoners, they had still been unable to influence substantial sections of the Irish and British establishment. Strategists concluded that the armed struggle needed to be supported by a more subtle attack on the political pillars that held up the Northern state. While Morrison's "ballot box and Armalite" speech captured all the newspaper headlines, lost in the column inches was a new Sinn Féin policy. Whereas republicans would continue the abstention policy when it came to the Dail, Westminster and any Stormont Assembly, the party would now stand candidates in future council elections and take their seats if successful.

As one of the growing number of converts to the "ballot box and Armalite" strategy, as it was to become known, Maskey was included in the ranks of those trusted comrades tasked with persuading the grassroots that taking part in elections was not selling out the republican ideal.

"There was quite a lot of debate within the movement at that stage about an electoral strategy," he explains. "I took part in the debate and supported the changes wholeheartedly and, probably just as importantly, worked to defend them and get them adopted within Sinn Féin and the wider republican family."

The new generation of "politicised" republicans were to become the foot soldiers of a rapidly growing Sinn Féin. Prior to 1981, many had seen the party as something of an irrelevance while their time was taken up with the armed struggle and street protests. While the prime motive for the electoral strategy was to broaden the struggle, a second was to tackle the repeated claim that republicans had no mandate from the nationalist community for its actions. The battle was now on to develop a political machine and mandate which the governments and unionists simply could not ignore.

Alex Maskey outlines the philosophy that now permeated down

through the ranks.

"I have always believed that armed struggle is a rather exclusive activity. By its very nature, only a relatively small number of people can be involved in it. There needed to be something bigger. When the band starts to play, there's always a bigger audience. We had to find a part for everyone to play."

While the electoral successes achieved during the hunger strikes had given a new momentum to republicans, there was still a realisation that the new assault on the political front would be long and difficult.

Maskey was one of a small number of influential republicans who were brought together around this period to draw up the new strategy. The group, which was dubbed the "Falls Road Think Tank", was made up of Gerry Adams, Danny Morrison, Derry's Martin McGuinness, Richard McAuley and Donegal's Pat Doherty. Also included were Tom Hartley and Joe Austin, both of whom were to follow Maskey into Belfast's City Hall. Others were later brought into the Think Tank but the nucleus remained largely unchanged. From 1981, the small group busied itself with widening the republican support base, fighting to retain the radical nature of Sinn Féin and countering criticism that the party was allowing itself to be "bought off by the Brits".

By the beginning of 1982, the public face of the new Sinn Féin machine was well established. Adams, McGuinness and Morrison were the frontline voices whose role was to articulate the movement's new electoral policy. All three stood in the October assembly elections of that year which the party contested on an abstentionist ticket. Republicans had no intention of taking any seats they might win but the assembly elections taught Sinn Féin valuable lessons in the subtlety of politics. The party had initially called on nationalists to ignore the elections but when the SDLP said it would participate in the poll but boycott the assembly itself, republicans followed suit. The decision was to prove fortuitous. The party was now fighting against the larger SDLP for the hearts and minds of the nationalist community and many Catholics took the opportunity to vote for the new Sinn Féin alternative.

Republicans fielded twelve candidates with Maskey chosen as

running mate to Gerry Adams in West Belfast. Sinn Féin was quietly confident that Adams, McGuinness and Morrison would win seats. In fact, the party won five in total with Owen Carron in Fermanagh-South Tyrone and Jim McAllister in Newry-Armagh also being elected.

There was, however, an acknowledgement that the party desperately needed to develop a new tier of "middle management" to fight the day-to-day battles in the North's 26 council chambers. While the morale of republicans had been boosted by the ten per cent of the vote achieved in their first real election campaign, they also learned a harsh reality: although Sinn Féin had won five seats, the Alliance Party received less first preference votes yet garnered ten seats. Under the North's system of proportional representation, Sinn Féin candidates could top the poll on the first count but because other parties refused to transfer votes to them, they were often overtaken in successive rounds.

Maskey admits that the fledging restructured Sinn Féin was sailing in uncharted waters and missed out on a number of seats because they had not realised the full strength of their vote. The party's political naivety meant he lost out on a second seat in West Belfast, by just 244 votes, to Alliance's Will Glendenning. In North Belfast, the subtle nuances of the proportional representation system of voting was displayed even more starkly. After the initial count, Sinn Féin's Joe Austin picked up 4,029 first preference votes while Alliance's Paul Maguire bagged 2,527. By the fourteenth count, Maguire had picked up a further 2,230 transfers and Austin only 544. The Alliance candidate eventually took the seat ahead of Austin by just 184 votes.

While Maskey was content to be Gerry Adams' running mate, he readily agrees that he had no expectations of being elected.

"We were confident about doing well in the assembly elections but we couldn't be overly confident. We had to test the vote. We did this on the understanding that, come future elections, I would be a candidate. Because we were cautious we probably failed to take second seats in Fermanagh-South Tyrone and West Belfast. We weren't sure we were capable of winning second seats when, in actual fact, the results showed that we could have.

"But we weren't ready to take that risk. Owen Carron was an MP and Gerry Adams was a party leader so we weren't going to put that in jeopardy. When it came to the electoral strategy it was one step at a time. Defeat at that stage was too much of a danger to the future building of the party."

By 1982, Gerry Adams was a national figure but Alex Maskey was relatively unheard of outside republican circles. Tom Hartley explains why the little-known Maskey was chosen to become a public face for republicans: "There was already a well-established leadership in place but there was a realisation that there needed to be a second tier. Sinn Féin still had the abstention policy against the Dail, Westminster and whatever Stormont assemblies the Brits would come up with from time to time. But we had taken the decision that, to be able to build the party, we needed to go into council chambers and take on the unionists and the SDLP. That meant going in and working the system but on our terms."

The individuals tasked with doing this were carefully chosen. The new "middle management" had to be trusted not only by the party but, more importantly, by the IRA. Those who were to go into the council chambers had to have a proven track record within the movement and had to be relied upon to carry out difficult and dangerous work.

"We needed people who were confident, could think on their feet and, probably more importantly, were prepared to take the serious pressure which they would inevitably come under," says Hartley. "These would be the first republicans that unionists and the Brits would ever have come face-to-face with on a daily basis. It was obvious that the loyalists and the Brits were going to try to knock us out at the first stage by destroying or killing whoever was chosen to go into the councils. This was a serious job which needed serious people. Alex Maskey personified what was needed for the job."

While the North Belfast docker agreed to be the first Sinn Féin representative to enter Belfast's council chamber, he was also aware that the decision to become the public face of republicanism in the stronghold of unionism would make him a target for not only loyalists but also the state and its covert agencies.

The warning that he would now be viewed as a "legitimate target" was no empty threat. In October 1976, mother-of-five and Sinn Féin vice-president Máire Drumm (57), was shot dead by UFF gunmen in her North Belfast hospital bed where she was awaiting a cataract operation.

In June 1980, former Irish Independence Party founding member, John Turnly, who was also a member of the National H-Block Committee, was shot dead in front of his wife and two sons in Carnlough, County Antrim.

Later that month, university lecturer and former IRSP leader Miriam Daly was shot dead in her Andersonstown Road home. Nationalists believed that the 45-year-old Daly, another member of the National H-Block Committee, was murdered by operatives of the British army's covert Special Air Service (SAS).

In October that same year, Ronnie Bunting and Noel Lyttle were shot dead in Bunting's home in West Belfast. Because of the military nature of the murders, nationalists again pointed the finger of blame at the SAS. Like Miriam Daly, Bunting and Lyttle had been members of the IRSP and the National H-Block Committee

On February 16, 1981, the prominent socialist republican Bernadette McAliskey and her husband were shot and seriously wounded after UFF gunmen burst into their isolated farmhouse outside Coalisland, County Tyrone. Soldiers of an undercover British army unit, who had been covertly observing the McAliskey home, arrested the gunmen as they emerged from the premises after shooting the couple.

Maskey was under no illusion about the personal dangers that lay ahead of him when he assumed the role which was to make him one of the leading hate figures for Northern Ireland's loyalists.

"When I agreed to become a public figure, I told my family I would be fighting elections as a Sinn Féin candidate and that would inevitably draw public attention on myself and the family as a whole. It was okay me deciding that I was going to put myself in the firing line but I knew there was a danger that the rest of the family would also become targets. To be fair to my family, they were all very good about it and said I should do what I thought was right."

In June 1983, republicans were on a high after Gerry Adams unseated Gerry Fitt to become the MP for West Belfast, beating the former SDLP leader by 5,000 votes. While Maskey had stood as Adams' running mate in the previous year's assembly elections, he was not expected to stand again until the local council elections in 1985. The idea was that, if elected, Maskey would have had the protection of entering Belfast City Hall alongside other Sinn Féin councillors. However, the unexpected resignation of IRSP councillor Gerry Kelly in early 1983 brought the planned assault on the council forward by two years. A subsequent Sinn Féin election convention confirmed Maskey as the party's candidate.

"When Gerry Kelly resigned his seat, it was already taken as read that I would be the one to stand," Maskey says. "I had committed myself to going into City Hall and now I had to do it."

The motion for the June 29 by-election was put forward by People's Democracy councillor, Fergus O'Hare. Maskey picked up 7,858 first preference votes, just under 50 percent of the entire poll, to become councillor for Belfast's D Ward. The size of the majority meant Maskey was not to suffer from Sinn Féin's traditional Achilles heel of losing out to rival parties through lack of transfers. The new councillor was elected on the second count with a tally of 8,163 votes while SDLP candidate Tom Partland took second place with 6,831.

Speaking on behalf of Alliance candidate, Dan McGuinness – who had failed to turn up for the announcement of the results after receiving only 846 votes – colleague Will Glendenning admitted his party had been disappointed "that once again a party that supported violence had been elected".

However, the Alliance assemblyman warned: "Members of the unionist community should realise that if they continue to offer nothing to the minority this trend is likely to continue."

In a side-swipe at Sinn Féin's abstentionist policy, the SDLP's Joe Hendron said he "welcomed any elected representative who chose to take his seat". The West Belfast doctor nonetheless predicted that the Sinn Féin victory would "make little if any difference to political life" in the City Hall.

Challenged after the by-election count as to why he had chosen to take his council seat when Gerry Adams would not take his seat in Westminster, Maskey retorted: "There's no way even 17 nationalist MPs would bring about changes in the House of Commons. The City Hall has for far too long been the bastion of loyalism with a terribly cosy relationship between the SDLP, Alliance and the unionist parties."

Posting notice that Sinn Féin intended to be in City Hall on a permanent basis, Maskey told reporters: "We have stated before that, since the assembly elections, electoral politics in the British-occupied six counties will never be the same again. Those who have derided our electoral support in the past will ignore at their peril the trend towards Sinn Féin among anti-unionist voters."

Contrary to popular belief, Maskey was not the first member of Sinn Féin to take a council seat during the Troubles. That small footnote in republican history belongs to Carrickmore schoolteacher, Seamus Kerr, who beat the North Belfast boxer to the punch when he won a by-election to Omagh District Council three months earlier. Maskey, for his part, had more to worry about than losing a small place in northern political history. Within days of being elected, he had to face his first council meeting.

Newly-elected councillors in Liverpool, London or Dublin had only to worry about what suit and tie to wear for their first appearance in the chamber. Alex Maskey was more concerned with searching West Belfast for a protective vest.

On the evening of July 5, 1983, Belfast's newest councillor entered the City Hall. If he had been a member of any other party, Maskey could have brought his wife and children to witness his first steps into constitutional politics. For his inaugural council meeting, however, he was informed that it would be unsafe to have his family travel with him.

"It had already been decided that I would be brought to the meeting by some of our security people. At that stage the party had only one car with bullet-proof glass and it was commandeered for the night.

By no means were these bullet-proof windows state-of-the-art and we had no guarantees that they would save us if someone started shooting but it was better than nothing."

While Maskey may have joked about the reliability of the security measures taken to protect him, others within his party let him know in no uncertain terms that his safety on the journey into the city centre could not be guaranteed. Belfast City Hall had long been used as the venue for various election counts and republicans had regularly come into physical confrontation with loyalists, unionists and the RUC.

"I knew it wasn't going to be a sea of tranquillity when I turned up on the first night to take my seat but even I wasn't expecting it to be so bad," he recalls.

It had been agreed earlier that Maskey would take his seat and, on the first opportunity to speak, make a prepared statement before leaving immediately. Having arrived in relative safety, he first met the army of reporters and photographers there to see what the night would bring. As the novice Sinn Féin representative entered the council chamber, he was met with a chorus of jeers and boos from unionist councillors.

The next day's newspapers recorded a palpable sense of tension emanating from the unionist benches and public gallery when it became clear that Maskey had not only slaughtered the sacred cow by entering the chamber but was now also intent on addressing the assembled representatives.

Following his party's advice to the letter, he chose to speak during a debate on the groundbreaking issue of grant funding for the Ulster Orchestra. He raised his hand, signalling to Ulster Unionist Lord Mayor, Alfie Ferguson, that he wished to comment on the issue. As he rose to his feet, the room fell hushed. To unionist amazement, it appeared that the "Provo Pariah" now expected them to listen as he spoke. Caught in a quandary, Ferguson gave way and permitted Maskey to make his maiden address. As the former internee began to read from his prepared speech, the first few sentences of which were in Irish, unionists went into an uproar of heckling and stamping of feet.

Ignoring repeated requests from the Lord Mayor to sit down, Maskey told his irate audience that, while he was the first member of Sinn Féin to sit in the council, he was nonetheless "fully prepared to work alongside unionists". With that he left the chamber labelling it "a bit of a sham". His views on funding for the violinists and flautists of Northern Ireland's premier orchestra had been lost in the catcalls from the unionist benches.

Standing beneath the City Hall's imposing dome, an exuberant Maskey gave his verdict on his first experience of council politics to the assembled media: "Before I could open my mouth, they were shouting and jeering."

Asked if he was concerned at the uproar that his few sentences in Irish had caused on the unionist benches, Maskey retorted: "If I had been speaking in English, they would have done the same thing."

SDLP councillor Brian Feeney, who was to become one of Maskey's toughest sparring partners in the council chamber, recalls unionist reaction to the Sinn Féin councillor's inaugural meeting.

"Unionists gazed at him in horror. They had never seen a republican up close and the sight was more frightening than their worst nightmare."

Looking back on his first night in City Hall, Maskey remembers: "The unionists seemed to be in total shock when I walked into the chamber for the first time. They couldn't fathom that I was there. What I couldn't fathom is that they were so surprised that I had turned up. I had said through the election that I would take my seat and intended treating this job with the utmost seriousness. At one stage, they actually protested to the Mayor that I was even in the chamber. These were intelligent people who had been told repeatedly that I was going into City Hall and that I wasn't going to be scared away."

So it was that the new battle lines in the City Hall were drawn. From that point on, Sinn Féin would have a voice in the building that had, over the decades, epitomised loyalism. But while unionists were forced to accept a republican presence in their citadel, in the form of a solitary Belfast docker, they were determined that his ordeal would not end with this baptism of fire. Maskey would continue to feel their displeasure until he admitted defeat, they reasoned.

Just like the battle between Margaret Thatcher and the blanket men, there was a belief amongst unionists that, if they could break Maskey, they could smother the republican attempt to open up a second political front in its infancy. With little hope of any other Sinn Féin councillors joining him until the next council elections two years away, Maskey was aware he was going to have to brave it out as he sat alone on the opposition benches.

He may not have known it, but the battle to break his will was about to intensify dramatically – and it wasn't just the unionists who were determined that to cut short his stay in City Hall.

Loyalists would later say that when Alex Maskey walked into the maelstrom of local government that July evening, he not only became the first Sinn Féiner to enter Belfast's council chamber for 70 years – he also moved into the category of people they most wanted to kill.

CHAPTER THREE

A VOLCANO ERUPTS IN CITY HALL

T HE morning after his stormy first council meeting, Alex
Maskey walked back into City Hall for an appointment with the
town clerk Cecil Ward. Once again, he travelled to town wearing a
protective vest and was accompanied by three minders. Because of
the threat of loyalist attack, he knew that he would have to get used to
varying the timing and route of his journey to the offices. Council
and committee meetings were always at pre-arranged times and the
danger remained constant.

"I had gone to see Cecil Ward so that he could explain the council's
procedures to me," Maskey says. "I had become an elected councillor
but, because we had no real history in day-to-day politics, I didn't
actually know what really went on. I went into City Hall that morning
to start learning the ropes."

As he entered the marble foyer under the imposing dome,
firebrand veteran unionist Frank Millar Sr unexpectedly confronted
him. The Shankill councillor would later become infamous for, among
other things, branding Nelson Mandela a "Black Provo". Indeed, when
nationalists in turn sarcastically labelled Millar "Super Prod", he
accepted the nickname as a compliment.

The altercation that ensued was the first of many verbal exchanges
between Maskey and the 40 or so unionist councillors who opposed
him on Belfast council, all of whom he believed were determined to
break his political will.

"As I walked into the foyer, Frank Millar was on the marble staircase
which leads to the first floor and the council chamber. When Millar
spotted me, he started hurling abuse about what he was going to do
and what was in store for me. I was very conscious that it was my first
day and that I was there to do a serious job of work. At the same time,
I wanted to lay down a marker that I wasn't going to be pushed around
by anyone."

On the spur of the moment, Maskey bounded up the staircase and confronted the startled councillor. However, the former champion boxer refuses to reveal the precise detail of the exchange that followed.

"All I will say is that I advised Frank Millar that if he had any thoughts about anything other than dialogue, he was picking on the wrong man. Frank might have worked in the shipyards but I think he knew there was only going to be one winner on this particular occasion and it wasn't going to be him."

Ironically, Frank Millar Sr had a friendly relationship with Alex Maskey Sr. The pair had known each other for many years in North Belfast.

It was not the last time the republican and the unionist would "butt heads" both inside and outside the chamber. With the first confrontation of the day dealt with, Maskey proceeded to his appointment with Cecil Ward. He asked the town clerk to deliver a message to the other parties on the council: he was in City Hall to work and was not looking for trouble. However, it was also to be made crystal clear that he was not prepared to be become a whipping boy for unionists.

Maskey recalls that, nearly a decade later, Ward privately admitted to him that he had recognised that City Hall politics had changed forever on that first day.

"I was in Belfast City Hall to stay and I would be playing a full part in every aspect of the council. Cecil Ward was perceptive enough to know that, once Sinn Féin arrived, things were never going to be the same again. He told me he realised the day I entered City Hall that local government, as unionists had known it, was going to become a thing of the past. He knew they were going to have huge problems dealing with this simple fact. I assured him that I wasn't there to threaten anyone but we both knew that, for unionists, the issue of my being there was a volcano which was always going to erupt."

While unionists would hold the majority on the council for the next 15 years, the sand in the political egg timer had already begun to slip away. In 1981, the four republican councillors from the People's

Democracy and the IRSP had entered City Hall on an anti-H-Block protest vote but had little or no real interest in taking part in the day-to-day running of the council. They had managed to get their collective foot in the chamber door but showed little concern for pushing it open any further. For their part, republicans had been content to abstain from state politics during the previous 14 years. With Maskey's election, however, Sinn Féin signalled that it was not only entering the unionist-dominated chamber but was determined to get a piece of the action.

The vast majority of the North's 26 councils had traditionally been controlled by unionists due to the fact that republicans had opted to leave the political stage, even at local government level, to the moderate nationalist SDLP while they "got on with the war". Buoyed by Bobby Sands' Fermanagh-South Tyrone victory and the 1982 assembly elections, Sinn Féin strategists now saw the advantages of a political mandate in terms of forcing the British government and the unionists to deal with them face-to-face.

Maskey's election was important on two levels. First, it publicly flagged up his party's mandate from nationalist voters, which their opponents had long argued they could never achieve. Second, Belfast City Council was, by default, the biggest political platform available for all the northern parties. The fact that successive British administrations had tried and failed to establish institutions at Stormont meant that local government in Northern Ireland had an exaggerated importance. Unlike their counterparts in Britain and the Republic, there were no institutions open to northern politicians other than Westminster and the European Parliament. An assembly had been formed by the then Secretary of State, Jim Prior, but it was boycotted by Sinn Féin and the SDLP and quickly degenerated into a unionist talking shop. The 26 council chambers, therefore, provided an opportunity for the various parties to flex their political muscle and allowed them to justify their existence.

Northern Ireland had 17 MPs at Westminster and three MEPs in the European Parliament. The consequence of this was that there were always many more prospective politicians than there were available seats. As the first city of the state, therefore, Belfast's council took on an added significance in the municipal life of the region.

After Maskey's election, all of the parties were gearing up for the inevitable fireworks that were to come. He was well aware that his new role as the only Sinn Féin representative on the council would have an impact way beyond the marble walls of City Hall.

Unionist opposition to the "Provo Pariah" who now sat amongst them was not solely based on their much-publicised antipathy to anything and everything that didn't conform to their viewpoint. The ex-docker's time in City Hall coincided with a period in which the IRA was escalating its campaign of attacking "economic targets" across the North, especially in Belfast's city centre. Throughout the 1980s, car bomb after car bomb exploded in the heart of Belfast in a bid to show the outside world that the city was not as "British as Finchley", as Margaret Thatcher had claimed. This provided unionists with ample ammunition to use against Sinn Féin. Subsequently, Maskey was to be cold-shouldered by his council colleagues for the duration of these attacks and continues to be shunned by some to the present day.

Initially, unionist attempts to isolate the new and unwelcome member bore all the hallmarks of schoolboyish behaviour. Each of the 51 councillors were entitled to use a common room where they could carry out constituency work or, more often than not, simply meet for a cup of tea. Maskey soon discovered that, when he walked into the room, the DUP and Ulster Unionist Party (UUP) councillors would automatically get up and leave. He laughed off this snub, concluding that it merely handed him an effective veto on the use of the room whenever he wanted. If unionists wished to voluntarily bar themselves from such facilities, then so be it.

But it was not only the unionist parties who were concerned at Maskey's unexpected arrival in City Hall. SDLP councillors knew that, while he was on his own in 1983, by the time full council elections came around two years later, the story was likely to be very different. The moderate nationalist party had a 15-year head start on their republican rivals in the battle for the hearts and minds of Catholic voters. They were well aware that the newly developed Sinn Féin political machine, although virtually untested, had a huge head of steam building up behind it. John Hume's party had a wealth of political experience to draw from but they were becoming increasingly concerned at the apparently unstoppable momentum of Sinn Féin's progress. Some SDLP councillors were simply perplexed that the relative tranquillity of the status quo in City Hall was about to be hit by the republican cyclone.

While a number of SDLP councillors, namely Brian Feeney and Joe Hendron, were prepared to mix it with their political opponents on the floor of the council chamber, unionists were content for the most part to tolerate moderate nationalists, safe in the knowledge that their overall majority guaranteed total control.

"The SDLP was a mixed bunch," recalls Maskey. "Some would speak to you, others would shun you. I wasn't really concerned if someone refused to talk to me. I would have preferred if people were prepared to work with me rather than against me but I knew I was primarily there to learn how things worked and to prepare the ground for 1985. If we had our calculations right that was when the political floodgates would be breached for the first time."

If he thought that his electoral mandate from the West Belfast voters meant that he was going to be entitled to a share of power in the council, Maskey was to learn very quickly that this would not be the case. Unionists used their overall majority to block the SDLP, Alliance and independent councillors from all but the most irrelevant of committees. Non-unionists might be tolerated in the inner sanctum of local government but sharing political power was not on the agenda. Even when there was a blip in the "unionist-take-all" policy, the DUP-UUP monopoly had a built-in safeguard: any "faulty" decisions could simply be overturned at the following full council meeting where their overwhelming majority meant that any "mistakes" were duly corrected.

Maskey was soon at the sharp end of the *real-politik*, City Hall-style. In the autumn of 1983, the innocuous Community Services Committee appointed him as its representative to the governing board of Community Technical Aid. This was a body that advised community groups throughout the city. At the same meeting People's Democracy (PD) councillor John McAnulty was voted onto the steering committee of the Citizens Advice Bureau. The two nationalists had managed to "sneak" into their respective positions because unionist committee members had left the meeting early, entrusting the other members to deal with the remaining appointments on the agenda. Convinced that everyone was aware of the unwritten rule that neither Maskey nor PD councillors were entitled to represent City Hall on outside bodies, unionists had departed, confident that the status quo would be maintained.

The DUP-UUP hierarchy flew into a rage when they realised what had happened. Maskey and McAnulty representing the council, no matter at how irrelevant a position, was a public embarrassment that unionists were not prepared to accept. The Sinn Féin and PD councillors' new appointments were first on the agenda at the next full council meeting. The DUP immediately proposed that both nominations be rejected. With a show of hands, Maskey's career as an advisor to Belfast's community groups and John McAnulty's days as a director of the Citizens Advice Bureau were over before they began.

Maskey castigated unionists for the decision. Outside the chamber he told journalists: "These activities show that the unionists feel democracy is fine as long as the correct people, as they judge it, are elected."

Maskey may have felt somewhat downhearted after his first year as an elected representative but, at the beginning of 1984, his party found an unexpected ally in the establishment. Cardinal Tomás Ó Fiaich publicly stated that Catholic voters could be morally justified in joining Sinn Féin if the reason was to work on community issues.

The IRA's campaign was in full flow and other members of the Catholic hierarchy did not share Ó Fiaich's views. The British and Irish governments also distanced themselves from the Cardinal's remarks. Regardless of the criticism Ó Fiaich's statement received, republicans saw it as a welcome endorsement of their political mandate.

For his part, Maskey recalls that the most important lesson learned during that first year as a councillor was to enter and exit City Hall as quickly and quietly as possible. Wearing a protective vest and being accompanied by Sinn Féin security was no guarantee that he would come home alive from his meetings.

"In those days, there was only one way to get into City Hall and that was through the back entrance. You travelled in and out of the council at some risk because it was a perfect place for loyalist attack."

The anxiety over travelling to and from the city centre was well founded. On the afternoon of March 14, 1984, Gerry Adams and future councillor Sean Keenan were shot and seriously wounded in a gun attack on Howard Street less than 100 yards from the City Hall entrance. Adams, Keenan and three others were returning to West Belfast after a court appearance when their car was riddled with bullets fired by UFF gunmen standing at the side of the road. The Sinn Féin president was shot five times and received wounds to the neck, shoulder and chest. Keenan was shot three times with one bullet passing through the back of his head and out through his face. The lives of those in the car were almost certainly saved by the quick thinking of the driver who managed to speed away from the attack, only stopping when he reached the Royal Victoria Hospital a mile away.

Three men were arrested at the scene, reportedly by an off-duty UDR man and two members of the Military Police who had been sitting in an unmarked car parked nearby. In 1985, the attackers were each sentenced to 18 years imprisonment for attempted murder while a fourth was given a twelve-year sentence for driving the would-be getaway car. It was later claimed that the soldiers present were, in fact, members of the British army's shadowy Force Research Unit (FRU). Evidence would later suggest that the soldiers had permitted the gun attack on Adams and the others to take place and only arrested the UFF gang afterwards. These claims would later be borne out by what was to befall Alex Maskey himself.

One of those convicted of the assassination attempt on Adams was John Gregg, who went on to become a leader in the UDA, the parent body of the UFF. Gregg and a colleague were shot dead in a taxi as they left a ferry terminal at Belfast docks in February 2003. Their deaths were the result of an internal feud in the UDA.

The attack on Adams and Keenan was a timely reminder for Maskey and Sean McKnight, who, that same month, had become the second Sinn Féin councillor to be elected to Belfast council. McKnight joined Maskey when he won a West Belfast by-election caused by the expulsion of the IRSP's Sean Flynn who had been unable to attend three successive meetings for security reasons. An attempt had been made on the republican socialist's life during an internal feud within the INLA and IRSP and he was forced to live in Dublin for a period. Local government rules meant that failure to attend three council meetings, in the absence of extenuating circumstances, resulted in automatic de-selection.

McKnight, from the Markets area, was one of the new breed of Sinn Féin politicos who had been drafted in to join the ranks of those willing to put their heads above the political parapet in City Hall. The pair's presence in the council chamber was not always the main bone of contention. Within a month of McKnight's election, a political storm blew up over controversial comments by DUP stalwart George Seawright who called for Catholics and their priests "to be publicly incinerated".

The fiery Shankill councillor's remarks caused uproar during a meeting of the normally sedate Belfast Education and Library Board in May 1984, at which the board had been debating objections by Catholic parents to the playing of *God Save the Queen* at a cross-community schools' concert. Seawright, who had successfully campaigned for a seat in the Stormont assembly in 1982 with the slogan "a Protestant candidate for a Protestant people", had his own form of reprimand for the "ungrateful Catholics who refused to stand for the Queen".

"Taxpayers' money would be better spent on an incinerator and burning the whole lot of them … the priests should be thrown in and burnt as well," he roared in his distinctive Glaswegian accent.

While the DUP leadership attempted to distance itself from the councillor's comments, it did not go unnoticed by nationalists that a few days later Seawright joined party leader Ian Paisley on the Shankill Road during campaigning for elections to the European Parliament.

By the end of the year, the DUP was forced to ditch Seawright when he refused to withdraw his incinerator comments to the council. He was later charged under the Incitement to Hatred Act and received a three months suspended sentence and a £100 fine for his outburst.

Seawright remained as a council member until October 1986 when he was jailed for nine months after an attack on Secretary of State, Tom King, as he made his way into the City Hall at the height of unionist protests against the Anglo-Irish Agreement. Nationalists highlighted the fact that Seawright received only a suspended sentence for advocating the burning of Catholics yet was jailed for "pushing Tom King into a flowerpot".

Ironically, Maskey recalls that George Seawright was the one unionist who was happy to talk to Sinn Féin councillors.

"I remember a debate over where leisure centres should be built in Belfast. One of Seawright's DUP colleagues told him to block funding for a leisure centre in a nationalist area, citing finances. But Seawright was a renegade. He stood up and embarrassed the DUP, saying he would block funding for the leisure centre simply because he didn't want nationalists to get a leisure centre. He said he would prefer to be an honest bigot unlike the rest of his unionist colleagues, who preferred to be secret bigots."

Sean Keenan, who joined Maskey and McKnight in the council chamber in 1985, remembers the Scottish loyalist being equally happy to antagonise unionists as well as his nationalist opponents.

"The first time I met Seawright," says Keenan, "he told me he would happily shoot me dead. Then he said: 'Now we've got that out of the way, how are you doing anyway?'

"The unionists had a policy of not speaking to us but Seawright would actually go out of his way to chat to you in front of them. He once joked to Fergus O'Hare, after they had been ordered out of a meeting together, that they should set up a club for expelled councillors. That was just the man the kind of man he was, a bigot with a sense of humour."

Seawright retired from political life in 1987 after failing to win an assembly seat in North Belfast. In November that same year, he was shot and fatally wounded by the Irish People's Liberation Organisation (IPLO), a republican splinter group, as he sat in a taxi on the Shankill Road. He died from his injuries on December 3.

If the republican councillors had found someone to chat to in George Seawright in 1984, the other unionist councillors were not so talkative. Maskey recalls that, throughout 1984 and the following year, they made repeated attempts to freeze him and Sean McKnight out of life in City Hall.

Standing orders permitted each councillor to sign three guests into the public gallery for the monthly council meeting. Because of the threat of loyalist attack, Maskey and McKnight's guests were always security staff. Unionists' calculations based on voting projections showed that Sinn Féin was likely to take seven seats in the 1985 council elections. That would mean 21 republicans being allowed into the small public gallery. The standing orders were quickly amended so that each councillor was only entitled to sign in one guest.

Unionists also managed to force a motion through, banning Maskey and McKnight from attending any civic function organised by the council. The DUP's Sammy Wilson even attempted to stop the two republicans from using the council's car park at the back of the building.

They were to fare no better when it came to meeting British ministers at the Northern Ireland Office (NIO). If either Maskey or McKnight were part of a delegation due to meet with a government minister, the appointment was duly cancelled. The Sinn Féin duo's argument – that they were elected representatives and were entitled to the same access to NIO ministers as their unionist counterparts – cut little ice. They did, however, manage to have the RUC ejected from council premises around this time.

"The RUC set themselves up in an office at the back doors ... and they logged our movements in and out," Maskey remembers. "Very often, they stopped and searched us, just for the sake of harassment.

On one occasion, they stopped me and hauled me into a room where they tried to arrest me. They only backed off when I threatened to phone my solicitor. I eventually protested to the town clerk and they were removed from City Hall."

In one of the rare lighter moments amid ongoing tension in the council, Maskey recalls that it wasn't always "nationalists against unionists". During the council meeting of September 1984, a bizarre incident took place when PD councillor Fergus O'Hare approached the SDLP benches with a petition condemning the RUC after Andersonstown man Sean Downes was killed by a plastic bullet.

"Fergus approached the SDLP's Cormac Boomer, who was an independent-minded man at the best of times," says Maskey. "Out of the blue, Boomer hauled Fergus over the benches while, at the same time, taking a swing at his own party colleague Paschal O'Hare who had tried to intervene to cool things down.

"While this was happening, Ulster Unionist John Carson came across the chamber and tried to separate the men involved in the melee but, in the middle of the commotion, he managed to slip and fall. The unionists went into uproar thinking that Fergus had floored Carson. The whole thing ended with Fergus O'Hare being hauled out of the meeting by the RUC. If it had been part of a *Carry On* film, it would have been thought too far-fetched to be believed."

It was, however, the ejection of O'Hare's party colleague John McAnulty from the chamber in December 1984 that was to impact on the way council confrontations would be handled in the future. McAnulty found himself thrown out after branding the Union Flag as the "Butcher's Apron" – an old nationalist taunt which suggested that Britain's colonial policy was represented by its flag which they likened to a blue and white-striped apron streaked with blood.

Called upon to withdraw his comments, McAnulty refused and was banned from City Hall until an apology was forthcoming. Insistent that he would not withdraw the comments, McAnulty went to the High Court to challenge the ban.

"The way standing orders are being used at the moment, the unionists can say what language is permissible," McAnulty told reporters. "Insulting references to Catholics or nationalists are ignored or defended. Every opportunity is availed of to belittle nationalists and to hammer home the message that they have no role to play."

The court ruled that the ban on McAnulty taking part in council activities was indeed illegal. The council was ordered to pay the PD representative's £5,000 legal costs.

McAnulty was the first nationalist to use the courts to challenge sectarian policies but Sinn Féin soon came to adopt the strategy as their own and, in subsequent years, would regularly use the courts to force unionists to reverse controversial decisions. In the late 1980s, when the party's use of the strategy was most prevalent, Ulster Unionist councillor Fred Cobain highlighted the irony that republicans, who had traditionally refused to recognise the legitimacy of British courts, were happy to use the judicial system when it came to challenging City Hall policy.

Maskey, who was Sinn Féin leader in the council and frequently encouraged newer Sinn Féin councillors to initiate cases, makes no apology for using British courts to force unionists into line.

"The unionist majority was passing motions which were patently sectarian and the best way to show that these policies were clearly anti-nationalist was through the courts. That was a period when the atmosphere in the council was absolutely venomous. These were businessmen, schoolteachers and barristers but they were filled with such hate and poison. They were constantly taking sectarian decisions. Discrimination was endemic, absolutely systematic, in City Hall. Employment practices were blatantly sectarian. Employees were taking the council to court; ratepayers were doing the same. Even councillors were taking the council to court.

"For us, it was irrelevant that we were using a British court to break down what were bigoted policies. What unionists couldn't take was the fact that it was their own legal system which was showing them up to be bigots and we were prepared to use anything and everything available to us to show them up for what they were. The record of repeated legal judgements against the council backed up what we were saying."

There may have been little sign of consensus in Belfast City Hall but, outside the chamber, people were beginning to talk. In January 1985, there was hope of a breakthrough in the Troubles when SDLP leader John Hume announced he was accepting an invitation to meet the IRA. Hume said he would be urging the republican leadership to end its campaign but he was, nonetheless, heavily criticised by unionists and Fine Gael Taoiseach, Garret Fitzgerald. While Fianna Fail leader Charles Haughey supported the Hume-IRA meeting, Fitzgerald maintained that republicans would use the discussions for propaganda purposes. Little was to come from the talks but a line of contact was established that would bear fruit a decade later.

In May 1985, republicans received a boost when Sinn Féin won 59 council seats, establishing representation on 17 councils. Seamus Kerr, who had been his party's first councillor in the North, was elected chairman of Omagh District Council.

In just two years, Sinn Féin had become the biggest nationalist party in Belfast. Another five colleagues joined Maskey and McKnight in the council chamber while the SDLP retained six seats. The SDLP remained by far the largest nationalist party in the North, having won 102 seats.

The fact that republicans had seized dozens of seats was not lost on the unionists or the British and Irish governments. On the day of the election count in Belfast City Hall, Ian Paisley and Jim Molyneaux signed a unionist pact, pledging a total boycott of all republican councillors. Unionists, the pact proclaimed, would leave their seats every time republicans rose to speak. Furthermore, they would do their utmost to prevent Sinn Féin representatives from holding chairmanships of any committees. A new hard-line slogan, "Smash Sinn Féin", was created for the campaign. Paisley and his party deputy Peter Robinson were photographed at a press conference holding sledgehammers to illustrate their intentions.

At the first meeting of the new council term, the DUP's Rhonda Paisley, daughter of the party founder and leader, produced a toy trumpet which she blew whenever republicans attempted to speak. Party colleague Sammy Wilson proposed that Sinn Féin councillors should be excluded from the councillors' common room and banned from the car park. Chief Executive Cecil Ward was ignored when he warned that such motions were technically illegal

By October, the level of unionist disruption in the chamber led to Sinn Féin issuing a warning that it would cause its own chaos unless steps were taken to ensure that its councillors were allowed to speak.

"Sinn Féin members must take measures to ensure the right to speak," warned Maskey at the time. "The responsibility for the resulting disruption lies with the unionists."

While attempts were being made to marginalise Sinn Féin in the council chambers, the British and Irish governments had been working hard themselves to produce a strategy that would curtail the party's dramatic rise. The result was the signing of the Anglo-Irish Agreement at Hillsborough Castle on November 15, 1985. Republicans later claimed that the Agreement was designed to bolster the SDLP against Sinn Féin's electoral successes but it was unionists who turned out to be its most vociferous opponents. They flew into a collective frenzy, insisting that the Irish government had been handed an "illegal" say in the running of Northern Ireland.

That month, the 18 unionist-controlled local councils, including Belfast's City Hall, voted to adopt a policy of adjournment in protest against the Agreement. The 15 unionist MPs at Westminster resigned their seats, forcing by-elections that, they insisted, would be an unofficial referendum showing the Protestant population's total opposition to the Agreement. The tactic resulted in something of a pyrrhic victory with unionists losing the Newry and Mourne seat to the SDLP.

The unionist majority in City Hall immediately passed a motion suspending all council meetings until the Agreement was scrapped. On November 20, when the Secretary of State Tom King arrived at City Hall, he was physically manhandled by loyalists in the incident that culminated in George Seawright pushing him into a concrete flowerpot.

Three days later, 100,000 people took part in an anti-Agreement rally outside City Hall. Unionist councillors further voted to cut all contact with Northern Ireland ministers in protest against the Agreement. Ironically, by barring government ministers from council property and civic events, they were using the same tactic that had been used against Sinn Féin.

In following weeks, the UUP and DUP stepped things up by refusing to allow any day-to-day council business to take place. With local government threatened with collapse, the situation was brought to a head when unionists refused to permit the holding of a meeting at which the annual rate was due to be struck.

Faced with the scenario of council meetings being adjourned *ad infinitum*, the Alliance Party went to the courts to challenge the adjournment policy. In February 1986, Belfast High Court ordered the council to end its adjournments and remove the huge "Belfast Says No" banner that had been erected, without the required planning permission, at the front of the City Hall. The court also ruled that a rate should be struck for the city no later than midnight on February 15. Undeterred, unionists voted to appeal the decision but promptly lost for the second time. With each unsuccessful court case, the council was faced with a mounting legal bill. The courts were consistently ordering City Hall to meet the Alliance Party's costs as well as its own.

Unimpressed by the wisdom of the courts, unionists continued to adjourn meetings, thereby refusing to strike a rate. Belfast ratepayers were left in the bizarre position of having to foot the legal bill for a unionist-dominated council that repeatedly prevented normal business from operating.

By March 8, a rate had still not been struck. A fortnight later, faced with the complete collapse of the city's infrastructure, NIO Minister Richard Needham announced the appointment of a commissioner who would go into City Hall to set the rate. Needham also sent commissioners into the 17 other unionist councils. Refusing to accept defeat, the unionist bloc adopted a new policy of "deferring business". By June, Ian Paisley was declaring that Northern Ireland was "on the verge of civil war". Later that month, the British government dissolved the Stormont Assembly in near farcical circumstances – unionist members were the sole occupants of the debating chamber when the Alliance Party resigned because of the UUP and DUP's use of the forum to protest against the Agreement.

Undaunted, unionists established their own assembly in City Hall that July. By September, the DUP and UUP leaderships were urging councillors to resign their seats in protest at the Agreement and to force the NIO to appoint commissioners to run the councils on a permanent basis. Splits began to appear in the unionist ranks the following month when, against the wishes of their party leaders, the councillors themselves decided against mass resignations.

By November 1987, Belfast Lord Mayor and DUP councillor Sammy Wilson had banned government ministers from attending the city's annual Remembrance Day service. Ironically, nearly two decades later, it was the DUP who accused Maskey of showing disrespect to those who had died in the First World War by "turning Remembrance Day into a political football" when he became the first republican to lay a wreath at the Cenotaph.

Tension rose by several degrees when, a week later, Wilson appeared with his party leaders Ian Paisley and Peter Robinson on stage at the Ulster Hall for the formation of a new organisation, the Ulster Resistance Movement. The invited audience was told that the paramilitary group had been formed to "take direct action as and when required" to end the Anglo-Irish Agreement.

Nationalist fears that the group had sinister undertones were justified the following year when Ulster Resistance joined forces with the UVF and UDA to import weapons into Northern Ireland from South Africa. The DUP leadership insisted it had already severed its ties with the organisation by the time of the arms shipments.

In February 1987, Belfast City became the latest in a line of councils to be penalised for failing to conduct normal business and was fined £25,000 for refusing to carry out its stated duties. The Local Government Auditor later ruled that unionist councillors should pay the fine. Cracks appeared in the solidarity when, in early May, five Ulster Unionists performed an about-face and voted to resume normal business.

While protests against the Agreement would trundle on in later years, unionists gradually returned to the chambers. Somewhat surprisingly, however, the ban on Northern Ireland Ministers entering City Hall was not lifted until 1991 when Richard Needham became the first government official to visit Belfast council in the six years since the protests against the Anglo-Irish Agreement began.

As 1986 drew to a close, Alex Maskey was to learn that hostile sentiments towards Sinn Féin were not restricted to Belfast, or even Northern Ireland for that matter. In August, he had been summoned to court for taking part in an anti-internment march but the action against him was later dropped. In October, he led a ten-strong delegation of Sinn Féin representatives on a speaking tour of English councils. The trip had been organised by pressure groups including the Troops-Out Movement, Irish In Britain Representation Group and the Labour Committee on Ireland. While supported by prominent Labour Party left-wingers Ken Livingstone, John McDonald, Bernie Grant and Jeremy Corbyn, the trip was widely condemned. Criticism came not only from Ulster Unionists, but also from Conservative (or Tory) and Liberal councillors in Britain. Andersonstown councillor Tish Holland received a death threat as she was due to address the chamber at Leamington-Spa.

When Maskey arrived at Harringay Council's premises, he was met by protestors from four different groups.

"It was quite funny because there were people there to support us. Others were there to protest at our presence. But then there were two other groups outside the council protesting and supporting the Clause Four campaign, which they claimed promoted homosexuality through education. When I got into Harringay Town Hall, I had to use a loudhailer to address the council because the Tories were trying to disrupt the meeting and all the microphones in the hall had been turned off. I remember thinking that the meetings back in Belfast were bad but I'd never had to use a loudhailer just to be heard."

On October 23, Maskey was waiting to address London's Hackney Council when Tory and Liberal councillors walked out of the chamber in protest at his presence. Only one Liberal remained with the Labour

75

councillors to hear the republican's address. Maskey remembers that, as he prepared to make his address, he became convinced that Liberal councillor Pierre Royan was determined to cause a scene.

"I remember pointing this one guy out to the Labour group leader, Andrew Pudephatt. I told Andrew that I was sure this guy was going to pull some stunt when it was my time to speak. I informed him I wouldn't be getting involved in any row and it was up to him to decide which way he wanted to handle it. I remember this guy kept fiddling around with a bag he had in a drawer in front of him. I thought he probably had some eggs to throw at me."

But, as Maskey rose to speak, Pierre Royan pulled a pistol from the bag and fired three shots in his direction. The sound of gunfire sent the chamber into a state of complete pandemonium. Maskey was transfixed, as was his colleague Bairbre de Brún, later to become Minister for Health in the Stormont power-sharing assembly.

"In the middle of the commotion, Royan ran towards Bairbre as he was being chased by the Labour councillors."

They eventually managed to grab Royan and wrestle him to the ground, disarming him in the process. When police arrived, it was discovered that Royan's gun was, in fact, a starting pistol.

"For a split second," says Maskey, "I thought the weapon was real but it was a timely reminder of just how dangerous things were for us."

Journalists would later remark that the Sinn Féin pair "must have been used to such happenings". Royan defended the shooting incident, insisting he had been forced into such "extreme behaviour" by the presence of Maskey and his colleagues. He claimed he had only fired the pistol to stop the republican from addressing the council. When order was restored, Maskey continued with his address.

Outside the chamber, a defiant and unrepentant Royan declared: "If I frightened the Labour Party then that was to good effect."

Security was stepped up around the Sinn Féin delegation in the aftermath of the Hackney incident. The lesson learned was that the threat to Sinn Féin councillors was not restricted to Belfast. Maskey could not afford to let down his guard for an instant. Less than a month later, he was to face a more serious bid on his life – but this time his wife and two young children were also targeted.

On November 21, Maskey was alone in the living room of his home at Gartree Place in the heart of West Belfast. Ironically, the living room windows in the house had been removed that day to allow for reinforced glass to be installed. This was a measure being taken to protect Maskey, his wife and their two young sons – Sean, aged six, and nine-year-old Niall – against loyalist attacks.

With the strengthened glass not due to be fitted until the following morning, Maskey had nailed heavy blankets across the window spaces to shelter the living room from the persistent rain. Shortly after midnight, and now more security-conscious than ever, he was concerned to hear a vehicle pulling up outside the house. He recalls someone getting out of the car and jumping over the garden wall.

Seconds later, two petrol bombs were hurled at the exposed window. The heavy blankets took some of the force but there was enough impetus to carry the firebombs into the living room. The devices shattered on the floor and exploded into flames, setting fire to the curtains and threatening to engulf the room.

"I was sitting in front of the windows," says Maskey, "when the petrol bombs landed on the floor. I managed to get the curtains pulled down and ran up the stairs to get the children out to safety. Luckily, because Liz was not home at the time, I had not yet gone to bed. While I was carrying the boys down the stairs, the flames and smoke were coming through the open door of the living room. If it hadn't been for the neighbours rushing in to help, the house would have been destroyed. Looking back on it now, we were lucky that we weren't asleep in bed because I don't think we would have got out of the house alive."

It was a timely reminder, if indeed one was needed, that the Sinn Féin councillor and his family were under the constant threat of death. Maskey says that the NIO not only refused to provide security for the house after the attack but also turned down the family's claim for compensation for the damage caused to their living room. While the government funded a security programme called the Key Persons

Protection Scheme (KPPS) for important public figures whose lives were at risk, Sinn Féin politicians, unlike their counterparts in other parties, were not permitted to participate. The reason given by officials was that Sinn Féin "was affiliated to the IRA". The issue was to become a running sore that lasted for more than a decade.

A number of Sinn Féin councillors and family members were shot dead in subsequent years with the party claiming the deaths were a direct result of the NIO's refusal to provide even the most basic security measures to protect republicans.

"At that time, we got no help whatsoever from the NIO," Maskey explains. "At least twelve members of Sinn Féin and their families were killed in that two-year period, yet every single security measure on our houses or advice centres had to be carried out by ourselves because the NIO basically told us to clear off.

"Security on our homes in those days was makeshift. Very often there was nothing stronger than Perspex on the windows to stop gun or bomb attacks. We couldn't afford bullet-proof windows even though our houses were coming under attack more frequently. It is a simple fact that there would be people alive today if the NIO had provided us with even the minimal form of protection. That, for me, is one of the biggest tragedies of that whole period."

As 1986 drew to a close, there were people plotting to assassinate Maskey – not just loyalist paramilitaries, but the state itself.

CHAPTER FOUR

A TARGET FOR THE STATE

THREE years after the hunger strike ended, the IRA took a terrifying revenge. In October 1984, a bomb containing 25 pounds of high explosives ripped through the Grand Hotel in Brighton where Margaret Thatcher and leading members of the Tory cabinet were staying during the Conservative Party Conference.

Five people died and another 30 were seriously injured in the no-warning attack. Admitting responsibility, the IRA in a statement warned: "Mrs Thatcher will now realise that Britain cannot occupy our country and torture our prisoners and shoot our people in their own streets and get away with it. Today we were unlucky, but remember we only have to be lucky once – you will have to be lucky always."

By 1986, the war between the IRA and the British government had reached an effective stalemate. As the year came to an end, the number of people killed during the Troubles passed the 2,500 mark. Since 1969, the IRA had killed 750 British soldiers and members of the RUC with another 6,000 wounded.

In the same period, republicans, loyalists and the security forces had collectively been responsible for the deaths of 1,300 civilians. Loyalists had killed 587 civilians, republicans 524 and the British army and RUC, 166.

A combination of Sinn Féin's entry into electoral politics and internal reorganisation of the IRA saw a comparative lull in the period between 1984 and 1986 with republicans inflicting 15 fatalities on the British army.

Behind the scenes, however, both the IRA and the British government were preparing in their own respective ways for major offensives. By the beginning of 1987, the IRA had already landed four shipments of arms from Libya, totalling an estimated 110 tons of weapons and explosives. This arsenal was to be used in a serious intensification of the armed struggle.

In April 1987, one of Northern Ireland's most prominent judges, Lord Justice Maurice Gibson, and his wife Cecily were killed when the IRA detonated a 500-pound landmine under their car as they crossed the border from the Republic. The couple had been returning from a holiday in France. They had been in sight of their RUC protection cars when they were killed.

As the North's second most senior judge, Gibson had presided over a number of the controversial trials that came to be known as the "shoot-to-kill" cases. These involved members of the security forces who had taken part in a series of ambushes in which they had killed unarmed republicans. In one case, the Lord Justice dismissed charges against RUC officers who had shot dead three unarmed IRA volunteers. Clearing the defendants of any wrongdoing, Gibson went on to commend them for bringing the dead men to what he described as the "final courts of justice".

Margaret Thatcher was outraged at the killing of the Gibsons. It was speculated that the IRA had received details of the their journey from a mole within the Garda Siochana, the Republic's police force. However, along with the IRA's increased capability to strike at the highest level came significant setbacks. A month after the Gibson killings, the IRA suffered its single biggest loss of personnel since the 1920s when eight members of its east Tyrone brigade were killed in an SAS ambush as they attacked an RUC station in Loughgall, County Armagh.

A civilian, father-of-three Anthony Hughes, who had been driving through the village with his brother when the ambush was launched, was killed when the SAS fired 40 shots into his car. The mechanic died immediately while his brother survived despite being hit 14 times. Neither had anything to do with the IRA but had been targeted by the undercover soldiers because they had been dressed in overalls similar to those worn by the IRA unit. The SAS seldom took prisoners.

It was later claimed that the eight IRA men had been killed following a sophisticated British military undercover operation. The message appeared clear for both the IRA and the British government – the gloves were now off. Among its more overt measures, the

Thatcher government in October 1988 imposed a broadcasting ban which barred Sinn Féin from the airwaves. In an attempt to circumvent the gagging order, some broadcasters replaced the voices of Sinn Féin representatives with the voices of actors. The ban remained in place until September 1994.

In the mid-1980s, Maskey had been tipped off by a public figure about another loyalist plan to kill him. At the time, he regularly travelled to Dublin by train for Sinn Féin Ard Comhairle (party executive) meetings and often parked his car at Belfast's Central railway station. He was contacted and informed that loyalists planned to place a bomb underneath his vehicle while it was parked there.

"Because of where the information came from, I had no doubt that it was a real threat and immediately changed my travelling patterns," he says.

What did not become public for another five years, however, was just how far the British government itself was prepared to flout the rules of law and order in Northern Ireland. The next three years were to prove that the establishment had embarked on a dirty war. While the government could publicly show its determination to fight fire with fire by pitting the SAS against the IRA, by 1987, senior figures within its military had decided that an even higher level of lethal force would be used, in the form of the shadowy Force Research Unit (FRU).

The British army had used undercover units from the early 1970s but the introduction of the FRU and the use of an agent, codenamed 6137, would lead to some of the most controversial killings of the Troubles, details of which are only now coming to light.

In 1965, 17-year-old Brian Nelson joined the British army's Black Watch regiment. Born and raised in the loyalist Shankill Road area, Agent 6137, as he would later become known, was the only son of Adam and Maisie Nelson.

A glance at Nelson's employment record suggests that his career as a soldier lasted barely four years. While he was officially discharged on medical grounds in 1969, it is open to question as to whether he actually left the British army at all. It is known, however, that he joined the loyalist UDA a year after it was formed in 1972. Joint membership of the British army and the UDA was not then illegal. Unlike the IRA, UVF and INLA, the British government refused to proscribe the UDA until 1992, when it was forced to do so by outraged public opinion. During the first three years of its existence, the UDA was responsible for 160 murders. Quite why the group was not proscribed for 20 years remains a mystery to many people.

In 1973, Nelson was one of three UDA men who kidnapped a Catholic, Gerald Higgins, as he was walking along North Queen Street in North Belfast. The partially sighted Higgins was an easy target for the loyalist trio. Nelson and his accomplices took their captive to a UDA club in Wilton Street off the Shankill Road. There the gang removed Higgins' powerful spectacles, leaving him almost blind. Nelson soaked the Catholic man's hands in water and then forced him to hold two wires connected to a battery resulting in electric shocks being sent through his body. The victim suffered from a heart condition but Nelson refused to allow him to take tablets found in his pockets. Higgins died just weeks after his kidnap ordeal. His family blamed his premature death on the torture he suffered at the hands of Nelson.

Despite Gerald Higgins' death, Nelson and his accomplices did not face murder charges but were convicted of kidnapping and possession of a revolver. Nelson was sentenced to seven years imprisonment and was freed after serving four years in the loyalist compounds in Long Kesh. When released in 1977, he immediately resumed his activities with the UDA.

The British army later claimed that Nelson first began working for the FRU in 1983. However, reliable UDA sources have suggested that he had in fact been working for British military intelligence from a much earlier date. One UDA source recalls how Nelson regularly supplied pistols and ammunition to loyalists during the 1970s, telling them he had obtained the weapons from former soldiers and Royal Air Force men.

"Looking back on it now, we should have suspected something was wrong even at that early stage," says the UDA source who knew

Nelson well. "Most of the gear he brought to us never worked and men were getting caught because these guns were always jamming. It wasn't until much later that we put two and two together and came to the conclusion Nelson had been an agent all along."

What is certain is that Nelson was working for the FRU in 1985 and, by that time, had become the West Belfast UDA's Intelligence Officer.

It would later emerge that a favourite FRU tactic was to plant moles into both loyalist and republican organisations as intelligence officers and quartermasters. With agents working in these roles, the FRU could effectively control the information flowing into and out of an organisation. By having an agent as the quartermaster, who was in charge of weapons, they could control and monitor the movement of arms and the identity of the gunmen who were using them. As an instrument of the state who had infiltrated the inner sanctum of the UDA, Nelson was not only a valuable source of information on the day-to-day workings of the loyalist organisation. He also could have, presumably, even at this early stage, been used to provide his army handlers with enough information to charge and imprison the UDA leadership.

For reasons that remain shrouded in mystery, Nelson and his family unexpectedly moved to Regensberg, Germany in late 1985. Quite why he was allowed to leave Northern Ireland when he was clearly a valuable agent for the British army has never been properly explained.

During interviews carried out for this book, a UDA source points to the compromising of an arms deal in South Africa involving the paramilitary grouping in 1982-83 as the reason for Nelson's unexpected departure.

"Four of the organisation's most senior people had travelled to Bloomfontaine in South Africa to buy a large consignment of weapons. The South Africans had recovered the guns in Namibia or one of the African countries and were willing to sell them on to us without any questions being asked. The deal was actually being done through a South African government minister. The South Africans obviously couldn't sanction the deal officially but the fact that a government minister was the middleman said it all.

"Our lads were actually leaving their hotel in Bloomfontaine to go to see the weapons when they got a last minute phone call from Belfast to tell them that the operation had been compromised and to get out of there. The four split up immediately and went their separate ways. Eventually they made it back to Northern Ireland with the money. While we weren't totally sure, the finger of suspicion was pointing in Nelson's direction, even at that stage."

In June 1985, just months before he left Northern Ireland, Brian Nelson himself travelled to South Africa to set up another arms deal for the UDA. This time, the agreement was that loyalists would supply the South Africans with plans for the Starstreak missile system that had been developed by Short Brothers engineering company in Belfast. The UDA would hand the Starstreak plans over to the South Africans in exchange for weapons.

It later emerged that Nelson's trip had not only been sanctioned by his army superiors but had also been cleared by an unnamed British government minister.

In October 1985, Nelson, his wife and their three children left Northern Ireland for Regensberg with the apparent blessing of the UDA and the British army. It was later claimed that he worked as a builder during the two years he spent in Germany before being brought back to the North by the army.

A former FRU handler, who uses the pseudonym Martin Ingram, insists that Nelson actually worked for another branch of military intelligence for the entire period he was in Germany. Whatever the truth, by January 1987, a decision had been taken by army chiefs to bring Nelson back from Regensberg to re-insert him into the UDA. This time, Nelson had a very specific brief from his FRU superiors. Agent 6137 was given the task of refocusing the killing power of the loyalist organisation. He was to move the group's gunmen away from random sectarian murders and towards what were regarded as "legitimate" republican targets. In effect, a decision had been taken at the highest level to permit an arm of the government, not only to step outside the law by targeting citizens of the state, but also to use loyalist paramilitaries to carry out the killings. The tactic of "murder-by-proxy" had begun.

Over the next three years, Brian Nelson and the FRU went beyond isolated acts of collusion and into the murky waters of state-sponsored killings. Nelson's role of directing loyalists towards attacking the "right people" was made easier by the fact that his army handlers systematically worked through the UDA's lists of nationalist targets and made them "more selective".

Nelson's handlers arranged for two computers to be bought – one for their agent and one for the FRU. Information on the military computer could then be downloaded and handed over to Nelson on floppy disks, which he could study in the flat provided for him. The FRU had made sure the flat was "red flagged", which meant that it would never be raided by the security forces.

With the help of his handlers, Nelson built up a card index system that contained the personal details of hundreds of nationalists. He had little difficulty in building up a comprehensive set of dossiers – the FRU provided most of the information for their agent. In the three years before Nelson began to feed security force intelligence files to the UDA, the loyalist paramilitary group had been responsible for ten murders. In the period between 1987 and 1990, during which Agent 6137 operated, the UDA killed more than 30 Catholics and attempted to murder dozens of others.

Alex Maskey was a special case for Brian Nelson and the FRU. Nelson and his handlers were to attempt to kill the Sinn Féin councillor on no less than four separate occasions.

In 1999, English journalist Nicholas Davies published the book, *Ten Thirty Three*.

Davies set out, with the assistance of two former FRU handlers, to reveal the extent of Nelson's activities. His home was raided during the writing of the book and British police seized a laptop computer and other material. A court injunction subsequently led to a ban on publication of the work. Davies was eventually permitted to publish an "amended" version that had been "viewed" by the Ministry of Defence before it went to print.

Ten Thirty Three reveals how Nelson's handlers suggested that Alex Maskey be killed almost as soon as their agent had returned to the North. The book went further, claiming that Nelson's FRU handlers not only implied that the UDA should target Maskey, but actually came up with a plan to kill him.

The authenticity of some of what is alleged in *Ten Thirty Three* has been called into question. However, a journal written by Brian Nelson while he was in jail awaiting trial in 1990, confirms beyond doubt that he was, in fact, involved in the May 1987 attack in which Maskey was shot and seriously wounded.

The former army agents who assisted Nicholas Davies with his book claim that Maskey was suggested as a target for assassination during a meeting between Nelson and his FRU contacts in early March 1987. Indeed, Nelson records in his journal that the murder bid on Maskey was only the second UDA operation in which he was involved after his return from Germany.

Nelson's handlers are said to have passed him Maskey's personal details at the March meeting. These included his address, telephone number, the make and registration of his car and up-to-date black and white photographs of their target. Armed with the dossier, Nelson went back to the UDA to put forward the plan to kill Maskey. The FRU operatives were confident that the loyalists would not pass up the opportunity to kill the individual who was, for them, the most hated man in Northern Ireland after Gerry Adams. But weeks later, with still no attack having taken place, Nelson complained that the Sinn Féin councillor's constant observance of security precautions made a murder bid virtually impossible. However, the FRU then took the initiative and, a week later, produced their own plan for the UDA to kill Maskey.

Faced with the difficulty that Maskey was suspicious of even the smallest sign of apparent danger, the handlers concluded that he had to be caught completely off-guard if the assassination attempt was to succeed. The FRU suggested that the UDA hijack a car from a republican area and take it to a "friendly" loyalist garage where the vehicle would be fitted with the bogus sign of a local taxi company regularly used by Maskey. Nelson was said to have been ecstatic that his army handlers had come up with their own plan to assist the UDA.

Friday May 22, 1987 started like any other morning at the Maskey home. With her two sons already sent off to school, Liz Maskey was babysitting her three-year-old nephew Colm. The couple were enjoying a cup of tea in the front living room that morning, discussing their plans for the day. Maskey's sister, Geraldine, had complained of a heavy British army and RUC presence in the area as she dropped her son off at her brother's that morning.

By 9.30am Maskey, still dressed in his pyjamas and complaining that he was running late, noticed a taxi pulling up outside the house. He did not initially think the unexpected arrival strange because he regularly used the same West Belfast firm to ferry him to meetings. From time to time, drivers from the same depot would deliver documents from Sinn Féin's Connolly House headquarters for him to sign.

While he would have normally received a phone call to tell him that a taxi was about to make a delivery, the fact that the car had a familiar sign on its roof lulled him into a false sense of security. Maskey had not ordered a cab and didn't recognise the man, in his thirties and wearing a peaked cap and light blue jerkin, who got out of the vehicle. He watched as the lean, unfamiliar figure walked up the garden path towards the front door. After the attack on their home the previous year and the assassination bid on Gerry Adams in 1984, Sinn Féin had warned party members to step up their personal security. Maskey, however, admits to ignoring his instincts, an omission that almost cost him his life. He now recalls that while he was fully aware of the danger as he walked to the hall to answer the knock on the door, he was "simply caught off guard".

Peering through the spy-hole, he called out: "Hello, what do you want?"

"Taxi, Alex," came the reply from the man whom, at close range, Maskey could see was wearing a moustache.

Maskey says it was at that moment that he made the potentially fatal mistake of opening the door to question the stranger further. As he edged the door open several inches, the man produced a double-barrelled sawn-off shotgun from beneath his jerkin and fired a shot at point-blank range.

"I remember thinking when I opened the door, 'Alex, you stupid bastard'," he now recalls.

The main blast, fired from less than twelve inches, caught him in the chest. Bleeding and in shock, he nonetheless had the presence of mind to attempt to slam the door shut. Rapidly weakening, he grappled with his attacker as the gunman pushed forward, forcing the shotgun through the gap. With the aid of the waves of adrenaline pumping through his body, Maskey succeeded in crashing the door against his attacker's arm, forcing the gunman to pull back in pain.

"I felt as if I had been hit with a sledgehammer and my chest was on fire. It was the most intense feeling of burning imaginable," he says.

Hearing the sound of gunfire Liz Maskey ran towards the hall but her husband yelled at her to stay back. Maskey said he feared the gunman was at that moment reloading his weapon and preparing to fire more rounds through the door at any second. Bleeding heavily, he stumbled to the staircase, pulling a heavy wrought-iron security gate behind him as he desperately tried to get out of range of the shots he was sure were going to come.

"I knew I was badly wounded but the adrenalin had allowed me to slam the door shut and make it up the stairs," Maskey remembers. "I made it to the top of the stairs and then the trauma of being shot just hit me and I collapsed. I could just about hear Liz calling out my name and Colm screaming in terror."

Unknown to Maskey, the gunman had been injured in the struggle. After managing to free his arm from the jammed door, the would-be assassin dropped the sawn-off shotgun on the doorstep where it came apart. The gunman ran back to the getaway car which then sped off towards Clonelly Avenue. Seconds later, Liz ran into the street to summon help for her husband who by now was slipping in and out of consciousness as he lay on the stairs. The entire shooting incident had lasted little more than a minute.

When Liz attempted to call an ambulance, she discovered that her telephone was out of order. Neighbours found her 35-year-old husband slumped at the top of the staircase with blood pumping from the wound in his stomach.

Recalling the moments when he thought he was dying, Maskey says: "I remember Liz and some neighbours covering me with a blanket and trying to comfort me and keep me from slipping into unconsciousness.

"I was freezing one moment and burning up the next moment. I remember imagining myself looking down at my family and wondering if they would be all right without me. I thought, 'I am going to die here on the stairs'."

An ambulance arrived within minutes and he was rushed to the Royal Victoria Hospital (RVH) on the Falls Road. Still slipping in and out of consciousness, he was admitted to hospital at 10.04am. Staff removed the bloodstained pyjama top to uncover a single gunshot wound to the chest and two exit wounds in his back. Doctors worked frantically for 40 minutes to stem the flow of blood gushing from the wounds. When part of the shotgun blast had ripped through the door, it had sent razor sharp splinters of wood and Perspex glass tearing into Maskey's chest, causing even further injury and contamination.

He had lost a dangerous amount of blood and his body's vital organs were starting to shut down. Shortly before 11.00am, surgeons began what was to be a four-hour operation to try to save his life. Maskey had sustained serious internal injuries and lost a substantial part of his stomach, kidneys and bowel. Now in deep trauma, his uninjured lung collapsed forcing him to attempt to breathe on a half lung.

After surgery, he was moved to an intensive care ward with his family being told that it was not certain he would survive. Shortly before midnight, his kidneys began to bleed and he was rushed back into the operating theatre. His condition stabilised only after four more hours of surgery. In the early morning, he was returned to the intensive care unit where the family was advised to maintain a bedside vigil such was the fear that he might not live. In the following days, doctors warned them that the extent of the injuries meant he would be left with lifelong side-effects.

Just days after the shooting, Liz was arrested as she travelled to hospital to visit her husband. Stopped at a checkpoint, the mother-of-two was taken to Woodbourne RUC station where she was charged with assault. The incident provoked an angry response from Sinn Féin president Gerry Adams who accused the RUC of harassing Liz while her husband was battling for his life in hospital. Mrs Maskey was found guilty, but on appeal the decision by the County Court judge was overturned by Mr Justice McCollum who described her as "a most impressive witness". Five years later, a Belfast court awarded Liz substantial damages for wrongful arrest. During the hearing, the judge referred to an "element of harassment" surrounding the incident which he described as "completely unjustified".

The getaway car used in the attack on Maskey was found four days later, submerged in a water-logged field close to Dundrod motorcycle racing circuit a few miles from West Belfast. It was highly unusual for loyalists to penetrate the very heart of the republican area where the councillor lived. The ditching of the car was also a departure as loyalist getaway vehicles were normally found burned-out on one of the housing estates in the Shankill area where gunmen had an easy escape route. No one was arrested or charged in the wake of the shooting.

A week after being shot and apparently out of danger, Alex Maskey's condition once again worsened.

"I remember waking up in the middle of the night because I was not able to breathe properly," he recalls. "My family kept a 24-hour vigil at my bedside and I remember my father sitting there when I woke up in panic. It was as if someone had dropped a concrete block on my chest. I thought at that moment that I was going to die. I felt my life slipping away. I looked at my father and whispered, 'I'm gone dad'. It sounds strange, but I remember thinking, 'Well Alex, you gave it a good go'."

The hospital monitors which Maskey was linked to were bleeping out an alarm as staff rushed to his bedside to discover that the remaining part of his lung had collapsed. Once again, Liz was told to prepare herself for the fact that her husband could die. Maskey's condition was again stabilised.

While the councillor was battling for his life, his family was becoming increasingly concerned that loyalists may have been preparing to launch a second attack on him as he lay in his hospital bed. But when they asked that the father-of-two be moved to a secure unit of the hospital with specially-installed bullet-proof doors, they were refused.

The Maskeys made further complaints after the RUC ordered relatives to leave the hospital's visiting rooms even though security staff at the RVH confirmed that they had received no complaints about the family's presence. Although it had been just 17 days since the gun attack and he was still seriously ill, Alex Maskey decided to discharge himself from hospital

"I have nothing but praise for the doctors, nurses and ambulance men who saved my life. But I will always believe that the health authorities bowed to pressure from the RUC to block my transfer into the secure unit where I would be safe. Because they refused me access to the secure ward I had no other option but to sign myself out of hospital."

Still unable to walk without the aid of crutches, Maskey, along with his family, was sent to Donegal to recuperate. However, he could not settle in the plush surroundings of the house that had been hired for them and he asked to be moved. The family were then given the use of a farmhouse in the heart of County Mayo, but with doctors warning that he could relapse unless he took total rest, they accepted an offer from childhood friend Eoghan O'Neill to travel to his home in the Channel Islands to recuperate properly.

"It seemed the perfect thing to go and see Eoghan and his family and get better in relative safety," he says.

Recovery, however, was proving difficult. With shrapnel wounds from the gun blast still embedded in his stomach, he collapsed again while in Guernsey and was rushed back into hospital.

"I was allowed out soon after but warned that my condition was still very serious."

At the end of November, he received a telephone call from Belfast to warn him that unionists were planning to unseat him at the next council meeting.

"City Hall standing orders meant that if you missed three meetings in a row you could be unseated. In the situation that a councillor was seriously ill, the rule was waived if a doctor's letter was put before the council. But I received a call from home telling me that the unionists were going to try to have me thrown out if I didn't make it to the December meeting of the council in person."

As the council had been suspended for the summer Maskey had only missed two meetings.

"This was the first chance unionists had to unseat me and they were determined to take it," he says.

Still heavily reliant on his crutches, he immediately made arrangements to travel home. Since there were no direct flights between the Channel Islands and Belfast, he planned to fly into London's Heathrow Airport and take another plane home. However, once he arrived in Heathrow he was stopped by police and placed under arrest.

"They knew exactly what they were doing. Once I set foot inside the Heathrow terminal I was arrested. They grabbed me by the arms and manhandled me through the whole concourse of the airport in front of hundreds of people who just looked on in amazement. Bear in mind, I was hardly going to escape on crutches."

After being held for a number of hours in cells at Heathrow, he was brought to Paddington Green police station where he was questioned for the next 36 hours. His family and solicitor were denied any information as to his condition or where he was being held. During questioning, he says he was offered large sums of money to become an informer. He firmly believes that there was only one reason for his arrest.

"They knew I was seriously ill and why I was travelling back to Belfast. I remember thinking to myself, 'do they really hate me this much?' I honestly believe the only reason I was arrested was to try to prevent me from getting to the council meeting so that I could be unseated."

Fortuitously for Maskey, the council meeting had been unexpectedly adjourned until the following week. When he was finally released from Paddington Green, he was handcuffed to a plain-clothes Special Branch officer and brought back to Heathrow.

Believing that he would be parted from his unwanted escort in the confines of the airport, Maskey admits to being a little surprised when he found himself still shackled to his untalkative companion as the plane took off for Belfast. He was only let go when the unlikely pair set foot on the runway of Aldergrove Airport. When the handcuffs came off, he was promptly handed a deportation order by his travelling partner who explained that he was excluded from entering any part of England, Scotland or Wales for the next three years with immediate effect. The exclusion order, however, was not rescinded for seven years.

"I think it would be fair to say that we didn't exchange home phone numbers and addresses when we parted. I presume he already had mine anyway," Maskey caustically recalls.

After the unexpected detour on his journey home, the Sinn Féin councillor eventually made it to the reconvened council meeting in time to save his seat. But if he had been expecting unionist colleagues to have erected "welcome home" banners for him in the City Hall, he was to be disappointed.

"When I walked into the chamber the unionists were disgusted. Despite the fact that I had been shot and nearly died, they were still determined to take my seat from me."

A number of DUP councillors taunted the Sinn Féin man by calling him "Leadbelly", a reference to the fact that he still had remnants of shotgun pellets lodged in his chest. Maskey says the unionists were not just angry that he had made it back in time to save his seat – they were totally disgusted that he been allowed back into the North at all.

"The unionists went absolutely berserk because I was back in Belfast. They knew that the British had banned me from Britain but there I was, sitting in front of them in a city that they had always claimed was as British as Finchley.

"It suddenly dawned on them that, while they may have believed that Belfast was a part of the United Kingdom, Margaret Thatcher obviously wasn't of the same opinion. The unionists actually argued that I should have been flown to Dublin Airport instead of Belfast and been forced into internal exile. It was a salutary lesson to them."

Having survived two murder bids in less than a year, Maskey says he was now becoming increasingly convinced that loyalist paramilitaries were receiving the assistance of the state in their attacks. It was only after another four years and three more attempts on his life that it was officially confirmed that an agent of the state, namely Brian Nelson, and the FRU had been actively conspiring to kill him.

While plans to kill Maskey had to be put on hold as he recuperated in the Channel Islands that summer, Nelson and the FRU busied themselves by targeting dozens of other nationalists. One of the first people Nelson selected for murder was father-of-three Michael Power. The 31-year-old Catholic was shot dead by the UDA as he drove his wife and children to Sunday Mass near his West Belfast home in August, 1987. The loyalists later claimed Power had been shot in retaliation for the IRA killing of UDR soldier Joseph McIlwaine in Lambeg two months earlier. Power's family said he was a deeply religious man and they rejected UDA claims that he was a member of the IRA. Two UDR men were questioned about the murder. It later became clear from FRU documents that Michael Power was killed for the most cynical of reasons – to help Brian Nelson ingratiate himself with his UDA superiors.

Two months later, on October 9, security force files supplied by Nelson led to the UDA murder of 66-year-old West Belfast grandfather Francisco Notarantonio. The killing hit the headlines 14 years later amid media claims that Nelson's FRU handlers had ordered the Catholic pensioner's murder to protect a British army mole within the IRA. Notarantonio's wife, who witnessed the murder, said at the time: "I don't know how the gang got into the estate because it was crawling with soldiers yesterday morning."

On January 25, 1988, Nelson was again heavily involved in a murder. Jack Kielty, a Catholic businessman from Dundrum, County Down, was gunned down at his building firm's office. He had been due to give evidence in a libel action brought by UDA leader Jim Craig. Craig, who was suing Central Television over a programme that had connected him to racketeering, ordered Kielty's death after it was learned that the businessman had agreed to act as a witness against him. Three men, one a former member of the controversial locally-recruited army reserve, the Ulster Defence Regiment (UDR), and another an ex-Royal Marine, were jailed for life for the murder. Three other men were tried for lesser offences connected to the killing. Two of the three convicted were members of the UDR.

On May 10, 1988, UDA gunmen burst into the Belfast home of 29-year-old Catholic man Terence McDaid. In the house with the father-of-two were his wife, Maura, their two young children and his mother. Showing remarkable courage, Maura McDaid fought with the gunmen as they opened fire on her husband. He died from gunshot wounds to his head and back. The victim's wife was lucky to survive after one of the gunmen fired two shots at her head. Her mother-in-law was shot in the leg.

In 1989, a corporal in the Royal Scots regiment and a female UDR soldier admitted passing security documents to loyalist paramilitaries. The papers included the personal details of Terence McDaid. The pair was given 18-month suspended sentences. While the female soldier subsequently resigned from the UDR, the corporal was allowed to stay in the army as a training instructor. It later emerged that Nelson meant to target the dead man's brother but had sent the killers to the wrong address.

Father-of-three Gerard Slane was his next victim. UDA gunmen shot him dead in his West Belfast home on September 23, 1988. A photograph of Slane, taken while he was being questioned in Castlereagh RUC interrogation centre five years previously, appeared in a UDA magazine shortly after he was murdered. The group claimed Slane had been involved in the killing of UDA man Billy Quee who had been shot dead by the IPLO weeks before. However, a detective at Slane's inquest said he had not been involved in that or any other murder. The policeman told the inquest the victim had been jailed for an arms offence in the 1970s but, after his release, had no involvement with republican paramilitaries. It subsequently emerged that Brian Nelson had passed on Slane's personal details to a well-known UDA gunman.

It was also revealed that the RUC had been aware that both Slane and McDaid were to be murdered by the UDA. The families of the two murder victims later received damages from the NIO.

On July 17 that same year, Nelson and the FRU again tried to have Maskey killed. It was a Sunday afternoon and the Sinn Féin councillor was back in his native North Belfast to visit his grandmother. Afterwards, Alex and Liz went for Sunday lunch to the Gregory Hotel on the Antrim Road, close to the British army's Girdwood barracks. An observation post on the perimeter of the fort provided a good view of the section of road close to the hotel.

When Nelson was finally arrested in 1990, he admitted his involvement in this murder bid on Maskey. Under questioning he insisted that the decision to launch yet another assassination attempt be taken after Maskey was recognised by a UDA man at the restaurant. According to Nelson, the loyalist, referred to only as 'B', then drove to Nelson's home to inform him of Maskey's presence in the restaurant. To this day, Maskey discounts Nelson's claim that he was spotted by 'B' and insists that either Nelson or his FRU handlers had in fact learned of the couple's presence at the hotel from soldiers in the Girdwood lookout post.

What is fact is that Nelson then began to set up a gun attack on Alex and Liz by contacting two known UDA gunmen. The pair was unable to obtain a weapon and Nelson contacted a third gunman who had easy access to a firearm. Unaware of the danger, the Maskeys escaped death only because they left the restaurant minutes before the attack was due to take place.

The UFF gunman found to carry out the attack had been Ken Barrett. In July 2002, Barrett was secretly filmed admitting his part in the murder attempt on the Maskeys.

"I mean I actually went into that place and stood and had a glass of beer, like. And he wasn't there," Barrett said, unaware that he was being covertly videotaped. "And yet with all … a couple of hours later

I was standing in Highfield Rangers (social club) having a drink. Brian comes in and says he's seen them there."

During police interviews, Nelson claimed he had been unable to contact his army handlers to alert them to the planned attack due to the fact that he was at home with his two sons when he was informed of Maskey's presence at the hotel. But it later emerged that Nelson had, in fact, made two separate calls to his FRU handlers before the murder bid, not to warn that the Sinn Féin councillor was to be killed but to seek their help in the attack.

In the first call, Nelson asked a British army handler to confirm that the registration number and details of Maskey's vehicle were correct. When Nelson called his handler 20 minutes later, he was told: "You're not wrong about the car."

What Nelson also failed to reveal during questioning was that he had subsequently telephoned his FRU handlers at 5.55pm that evening to inform them that the murder bid had been aborted.

"He just missed death by about twenty seconds," Nelson told his FRU contacts of Maskey's lucky escape. "I was involved up to my neck with a Mr Heckler (Heckler and Koch submachine gun). I'm mad, we only missed him by twenty seconds, it's because it took so long to set it up."

When Nelson's handler asked him what would happen next, he replied: "If he's there next Sunday, he's going down."

Despite the fact that Nelson had informed the FRU that a second murder bid was being planned for the following week, Maskey was never told that his life was in danger.

In the summer of 2002, Detective Sergeant Nicholas Benwell of the Stevens Enquiry team, which would eventually uncover the activities of Brian Nelson and the FRU, gave a telling insight into the lengths Nelson and his army handlers had gone to try to have Maskey killed.

"Nelson ... went around Belfast trying to recruit an assassination team and then, when one unit was unable to assist, he went on until he found another one," stated Benwell.

Asked if Nelson had acted as an *agent provocateur* rather than attempting to thwart the murder bid on Maskey, Benwell replied: "Absolutely."

Questioned as to whether Nelson had wanted the murder bid on Maskey to have gone ahead without security force intervention, Benwell confirmed, "Yes."

When queried about why the RUC had not been alerted to the murder bid, Benwell responded: "The conclusion must be that they did not want the police to be at the scene."

The detective was then asked if he believed the FRU had been prepared to allow the Maskey murder bid to go ahead unhindered. He replied: "In the absence of any other explanation coming from the army, that is the view I would take, yes."

Apart from Alex Maskey, the majority of those set up for death by Brian Nelson and the FRU were ordinary nationalists who had little or no interest in politics. One man who had become an increasingly painful thorn in the side of the British establishment was solicitor Pat Finucane. Maskey and Finucane were friends, with the solicitor's firm regularly representing the Sinn Féin councillor in legal battles against both the council and the British government.

"Pat Finucane was the solicitor we used more than most others in those days, simply because he was one of the best at what he did," says Maskey. "There were just a few solicitors willing to take on the state in those days. Pat's partner Peter Madden had been in the public gallery for the February 1989 meeting of the council to take notes for a court case we were taking against the council. Pat had won numerous cases against the council on our behalf."

The British government's frustration at Finucane's legal capabilities was not confined to his actions on behalf of City Hall councillors. The 38-year-old had represented republicans and loyalists in a series of high-profile court cases. Finucane had been solicitor to the hunger-strikers and had acted on behalf of the families of those targeted in the "shoot-to-kill" cases. Just weeks before he was shot dead in front of his wife and three children, Tory government minister Douglas Hogg caused uproar in the House of Commons when he claimed that unnamed solicitors in Northern Ireland were "unduly sympathetic to the cause of the IRA". When challenged Hogg added: "I state this on the basis of advice that I have received, guidance that I have been given by people who are dealing with these matters and I shall not expand on it further."

Hogg was referring to a meeting with senior RUC officers just days before. The SDLP's Seamus Mallon immediately called for Hogg to retract the statement, warning that solicitors' lives in Northern Ireland had now been put at risk.

On February 12, Pat Finucane was shot dead as he sat at Sunday dinner with his wife and children in their Belfast home. Allegations of security force collusion surfaced almost immediately after the murder. It emerged that Brian Nelson and his FRU contacts had played a central part in the murder, including supplying a photograph of the solicitor to be passed to the UDA gunmen.

Two different handlers were involved in three separate reconnaissance missions at the Finucane family home. It was later claimed that Nelson and an FRU operative drove past the house on two occasions days before the assassination. Another handler and Nelson were later reported to have posed as window cleaners to spy on the family.

"People knew straight away that some arm of the state had set Pat up for assassination," Maskey explains. "There were too many connections pointing in the one direction. Even Pat's clients were warning him that the RUC wanted him dead. Guys were coming out of Castlereagh and recounting how cops were boasting that Pat was going to be killed. No one could prove it at the time but everyone knew that something very dirty and squalid was going on. The state chose to kill Pat Finucane for no other reason than he represented the rights of his clients effectively in a court of law."

Less than five weeks after Finucane's murder, Nelson and the FRU were once again targeting Maskey. On April 3, the councillor and his father were parking their vehicle outside Liz's workplace in West Belfast when they saw two furtive-looking men in a car close by.

"It was my father who noticed the two men acting suspiciously. The car was right outside Liz's work so I drove straight at them and tried to block them in. They knew immediately that we had spotted them because they sped off with us chasing behind them. We lost them in the traffic which, looking back on it now, might have been just as well because they were probably armed. It was only at Nelson's trial that I learned that this was to have been another murder bid."

It was the fourth time in a little over two years that Nelson and the FRU had plotted to take Maskey's life. In April 1989, Nelson tired of the UDA's inability to kill Maskey and passed his personal details on to the UVF. An FRU document, dated April 4, 1989, confirmed that not only had Nelson set up Maskey for UVF assassination but that his FRU handlers had been fully aware of the change in direction.

"Although the UVF are not particular about their targets, they appear to be more aggressive," the FRU memo stated. "6137 has traded this information for explosives. This trading avenue may well be used on a regular basis."

In the summer of 1988, Maskey's son Sean was a patient in the City Hospital. His parents visited the eight-year-old boy every day, staying for as long as they could. However, Maskey was contacted by a public figure, the name of whom the author has agreed not to divulge, who told the Sinn Féin councillor that loyalists had learned of his daily visits to the hospital. The source warned that the UFF and UVF had met to discuss a plan to kill Maskey during regular visiting hours, when it was presumed he would be there with his son.

"I had suspected that something wasn't right beforehand," says Maskey, "But when I was contacted, I was told that the plan to kill me was very real and imminent. I told Liz I would have to vary my time and pattern of visiting Sean. It was hard on Liz, Sean and myself because the last thing you want to do is upset your child when he is ill. I have no doubt that they were serious about trying to kill me."

It emerged afterwards that the UVF killed or wounded at least six people whose names appeared in Brian Nelson's intelligence files. But, by the end of 1989, a series of events would lead to the eventual downfall of Nelson and reveal for the first time that an arm of the state had actively colluded to murder ordinary civilians, solicitors and elected politicians.

The level to which the public were becoming increasingly aware that soldiers and RUC men were actively colluding with loyalists was shown in September 1989 when Church of Ireland Bishop, Rev Brian Hannon, hit out at members of the security forces involved in passing documents to loyalists. The Church of Ireland bishop was the first leading Protestant churchman to publicly speak out against collusion, warning that such actions were not only undermining the rule of law but were lessening the standing of the forces of law and order in the community. Dr Hannon described those involved in the passing of documents to loyalists as "murderers by proxy".

The beginning of the end for Nelson and the FRU came with the UDA's murder of Catholic man Loughlin Maginn. The father-of-four was shot dead in his Rathfriland home in August 1989. Two full-time UDR soldiers and a third man were later convicted of the killing. When UDA claims that Maginn was a republican were rejected, the group attempted to justify the 28-year-old's murder by showing Nelson's security force montages to journalists. A photograph of Loughlin Maginn was included in one of the documents. It would later emerge that the photograph of Maginn had been taken as he stood next to Alex Maskey at an Easter Rising Commemoration in the County Down village of Castlewellan.

In a further, cavalier attempt to prove the authenticity of their information, the UDA pasted photocopies of security force pictures on walls across loyalist areas of Belfast. The paramilitaries had killed the goose that laid their golden eggs. As a result of the inevitable political uproar emanating from nationalist politicians, John Stevens, then a deputy chief constable of Cambridgeshire police, was brought over to Northern Ireland to investigate the extent to which members of the police and army were colluding with loyalists. Nelson's fingerprints were found on a number of the leaked files.

The British army at first denied that Nelson was one of their agents and, in January 1990, spirited Agent 6137 and his files out of Northern Ireland to Liverpool – the night before he was due to be arrested by the Stevens team. On the same night, FRU operatives set fire to the offices of the Stevens team, destroying files in a bid to keep the investigation from getting close to Nelson. But despite the FRU's best efforts, Stevens' detectives managed to arrest Nelson on his return from Liverpool. He immediately admitted his role as an FRU agent to detectives and not only revealed that he had passed on hundreds of British army and RUC files to the UDA but that his handlers had helped him pick targets.

At his first court hearing on June 15, Nelson faced 34 charges, including two counts of murder. It was publicly admitted for the first time at this hearing that he had been working for military intelligence. However, when he was finally brought to trial in 1992, a spokesman for the Attorney General revealed that fifteen of the most serious charges had been dropped, including two counts of murder. The Attorney General's spokesman said the charges had been dropped after "a rigorous examination of the interests of justice".

Nelson pleaded guilty to five counts of conspiracy to commit murder, including the attempted killing of Alex Maskey, plus eleven lesser offences. It was disclosed in court that the RUC, "at a senior level", had been aware that loyalists were targeting Maskey in 1987. Despite this knowledge, police failed to inform Maskey that he was in danger. Because Brian Nelson chose to plead guilty, the full extent of his role as an FRU agent in dozens of killings was kept from public scrutiny.

The court heard pleas for leniency from Nelson's FRU commander, Brigadier Gordon Kerr and Secretary of State for Defence, Tom King. The latter submitted a letter to the court declaring that Nelson "was a good agent". It was later revealed that in the week before the trial, discussions about the Nelson case took place at the highest levels of the British political and legal systems.

Brian Nelson was sentenced to 10 years in jail. He was moved to a prison in England and released in 1996. He was immediately given a new identity and was said to have been resettled by the British army in Canada. In April 2003, it was reported that he had died of a brain haemorrhage in either Canada or the United States. The announcement was made the day before John Stevens was due to publicise damning extracts from his report into collusion. In

September that same year, a Belfast newspaper claimed that Nelson had, in fact, died in Wales. Perplexed by the conflicting reports, relatives of some of his victims have demanded that authorities provide positive proof of the double agent's death.

The British establishment gave no sign of being embarrassed by the whole sordid affair. In 1993, the British army GOC for Northern Ireland, Sir John Wilsey, said he was in no way ashamed of the army's involvement in the Nelson case.

"If the Nelson episode taught us anything, it taught us that the relationship between the army and the RUC, and other agencies involved, was strong enough to withstand any pressures that came about because of that investigation," said Wilsey.

In fact, one of Nelson's two main FRU handlers, Captain Margaret Walshaw, was awarded the British Empire Medal at Buckingham Palace two weeks after he was sent to jail. Nelson's other main handler, codenamed "Geoff", later joined the RUC and is believed to have been suspended from duties pending the outcome of the ongoing Stevens inquiry.

Interviewed in 2002, Stevens' team detective Nicholas Benwell estimated that Nelson had been involved in more than 50 serious crimes, including murder and attempted murder. Contradicting Brigadier Gordon Kerr's claim that Nelson had been responsible for saving countless lives, Benwell said he could not think of one occasion when information provided by Agent 6137 had led to a single arrest or weapon recovered.

When questioned as to how the state had benefited from the actions of Brian Nelson and the FRU, Benwell replied: "You may well ask."

CHAPTER FIVE

THE DIRTY WAR

W HILE the British establishment was reluctant to publicly admit involvement in the targeting of nationalists throughout the late 1980s and early 1990s, no secrecy surrounded the open warfare between Sinn Féin and the unionists in Belfast City Hall during the same period.

In the six years before the IRA and loyalist paramilitaries announced their respective ceasefires in 1994, the City Hall was synonymous with the worst excesses of sectarian street politics. Sinn Féin councillors had achieved a number of important successes in the late 1980s, but a number of IRA mistakes outside the council did little to help their cause.

The unionist parties were able to justify their hardline stance against Sinn Féin, citing a number of IRA attacks that resulted in the deaths of innocent civilians at this time. On Remembrance Day, November 8 1987, a bomb exploded at the war memorial in the County Fermanagh town of Enniskillen. The no-warning device, which the IRA later said had been planted to kill RUC members and British soldiers involved in searching the area before the ceremony, went off as 200 people congregated around the Cenotaph. Eleven people were killed and another 60, aged between two and 75, were injured. Five of the dead were women. In a statement the following day the IRA said that it had not intended civilian casualties and "deeply regretted" the loss of life.

Sinn Féin's Gerry Adams said at the time that there was no justification for the deaths. Ten years later the Sinn Féin leader reiterated: "I hope there will be no more Enniskillens and I am deeply sorry about what happened in Enniskillen."

Over this period, nationalists repeatedly accused the unionist majority in the Belfast council chamber of working to an overtly sectarian agenda. Indeed the North's leading statutory watchdog, the

Fair Employment Agency (FEA), was also investigating the employment records of City Hall. In February 1988, the FEA informed councillors that it was invoking its legal powers to probe the religious make-up of the council's 3,000 employees. The move came after unionists blocked FEA attempts to investigate the council's employment record by adopting a policy of non-co-operation.

While unionists argued that criticism of City Hall was "nationalist propaganda", a series of religious discrimination cases brought against the council by Catholic employees in the 1980s appeared to reinforce nationalist claims. In October 1988, a Belfast court found that the council had discriminated against Catholic employee Alex Johnston after two Protestant colleagues had been promoted despite being less qualified than him. Mr Johnston was awarded £3,600 in damages.

Four years later, the Fair Employment Commission (FEC), which had replaced the FEA, ordered the council to pay Alex Johnston a further £7,500 for the victimisation he had suffered as a direct result of his original discrimination case.

In the same year, Belfast City Council was forced to pay £52,000 in compensation to five Catholic employees after a fair employment tribunal ruled that they had been overlooked for the post of senior officer in City Hall in favour of a Protestant candidate who was found to have been substantially less qualified for the job.

In April 1991, a Belfast High Court ruled that unionists had acted illegally against nationalist residents in the Whiterock estate in West Belfast by refusing to install swings and slides in a children's play park.

Delivering judgement, Lord Justice Nicholson stated: "I am satisfied that the unionists' hostility to Provisional Sinn Féin spilt over and led to the decision not to spend money at the playground."

The judge ruled that funding had been blocked for the play park solely on the grounds that the families who would use the facilities were likely to be Sinn Féin voters. It was estimated that such cases cost the Belfast ratepayer upwards of £500,000 in compensation and legal bills.

While Alliance, Sinn Féin, the SDLP and council employees were all turning to the courts to challenge City Hall policy, the chamber also came in for regular criticism from Belfast's two largest daily newspapers. In January 1990, the *Irish News* labelled Belfast City Hall as "little more than a gentleman's club for bigots" after unionist hardliners called for the boycott of a civic reception for recently released Beirut hostage Brian Keenan. Outrage had been caused by the fact that the Belfast Protestant, who had been held captive in Beirut for four years, held an Irish passport. Independent unionist Frank Millar Sr objected to the reception for Keenan, claiming: "When you go Paddy, you go all the way."

A year later, the *Belfast Telegraph* openly criticised unionists for denying "opposition" councillors the right to speak in City Hall. The newspaper's reproach came after nationalist and Alliance councillors were banned from speaking during a debate on a motion to invite newly elected Irish President Mary Robinson to City Hall.

Indeed the divisions ran so deep that both Sinn Féin and the SDLP made repeated calls for the British government to close down the council. In 1987, Alex Maskey had warned that "unionist misrule was so endemic" that nationalists were investigating the possibility of establishing their own independent council. The warning came after unionists locked the doors of committee rooms in November and December in an effort to stop Sinn Féin councillors attending meetings there.

Sinn Féin had two councillors elected in a November 1987 by-election, bringing their total to nine. SDLP numbers stood at six. However, the various unionist and loyalist parties had still overall control with 28 seats.

Sinn Féin again looked towards the courts for justice in City Hall, arguing that unionists were stopping republicans from carrying out their duties as elected representatives. When the courts ruled in favour of the republicans, the unionists decided to set up sub-committees from which Sinn Féin councillors were excluded. Maskey threatened that his party would occupy every room in City Hall unless unionists backed down. A five-year battle, involving countless court cases, ensued before the ban on republicans taking places on all council committees was overthrown.

While political "sparring" was an acceptable form of debate in council chambers across Britain and Ireland, in July 1988, Belfast councillors chose to mark the start of their summer holidays with a fistfight. The free-for-all started when Sinn Féin's Tish Holland tried to address the monthly council meeting. As was the norm when a Sinn Féin member indicated that they wanted to speak, the UUP and DUP councillors immediately walked to the door of the chamber where they attempted to make so much noise that the rest of the parties were unable to hear Holland speak.

In an impromptu move, which Maskey insists was not pre-planned, a number of the Sinn Féin bloc decided to confront their heckling colleagues at the entrance to the chamber.

"We had decided to confront them, but not physically. The council chamber was already tense," recalls Sinn Féin's Máirtín Ó Muilleoir. "But when Elizabeth Seawright (who had replaced her murdered husband George on the council) took out a can of deodorant and sprayed us with it, events took on a life of their own."

DUP Mayor Nigel Dodds twice adjourned the meeting but each time it restarted, hostilities resumed. Regarded as the "young Turks" of their respective parties, Ó Muilleoir and the DUP's Sammy Wilson were the first to engage. Ó Muilleoir and Wilson stood nose to nose at the entrance trading schoolboy insults.

"Eventually the vulnerable positioning of Sammy's stance proved too much and I found my knee rising sharply to where his manhood was resting at that time," Ó Muilleoir now recalls.

When Wilson doubled-up on the floor, the chamber went into uproar and a fracas ensued. Ó Muilleoir found himself being ejected from the room. Three councillors reported to hospital that night, including Ó Muilleoir. In a subsequent complaint to the RUC, Sammy Wilson described the physical and professional pain felt when the Sinn Féin councillor's left leg had "docked" with what he euphemistically described as "the mother-ship". While Ó Muilleoir later admitted to having adopted the tactics of a "Castlereagh interview", it was Lord Mayor Nigel Dodds who was blamed for allowing the brawl to develop on the floor of the chamber. The *Belfast*

Telegraph's report on the meeting recounted that Dodds had sat reading a newspaper each time a Sinn Féin councillor attempted to address the chamber.

SDLP councillor Cormac Boomer, a regular critic of Sinn Féin in City Hall, lambasted Dodds for allowing the meeting to descend into chaos.

"If it was possible, I would have him charged for what happened," said Boomer. "But of course, he was only following the traditional approach bequeathed him by previous lord mayors. He should do the people of Belfast a big favour by resigning now. He sat there reading the *Telegraph* when Sinn Féin was trying to speak."

Sinn Féin councillors regularly found themselves being escorted from the chamber by the RUC, but expulsions were not always one-sided. Before the February 1989 council meeting, party members issued Dodds with an ultimatum that they would initiate legal proceedings if he failed to prevent DUP councillors from jeering their speakers.

Minutes into the meeting, Alex Maskey rose to speak and Sammy Wilson and Rhonda Paisley duly started catcalling. However, an apparent mix-up in unionist tactics meant that the Ulster Unionist contingent had already left the chamber ahead of Maskey's address. To the surprise of the DUP, the non-unionist bloc found themselves in the majority. With the UUP absent, Maskey proposed that Paisley and Wilson be removed. The RUC were duly called to escort the two loyalists from the chamber.

"It was the only time I was happy to see the RUC," Maskey later joked.

Following the May election of that year, the ongoing competition between nationalists became even keener when Sinn Féin dropped one seat and were neck and neck with the SDLP with each holding eight seats. There were the odd occasions of amusement in the council chamber, but overall, nationalists were far from content with the way in which City Hall was being run.

In January 1990, the SDLP's Joe Hendron took the drastic measure of writing to then Secretary of State Peter Brooke calling for Belfast

City Council to be closed down and replaced with a local government commissioner. The call came after Ulster Unionists and the DUP had unveiled a behind-the-scenes deal for the running of City Hall which involved wholesale cutbacks in services. The fact that the unionists had not consulted with any of the other parties, or passed their proposals through any council committees, was seen as a clear indication of the blasé attitude they had adopted as a result of their overall majority.

In his letter to Brooke, the West Belfast doctor wrote: "I am starting to wonder if it's worth attending meetings at all because of the way unionists conduct business."

While nationalist and Alliance councillors were to have periodic victories on the floor of the chamber, unionist domination was never far away. At the first council meeting of 1991, a proposal was put forward by independent unionist John Carson to invite Irish President Mary Robinson to Belfast. Nationalists supported the motion in the certain knowledge that it would be defeated, but the actions of UUP Lord Mayor Fred Cobain were to mark a new low in City Hall relationships. Somewhat optimistically, the DUP said that it would support the invitation to Mary Robinson – once the Irish government had removed Articles 2 and 3 of the constitution, which claimed sovereignty over the island of Ireland.

Predictably, the motion was defeated but it was Cobain's role that caused the biggest uproar. Sinn Féin, SDLP, Alliance and Workers Party councillors collectively complained that the Lord Mayor had deliberately refused to allow members on the opposition benches to speak on the motion. Cobain subsequently denied the allegations. Despite the denials he still came in for severe criticism.

"It seems they have decided that non-unionists who sit on the council won't be allowed to express their viewpoint at all," said the Workers Party's Seamus Lynch.

Alliance's John Alderdice said that, while opposition members were used to being vilified by unionists, the denial of free speech in the debate on the invitation to Mrs Robinson was "quite an outrageous abuse of position". The following day, the *Irish News*, in an attack on unionists for gagging their political opponents, said: "Their past record speaks for itself. It is one of dismal, abject failure and quite open discrimination against Catholics. So unjust and so divisive was their rule in Northern Ireland that the British had to intervene to dissolve Stormont."

The unionist *Belfast Telegraph* went further: "The issue is one of freedom of speech, enshrined in every democratic forum in the world, but apparently unavailable in Belfast City Council."

Despite the public furore that the ban on non-unionists had caused, within a week, Deputy Mayor Eric Smyth re-instigated the gagging order on Alex Maskey and Sinn Féin. A special council meeting had been called by unionists to denounce an IRA firebombing campaign across the North during previous weeks. They had expected SDLP support for a motion condemning the firebombing. But when Sammy Wilson called for the RUC and British army to be allowed a free hand to go into the "nationalist lairs" to hunt out the IRA, the SDLP's Brian Feeney retorted that nationalists were neither animals, nor did they live in lairs.

As tempers flared, Frank Millar Sr called for Sinn Féin to be banned from speaking in the chamber. With Lord Mayor Fred Cobain absent, the meeting was being chaired by Eric Smyth who prevented Sinn Féin's Gerard McGuigan from speaking and agreed to put the gagging motion to a vote. Town clerk Cecil Ward twice advised the DUP preacher that the proposal was illegal, but the civil servant's words fell on deaf ears.

Outraged, Maskey approached Smyth who was seated on the council's political pulpit. Maskey snatched the order papers lying in front of Smyth. He later insisted that he had been trying to prove that his colleagues had their names down to speak but were being ignored by Smyth. In the melee, as Maskey snatched Smyth's papers, the DUP councillor grabbed the former boxer by the lapels of his blazer. As the pair tussled in front of a stunned council chamber, Maskey waved his finger at the Deputy Mayor.

"Let my coat go," he told Smyth. "Don't ever do that to me."

Sean McKnight and Cecil Ward intervened and tempers appeared to settle. However the lull was not to last with Smyth calling for a motion to prevent Maskey and the entire Sinn Féin group from addressing the council. The unionist majority quickly passed the gagging order. Sensing victory, Smyth then proposed a second motion: that Maskey should be ejected from the chamber. Once again, Maskey found himself being escorted from the room by the RUC.

After the meeting, Maskey and Smyth again "butted" political heads in the corridor outside. In a statement to the RUC, Smyth said the second incident occurred when Maskey confronted him as he left the Mayor's parlour.

"He came up to me and said, 'If you ever do that again, I'll knock your bollocks in'," Smyth complained.

In the aftermath of the incident in the chamber, Smyth alleged that Maskey's outstretched finger had in fact been an "imaginary gun" and that he had issued a "silent" death threat against him. As a result, some 40 councillors and council staff were interviewed about the alleged threat after Smyth lodged an official complaint with the RUC. Eight months later, Maskey was arrested at his West Belfast home and questioned at Strandtown RUC barracks. He was released without charge and later sued the RUC for wrongful arrest.

Maskey and his DUP rival did end up in court as a result of events at the January meeting, albeit in a different context. Determined that unionists would not be allowed to adopt the tactic of gagging Sinn Féin in the chamber, Maskey went to the High Court to challenge Smyth's actions.

High Court Judge Mr Justice Campbell ruled that unionist councillors had acted illegally in silencing their Sinn Féin counterparts.

"The debate was part of the democratic process," the judge told the court. "Those who elected a particular councillor were entitled to have their views put forward by him."

Mr Justice Campbell highlighted the fact that town clerk Cecil Ward had informed Smyth that the two motions were illegal, but that the DUP man "saw fit not to accept it". The council was ordered to pay Maskey's legal costs.

Speaking outside the court, Maskey warned: "The unionists tried to deny us our right to represent our voters. The judge ruled that they were wrong to do so. They now know they cannot ride roughshod over us or anyone else."

Within months, he was arrested once again in the midst of another City Hall scuffle. In the late 1980s, unionists had been allowed to hold "monster" rallies outside Belfast City Hall to protest against the Anglo-Irish Agreement but Sinn Féin repeatedly accused the RUC of upholding an unwritten ban on republicans holding their own parades to the building. The party argued that the refusal to allow republicans to parade in the same fashion as loyalists was an endorsement of "second-class" status for nationalists.

In June, women from the nationalist Right to March group staged a demonstration in the public gallery of the council as the monthly meeting got underway. The gallery was situated directly above the unionist benches and there was uproar when the demonstrators produced a banner proclaiming, "1969 – 1991: What Has Changed? Nationalists Demand the Right to March". The protesters then draped the banner over the ledge of the gallery, lowering it to within inches of the heads of unionist councillors. The DUP's Nigel Dodds, who was due to be elected Lord Mayor at the meeting, jumped up from his seat and grabbed hold of the banner and tried to pull it down. Other unionists joined in the tug-of-war with the women. When the combined weight of the unionist councillors succeeded in bringing down the banner, Sammy Wilson threw it onto the ground and proceeded to dance on it. As the meeting grew more raucous Rhonda Paisley called on unionists to follow as she headed off to confront the women in the gallery. The RUC was called to remove the demonstrators.

An hour after the council meeting, Maskey was arrested for having allegedly punched an RUC officer's flak jacket during jostling as the nationalists were taken from the hall. Sinn Féin's Gerard McGuigan accused the RUC of having used "unjustifiable force" in the dispersing of the female protesters.

Endorsing the claim that the RUC had been "heavy handed" in removing the protesters, the SDLP's Alex Attwood said: "People have the right to protest, but the RUC have no right to evict anyone from a public place with such aggression, disregard and unnecessary haste."

In January 1992, Judge Peter Gibson cleared Maskey of assault during the disturbance in City Hall, ruling that he couldn't be satisfied "beyond reasonable doubt" that the Sinn Féin man had assaulted the RUC officer. The six protesters who had been removed from the public gallery also successfully sued the RUC.

When the council resumed after its summer break in 1991, unionists were again accused of carrying out a sectarian policy against all things nationalist by voting to block a civic reception for the Down Gaelic football team who had just won the All-Ireland Championship. The dinner had been suggested because of the geographical fact that a sizeable part of Belfast was situated in the county of Down. Nationalists claimed that unionists' sectarianism was confirmed when Eric Smyth defended the refusal to host the dinner for the team on the grounds that the GAA was a "Catholic organisation".

In March 1992, the unionist ban on Sinn Féin attending civic functions led to councillors Tish Holland and Lily Fitzsimmons being barred from taking part in a council seminar with the Equal Opportunities Commission to mark International Woman's Day.

Ten months later, Maskey and Fra McCann were back in the courts to hear Lord Justice Murray rule that the unionist tactic of using sub-committees to exclude Sinn Féin from policy-making decisions in City Hall was both "invalid and illegal". In an ultimatum to unionists, the judge warned that Sinn Féin councillors were entitled to the "same rights and protection under the law as any other duly elected local government member".

"Unionist councillors may find this statement of the law very hard to accept, but accept it they must if they are not to fall foul of the law," said the judge.

Faced with another legal defeat, unionists were forced to abandon the sub-committee strategy. From the beginning of the new term in June 1993, the seats on all committees were shared according to party numbers within the council. The ban on Sinn Féin councillors attending civic functions had been lifted four months previously.

However the unionist grouping ensured that Sinn Féin was still barred from holding the chairmanships and vice-chairmanships of any committees.

Sammy Wilson, who remained unrepentant throughout, said: "Since October 1991, Sinn Féin have tried 151 times to put motions and 151 times they have been defeated."

Maskey, equally defiant at the way City Hall was being forced to change, replied: "It doesn't matter how many motions were lost. In 1983, we had one councillor and now we have nine. I'm confident that'll soon be ten."

Although tensions within City Hall were at a constant boiling point, there were times when the chamber appeared to be in danger of being turned into a circus. City Hall folklore has it that on one occasion when the council voted that a gondola be bought for the lake at Belfast Zoo, Ulster Unionist Tommy Patton suggested that two gondolas should be bought so that the pair could breed.

Máirtín Ó Muilleoir is thought to hold the record for the swiftest ever eviction from the council chamber. The 25-year-old rose to make his maiden speech in November 1987. A fluent Irish speaker, Ó Muilleoir was well aware that any attempt to deliver his maiden speech "as Gaeilge" (in Irish) would send the unionist benches apoplectic. Unionists had long been accused of an almost pathological paranoia against the Irish language, believing it to be part of a republican plot to undermine the cultural identity of everything British. So when Ó Muilleoir began addressing the council in Irish, there were instantaneous shouts for the newest Sinn Féin councillor to speak "in the Queen's English".

Sammy Wilson immediately demanded that Ó Muilleoir be censured for speaking in a "foreign tongue". Ulster Unionist Lord Mayor Dixie Gilmore scolded the fledgling city father for his misdemeanour and ordered him to retake his seat. When Ó Muilleoir refused, unionists immediately voted that he be ejected. The RUC was called to the chamber and the republican was promptly escorted from the hall. A stopwatch recorded that Ó Muilleoir had been in the chamber for just seven minutes.

On another occasion, Maskey recalls with amusement being approached by party colleague Tish Holland who complained that she was becoming increasingly frustrated by the abuse she was receiving from a number of unnamed councillors.

"I just told her privately to thump the next one who gave her trouble," Maskey says. "Two minutes later I looked around and she had just floored Máirtín Ó Muilleoir. It is a memory that always makes me laugh."

The sheer weight of unionist numbers meant that they controlled the council, but they found it virtually impossible to stop Sinn Féin and SDLP councillors from adopting other inventive methods to disrupt their dominance in City Hall. In January 1988, Belfast City Council began a year-long celebration to mark the city's centenary. The culmination of the planned events was to be a lavish City Hall banquet with invitations being sent out to the great and the good across Britain.

Unionist councillors were determined to put on the biggest birthday bash Belfast had ever seen, but there were others who were equally determined that the outside world would see a very different side to Belfast's City Hall. The SDLP's Brian Feeney, who was to prove a constant thorn in the side of unionists, mounted a one-man letter-writing campaign to all the invited dignitaries. Feeney advised the potential guests that they were unlikely to find themselves networking with either Northern Ireland Office (NIO) ministers or Irish government officials, as both were still barred from the City Hall as a result of unionism's ill-fated efforts to topple the Anglo-Irish Agreement. The SDLP man signed-off his letters by informing their recipients that their presence at the banquet would be seen as endorsing "100 years of oppression and bigotry" at City Hall. Feeney would later joke that he was not given the opportunity to see what effect the power of his pen had made on the celebrations as he had not been sent an invitation.

The strategy of publicly embarrassing unionists over their policies was something that nationalist councillors would increasingly adopt as their own in following years. In August 1992, Máirtín Ó Muilleoir wrote to Peter Brooke's successor, Sir Patrick Mayhew, to again demand that Belfast's council be shut down. Ó Muilleoir made the tongue-in-cheek request that a commissioner be appointed to City Hall for the last three months of the year, owing to the fact that half of the unionist grouping would be abroad on council trips. The letter may have been in jest, but it did highlight the fact that nationalists were all but barred from taking part in trips abroad, the validity of which were increasingly being called into question.

In October, the *Irish News* revealed that Belfast City Hall had spent £100,000 in that financial year on foreign excursions for councillors. Unionists took the lion's share of the various delegations, scooping up 108 places, with just two SDLP members and a single Alliance councillor being invited to join the sojourns. It was taken as read that Sinn Féin was excluded from all trips.

Criticising the exorbitant number of unionist trips abroad, paid for by Belfast ratepayers, the newspaper declared: "Of all the councils in Northern Ireland, Belfast's has become the laughing stock. Its monthly meetings are a source of constant embarrassment. The antics of some of its members would disgrace the monkey enclosure in the city zoo."

When Alliance's Tom Campbell questioned the benefit of sending independent unionist Frank Millar Sr on a three-week trip to Australia, the former shipyard worker defended the trip in his own colourful way, describing Campbell thus: "He is not big enough to get his head ducked. He is a know-all who knows f*** all."

A survey carried out by the *Irish News* the following month found that only six percent of Belfast ratepayers felt that their council provided a good service. None of those questioned felt that the council had succeeded in promoting the city in a positive light, either at home or abroad.

In 1993, Brian Feeney again sparked anger on the unionist benches when he blocked plans to twin Belfast with the sunny city of Caen in France. The North Belfast councillor said he would not only fight against the proposal, but he would "oppose any attempt to twin Belfast with any town in the universe".

The university lecturer's opposition to Belfast being linked with foreign shores was to become a constant; he had previously blocked attempts to twin Belfast with Berlin by writing to German civic leaders and informing them of the council's "colourful and dubious" history.

That same year, Eric Smyth was ejected from the chamber for continually interrupting and refusing to allow Maskey to speak. Lord Mayor Herbie Ditty had initially adjourned the meeting when the DUP preacher repeatedly disrupted what the Sinn Féin man had to say. When the meeting reconvened and Smyth still wouldn't let Maskey speak, the council voted 35-8 to have the Shankill pastor removed from the chamber. Smyth's protest lasted for 45 minutes before he agreed to leave.

While such antics helped fill the column inches of the morning newspapers, they had to vie with the shootings and murders that continued unabated on the city's streets. In June 1990, former Sinn Féin councillor Sean Keenan was shot and seriously wounded during a gun attack on his house in the heart of West Belfast. The 40-year-old republican had just returned to his Riverdale Park South address shortly before midnight when the UFF gunmen struck.

Keenan, his wife and three children were all at home when three loyalist gunmen used a sledgehammer to try and break down the kitchen door. When the would-be murder gang failed to get into the house, they opened fire through a kitchen window. Keenan, who was in the room at the time, dived for cover but was hit in the lower back as he tried to escape.

The circumstances surrounding the attack again led to claims that loyalists had been given security force assistance in mounting the murder bid. A red Vauxhall Cavalier car used in the attack had been parked on the M1 motorway on the edge of West Belfast, from where the loyalist gunmen walked the quarter of a mile through the nationalist estate to get to Keenan's home.

"They were confident enough to walk the whole way knowing they wouldn't be stopped by the RUC or British army, who had an almost permanent presence in the area," Keenan recalls. "Fortunately I had (steel drop) bars on the backdoor which stopped them getting into the house. We were lucky because if they had hit the door once more, it would have given way. They left the sledgehammer behind and I remember Alex telling me how the RUC didn't even bother to take it away for forensic tests."

The getaway car, which had been hijacked from Raleigh Street in the Shankill area, was later found burned out back in the loyalist heartland.

In October 1990, leading UDA men Jackie Thompson, Johnny Adair, Sam McCrory and Thomas Irvine were charged with the attack on the former councillor's home. The four were later released without charge when a witness withdrew her statement.

Sean Keenan explains the difficulties which being a public Sinn Féin figure brought, not only to councillors, but also to their families: "There was massive pressure on the families. You often thought about the real possibility of loyalists coming to your home and shooting your kids. The attacks were totally indiscriminate. They shot through windows or doors at anyone in a house when they attacked."

He insists that Alex Maskey was undoubtedly the one republican that loyalists wanted to kill more than any other.

"Out of all the republicans on the council, the biggest pressure was undoubtedly on Alex, simply because there were so many attempts on his life. The only attack on my life was in Riverdale. In the car with Gerry Adams, I was just there. But when it is personally directed at you, when you realise that someone is plotting to kill you, it is a very scary thought. Alex has lived with that pressure for more than 20 years and never once complained."

Just weeks before the various parties prepared for another round of local government elections in May 1993, loyalists again targeted Maskey for murder. He narrowly escaped death once more but was left devastated by the fact that a close friend was killed in the attack. Saturday, May 1 saw Maskey busy preparing for the elections which were just weeks away. With the increasing number of attacks on Sinn Féin members, councillors were warned to be particularly careful about personal security. Twelve members of the party had been killed in the four years since the last local government elections.

It was no idle warning. The UFF had carried out grenade attacks on the homes of councillors Gerard McGuigan and Joe Austin four weeks before. Convinced that he would be next, Maskey had asked his friend Alan Lundy to help him build a security porch at the front of his home. Maskey and Lundy had first met when they shared a cell in Crumlin prison in 1973. Locked up for 23 hours a day, it was easy for prisoners to get on each other's nerves, but Maskey insists that Lundy was the one man who could never annoy him.

"Alan was one of life's gentlemen. You couldn't meet a nicer guy and, when I needed help to build the porch, Alan was the first to offer it."

Maskey says that his friend had been eager to get started with the building on the morning of the attack.

"That morning Alan's wife, Margaret, had telephoned early to find out why I hadn't yet picked him up. He was always anxious to get on with the work."

Maskey recalls that two British army Saracen armoured troop carriers had been parked at the top of the street for most of the day. Soldiers had photographed and taken the personal details of the six people working on the porch in the days leading up to the shooting, but there had been no harassment on the Saturday. Around six o'clock, the men stopped work for the day. As the others left for home, Lundy stayed behind to finish and to have dinner with the Maskeys.

"We had finished dinner with Liz and the kids and were going back out to clean up," Maskey recalls. "I had gone upstairs to the bathroom when I heard two bursts of automatic gunfire."

As Lundy emerged from the porch, two UFF gunmen jumped out of a hijacked red Ford Orion car and fired at the 39-year-old. The gunmen sprayed the front of the house with automatic fire as the father-of-five tried to run back into the house.

"I could see Alan running towards the door with a hammer in his hands," recalls Liz Maskey. "Then there was a further burst of gunfire and Alan fell."

Liz screamed in terror and called out for her husband, believing that he had also been shot. She frantically tried to usher her sons through the back door, fearing that the gunmen were about to come into the house. The two boys refused to leave, repeatedly shouting out for their father who had run downstairs to find Alan Lundy lying dead in the living room.

"I still don't know if Alan was shot outside the house or was hit as he ran through the living room as the gunmen fired through the window," he says.

Still deeply affected by the death of his friend ten years on, Maskey describes Alan Lundy's murder as the darkest moment of his life.

"There is nothing I could ever do or say which could make up for the loss to Margaret and Alan's five children. I try to tell myself that I am not to blame, but you do feel guilt. Alan was protecting my home and he died for it."

The getaway car was later found at Mullhouse Lane not far from the Shankill area of loyalist West Belfast. The weapons used by the two UFF gunmen – a 9mm submachine gun and a 7.62 rifle – had been used in previous attacks, including murder. Admitting responsibility for the attack, the UFF claimed that Maskey had been its intended target. Alan Lundy was the thirteenth member of Sinn Féin to be killed since 1989. Maskey was scathing about the RUC investigation into the murder.

"What angered me most was the pathetic RUC forensic examination of the scene. They didn't even bother to pick up the bullets lying around the living room floor. They couldn't even be bothered to pick the bullet heads out of the chimney breast."

Gerry Adams immediately questioned how loyalist gunmen had been able to penetrate the heart of West Belfast without fear of arrest. Unionists dismissed Sinn Féin claims of collusion as "predictable", but the fact that the same allegations were made by the SDLP's Joe Hendron made it harder to ignore.

"It is more than a perception that there is collusion with some sections of the security forces," said Dr Hendron. "That loyalist gangsters can enter the heart of Andersonstown on a busy Saturday evening, firing shots with soldiers and police normally saturating the area, it does raise the question of collusion. I do believe this has happened and I point the finger at the security forces."

Maskey chose to go ahead with the council elections despite his friend's death. In June, Sinn Féin returned ten councillors to City Hall, while the SDLP picked up nine seats. On the unionist side, the DUP returned nine councillors, Ulster Unionists picked up 15 seats with loyalists filling another three seats. The Alliance Party returned five councillors.

In a sign of changing times at City Hall following the May elections, the Ulster Unionists attempted to broker a power-sharing agreement with the SDLP and Alliance. The UUP was prepared to jettison the DUP for their new non-unionist partners, but would still not entertain Sinn Féin in any such deal. Despite the new arrangement entitling Alliance and SDLP councillors to a share of the much-prized committee chairmanships, Ulster Unionists were not willing to surrender the top council posts of lord mayor and deputy mayor to either party.

The SDLP's Alban Maginness rounded on Ulster Unionists: "We thought sanity and civilisation would break out in Belfast City Council, but it has effectively got worse. Nothing seems to have changed. They've elected a unionist Mayor, a unionist Deputy Mayor and they have a majority of the most influential committees."

Sammy Wilson confidently predicted that nationalists would never be allowed to fill the top posts, adding: "We will ensure that there is never any non-unionist mayor or deputy in this council."

Outraged that Ulster Unionists had allowed the SDLP to take even the most irrelevant committee chairmanships, Eric Smyth refused to vote with the rest of his colleagues to elect Reg Empey as Lord Mayor. Despite blocking Sinn Féin from the chairmanships of council committees and refusing to allow any nationalist to become mayor, both the Ulster Unionists and DUP voted to elect Hugh Smyth from the Progressive Unionist Party (PUP) as Deputy Lord Mayor. This was despite the fact that the PUP was openly accepted as the political wing of the UVF, which was not to call a ceasefire for more than a year.

In August, the UFF attacked the North Belfast home of Sinn Féin councillor Bobby Lavery. Lavery's son Sean was shot and fatally wounded when two gunmen opened fire from a car, which pulled up outside the family's Antrim Road home. The 21-year-old student had been standing in the living room when the loyalists fired 25 times through the window. Nine people, including Lavery's five children, had been in the room at the time. Sean Lavery managed to stagger upstairs to his father, who did not initially realise that his son had been wounded until he collapsed into his arms.

Speaking after his son's death, Bobby Lavery insisted he did not hold any malice towards the killers.

"As far as I am concerned," he said, "the people who killed my son are ordinary human beings who have been brought up in a warped society which tells them that Catholics are evil and inferior. This state was founded on that principle."

In a plea that no one should carry out revenge attacks, he said that if anyone was to blame for his son's murder, it was the DUP leaders "who persist in telling people that they should hate us".

A month before his son's death, Lavery had been warned by the RUC that his home, which was in clear view of Girdwood army barracks, would be bombed. The home of a colleague, Lisburn councillor Annie Armstrong, had come under loyalist gun attack two weeks before the North Belfast murder. In December 1992, Lavery's brother Martin had been shot dead by the UVF as he sat in his Crumlin Road home wrapping Christmas presents.

The killing continued in 1993 when, in October, an IRA bomb killed nine Protestants on the Shankill Road. The republicans had been attempting to kill the entire UDA leadership at their headquarters above Frizzell's fish shop in the area. Thomas Begley was killed when the device he was carrying into the premises exploded prematurely. Two children and four women were among those who died in the blast. In all, 57 people were injured. It was later claimed that the UDA leadership had stopped using the building some weeks before. A day after the deaths, Gerry Adams described the bombing as "a tragedy".

"It was wrong. It cannot be excused," he said.

Three days after the attack, the UFF killed two Catholic workmen in West Belfast. But worse was to come. On October 30, UFF gunmen killed six Catholics and a Protestant in the Rising Sun bar in the County Derry village of Greysteel. Eleven others were injured. In the four-week period before the Shankill bomb, loyalists killed three people; in the month following the attack, their tally was 13.

Despite the fact that more than a dozen Sinn Féin members had been killed in four years, the NIO wrote to Maskey in December 1993 to inform him that the party's politicians were not entitled to protection for their homes. A spokesman defended the decision, stating: "The government will not provide public money to cover the installation of special security measures for Sinn Féin councillors."

Days after the NIO decision, Maskey's home was again attacked by loyalists in their first murder bid of 1994. Liz and her two sons narrowly escaped injury on January 2 when UFF gunmen fired up to 30 shots at the front of the house. The loyalists, who had been driving a Ford Orion hijacked earlier that day in Century Street in the Shankill area, fired into six other houses as they made their escape. When Maskey arrived home to check that his family were safe, he was arrested by the RUC after an alleged altercation with a policewoman at his front door. He was taken to Grosvenor Road station where he was charged with assault.

Maskey was cleared of all charges in October 1995 after television footage of the alleged incident was shown to the court. In March 1999, the RUC paid him undisclosed damages for wrongful arrest, false imprisonment and malicious prosecution. The court also ordered the RUC to pay his legal bill.

In May 1994, all parties in City Hall were provided with their own offices. As last minute work was being carried out on the new Sinn Féin suite, the UVF placed a two-pound bomb on scaffolding close to a window. The device exploded, causing serious damage and injuring two Catholic workmen, one of whom lost an eye. The party's Marie Moore had left the room just moments before the bomb exploded. The UVF later claimed it had used an electronic remote control receiver with the device but the City Hall's surrounding walls had blocked the signal. The loyalist group added that Maskey and another councillor had been the targets, but they had left the room by the time the bombers succeeded in setting off the device.

A fortnight later a death threat on council-headed notepaper was dropped into Alex Maskey's mailbox in City Hall. "Next time, be in the room," it warned.

In June, Bobby Lavery unexpectedly landed the deputy chairmanship of the Housing Liaison Committee. Although unionist policy was to prevent republicans holding any chairmanships, the North Belfast councillor had managed to "sneak" into the deputy's position due to the absence of a number of unionists from the committee meeting. Non-unionists took advantage of their absence to push the vote through. Support for Lavery and opposition to the unionist parties' ban on Sinn Féin came from an unlikely quarter. The *Belfast Telegraph* highlighted the fact that the party's democratic mandate entitled them to a legitimate say in the running of the council and warned: "They cannot be excluded. They are generally effective representatives, doing a good job for their constituents … councillors in Belfast should realise that the more they try to exclude Sinn Féin by dubious methods, the more support it may obtain."

Lavery's deputy chairmanship, however, was short-lived. His election to the post was overturned by the unionists in a move which, Maskey says, was supported by the SDLP.

By the end of 1994, things were changing both inside and outside City Hall. On August 31, the IRA announced it was calling a ceasefire and that it was determined to play its part in the new political climate. On October 13 the loyalist paramilitaries followed suit. On January 15, 1995 the NIO announced it was lifting its ban on ministers meeting with Sinn Féin.

As the council prepared to elect a new mayor in June 1995, UUP representatives tried to reactivate discussions with the SDLP in a bid to forge a pact. A key plank of the unionist attempts to secure a deal with the nationalist party was the hope that it would marginalise Sinn Féin and thwart its ambition to have a member elected as First Citizen.

The SDLP, however, shunned the UUP's advances, pointing to the fact that since the IRA's ceasefire, relationships with Sinn Féin had improved dramatically. What all sides realised was that the local government elections of 1997 held the possibility of a non-unionist majority for the first time in the history of City Hall.

Despite the SDLP being prepared to sit and wait for change in two years' time, its South Belfast councillor Alasdair McDonnell broke ranks by becoming the city's first Catholic Deputy Mayor, with the DUP's Eric Smyth taking the chair as Mayor. McDonnell's colleagues were scathing of the South Belfast doctor's refusal to toe the party line.

"It was self-seeking, wrong-headed and not in the best interests of either the council, the party or the city," said the party's leader on the council, Alex Attwood. "One swallow does not make a summer and Alasdair McDonnell as Deputy Mayor does not make for full partnership."

The SDLP responded by removing the party whip from McDonnell for a six-month period.

But ordinary citizens would quickly find that they had more to worry about when, on February 9, the IRA heralded the end of its ceasefire by exploding a huge bomb in London's Canary Wharf district. Two people were killed and another 100 injured. The IRA was widely condemned for resuming its "war", but a sizeable proportion of nationalists blamed British government intransigence for being largely to blame for the breakdown in the republican ceasefire.

In elections to the Northern Ireland Forum that year, Sinn Féin secured 15.5 percent of the vote. Despite the resumption of IRA activity, Sinn Féin managed to increase its numbers in City Hall to 13 in the May local government elections, becoming the joint largest party alongside the UUP. More crucially, with the SDLP picking up seven seats and the Alliance six, it signalled an apparent start to a non-unionist majority in the chamber.

The nationalist vote for Sinn Féin was widely seen as an endorsement of Gerry Adams' efforts to put the peace process back on track, rather than support for a resumption of the "armed struggle". By the time the IRA reinstated its ceasefire in July 1997, it had been responsible for eleven deaths. In the same period the UDA and UVF were responsible for an additional eleven killings.

In November that year, it was announced that the British government had finally accepted Alex Maskey onto its Key Persons Protection Scheme (KPPS). Maskey was the first republican to be allowed on to the programme, which funded security measures for politicians' homes and offices. Republicans saw the move as a "confidence building" measure by the British.

"It's a significant breakthrough," said Maskey, "since this is the first time a member of my party has been included in this protection scheme, which to date has been reserved for other parties and people such as judges, senior civil servants and MPs."

But the Sinn Féin councillor was soon to accuse the British government of reneging on the arrangements.

"In order for my family and me to qualify for protection I have been asked to give the RUC access to my home," he stated. "By including me in this scheme the British Secretary of State has affirmed that there is a real and immediate threat to my life. The British Secretary of State knows quite well the position of Sinn Féin in relation to the RUC."

Maskey highlighted the fact that Martin McGuinness and Gerry Adams had still to receive help with security for their homes, despite having been elected as MPs. In December, Maskey threatened legal action after Security Minister Adam Ingram refused to allow him on to the KPPS without first allowing the RUC into his home.

"I have been told that you are opposed to the involvement of the RUC because of past collusion between the RUC and loyalist paramilitaries," Ingram wrote in a letter to Maskey. "I have to make clear that I totally reject the suggestion that information gained by the RUC might be passed to loyalist terrorist groups. Such criticisms are totally unfounded. There has been no evidence to show that there is any collusion between the RUC and loyalist paramilitary groups."

Nationalists treated the statement with a high degree of scepticism. It would be another six years before Britain's most senior police officer,

Sir John Stevens, publicly acknowledged that members of the British army and RUC had colluded in the murder and attempted murder of dozens of nationalists.

Alex Maskey was to remark that the statement had come ten years too late to save his friend Alan Lundy and others.

Chapter Six
BREAKING THE MOULD

SHOCK waves ran through the benches in City Hall when the results of the May 1997 council elections were announced – for the first time in its history, the city's rate-payers had returned a non-unionist majority.

What had been the bastion of Britishness since the 1920s was in danger of being lost to nationalists. The fact that Sinn Féin was now the joint largest party on Belfast City Council alongside the UUP only added to unionist dismay.

The nightmare scenario seemed to have arrived. A combination of the SDLP's seven councillors, the Alliance Party's group of six and a Sinn Féin bloc of 13, meant that control of City Hall was no longer in the hands of the Ulster Unionists and DUP.

The first sign of change came on June 2 when Sinn Féin, Alliance and the SDLP combined to elect the city's first nationalist Lord Mayor. The SDLP's Alban Maginness defeated Harry Smyth of the DUP by four votes to become the first nationalist to break the 76-year tradition of unionist mayoralty in Belfast.

Another sign came when Maginness' nomination was seconded by Alex Maskey who helped the SDLP man don the heavy chains of office after his election. Ironically, while the institution of lord mayor had been kept exclusively within the hands of unionists since the 1920s, the antique chain itself bore the Irish inscription, "Eireann Go Brea" (Ireland forever).

Sammy Wilson refused to welcome either Maginness' ascension to office or Sinn Féin's increased electoral mandate.

"The DUP doesn't care about the 30,000 people who have voted to destroy this city," the East Belfast councillor told the chamber on the night of the election. "Sinn Féin are lepers and will remain lepers. We should lock them out. They should be squashed and kept outside."

In a statement which would come back to haunt him four short

Above: Alex Maskey (centre) with his aunt Jean, uncle Gerard and sister Marion (right) in 1955

Below: Alex, Patsy and Marion Maskey pictured in the grounds of Belfast Castle, 1960

Top left: Schoolboy boxer Alex trades punches with Anthony Hanna in the early 1960s

Above: Alex and his cousins Colette and Geraldine, and sister Patricia during a summer holiday to Minorstown, County Down in the mid 1960s

Left: Alex Maskey in the grounds of Belfast Art College in 1969

Above left: Liz and Alex on their wedding day, September 4, 1976 **Above top:** Alex Maskey photographed with internees in the republican cages in Long Kesh in 1974. **Above right:** Alex Maskey (right) with Kieran Doherty in Long Kesh, c. 1974. Doherty was later to die on hunger strike in August 1981 **Below:** Alex Maskey (right) helps to carry the coffin of IRA hunger striker Joe McDonnell in July 1981

Left: Maskey is carried by Sinn Féin supporters after becoming their first councillor to be elected to Belfast City Council in 70 years
Below: Maskey is watched by two armed RUC men as he poses for photographers at Belfast City Hall after his election in June 1983

Top left: Schoolboy boxer Alex trades punches with Anthony Hanna in the early 1960s

Above: Alex and his cousins Colette and Geraldine, and sister Patricia during a summer holiday to Minorstown, County Down in the mid 1960s

Left: Alex Maskey in the grounds of Belfast Art College in 1969

Above: Alex Maskey (centre) with his aunt Jean, uncle Gerard and sister Marion (right) in 1955
Below: Alex, Patsy and Marion Maskey pictured in the grounds of Belfast Castle, 1960

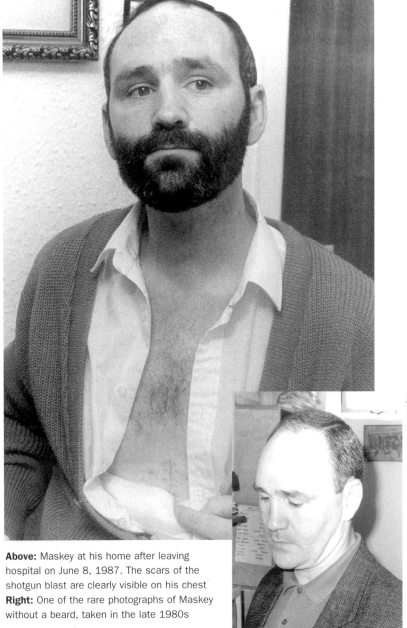

Above: Maskey at his home after leaving hospital on June 8, 1987. The scars of the shotgun blast are clearly visible on his chest
Right: One of the rare photographs of Maskey without a beard, taken in the late 1980s

Above: With former Sinn Féin councillor Joe Austin and Gerry Adams in 1985

Right: Liberal councillor Pierre Royan pictured brandishing a starting pistol in his right hand, which he had just fired at Maskey during the Sinn Féin man's address to Hackney Council in October 1986. Maskey's party colleague (and future Health Minister) Bairbre DeBrún is at the front of the picture

Above: Maskey confronts a senior RUC officer after republicans were blocked from marching to Belfast City Hall
Below: Maskey helps to carry the coffin of IRA volunteer Mairéad Farrell moments before the funeral was attacked by UFF man Michael Stone in March 1988. Directly behind Maskey is veteran republican Terry 'Cleeky' Clarke

Above: Maskey
welcomes veteran
republican Joe Cahill
back to Belfast for the
first time in twenty years

Left: Alan Lundy who was
shot dead outside Alex
Maskey's home in May 1993
pictured with his wife
Margaret and five children
Below: Maskey and Bobby
Lavery carry the coffin of Alan
Lundy to the Holy Cross
Church in Ardoyne after the
father of five was shot dead
outside Maskey's home

years later, he pointed towards the Lord Mayor's podium, predicting: "They will never occupy that chair."

While republicans were still excluded from the two most senior offices of City Hall, Maskey insists that Maginness' election was still an important victory. He had informed the SDLP man before the meeting that he would nominate him as Lord Mayor.

"We were the largest party in the council," says Maskey, "but we took the view that if we couldn't get the lord mayor's position ourselves, it should still have gone to a nationalist. It was the first time that unionists were seen to have lost control of City Hall and it would have been wrong for us to deprive the nationalist people of Belfast that long overdue victory. We wanted to be seen as being magnanimous."

Unionists had opposed Maginness' election and vowed to boycott his inaugural dinner in protest at a decision not to include the traditional toast to the Royal Family. Maginness, who had first been elected to the council in 1985, said that while he would not deny his nationalist roots, he was determined to work with unionists for an inclusive Belfast.

"I am aware of a great sense of history in the position I hold and in this building," he said. "But it is remarkable to think that no Catholic has ever been Lord Mayor of Belfast, that no nationalist has ever been allowed to be at home in these chambers."

When Maginness announced that he was removing the Union Flag from the Lord Mayor's parlour in a bid to depoliticise the office of Belfast's First Citizen, unionists reacted angrily, pledging a policy of non-cooperation throughout his year in office. They subsequently boycotted Maginness' Christmas dinner.

However, if nationalists thought that wholesale change was imminent, they were to receive a shock of their own. In October, the *Belfast Telegraph* revealed that the Alliance Party had brokered a behind-the-scenes deal with the Ulster Unionists to carve up the chairmanships of the council's 16 committees. Nationalists were outraged that their "victory" had been snatched away at the eleventh hour. When the Alliance-UUP pact was made public it showed that, despite Sinn Féin having captured more than a quarter of all first preference votes in the election, the party was to be excluded from holding the chairmanship of any committee. The SDLP fared only marginally better with one chairmanship. Alliance, with less than half the number of councillors of Sinn Féin and one less than the SDLP, found itself controlling four committees.

It was a similar story when it came to appointments to public bodies outside the chamber. Of the council's 76 nominations to these bodies, 66 came from either the unionist or Alliance benches. Although the SDLP and Sinn Féin held nearly 40 percent of the seats in City Hall, the pact meant that roughly 94 percent of committee chairmanships and deputy-chairmanships were held by the various shades of unionism. Maskey attacked the Alliance-UUP covenant, warning that it had ensured that discrimination was "alive and well", despite the fact that unionists were now technically in the minority.

"Unionists are opposed to equality within Belfast City Council," he said. "They are unable to come to terms with the political realities and conditions of Belfast, where Sinn Féin is the joint largest party."

The SDLP's Alex Attwood predicted that the pact would bring back the "bad old days" to City Hall and argued that the Catholic community would see it as rubber-stamping a unionist "agenda of exclusion" of nationalists.

Alliance councillor Tom Campbell, defending the deal, said: "The Alliance Party has sought to get the best deal it can for its electorate and we have sought to get the best deal for the city."

Rejecting nationalist claims that Alliance was endorsing an "exclusion pact", Campbell argued: "We felt the Ulster Unionists came up with the proposal that was most suitable. It envisages the sharing of all the top posts in the next four years between the constitutional parties."

The UUP's Fred Cobain was less diplomatic however, insisting that the deal would ensure that Sinn Féin were excluded from key positions of power for the following four years.

"I make no apology for that," said the former lord mayor.

The intrigue of Belfast's local government was soon to be overshadowed by events beyond the political boundaries of the city.

Talks between Gerry Adams and John Hume had stretched back more than a decade. The leaders of the two nationalist parties, in fact, had initiated a series of discussions in February 1985. Throughout 1987-88 Sinn Féin and the SDLP had engaged in face-to-face talks and even though the discussions ended in apparent failure in September 1989, Hume and Adams remained in contact. Both agreed on the right of the Irish people to self-determination, but differed hugely on the method used to achieve such an aspiration.

Within the republican movement, there was added pressure on the IRA to protect against unnecessary loss of life. On January 29, 1989, Gerry Adams told Sinn Féin delegates at the party's Ard Fheis that the IRA had to be "careful and careful again, to avoid civilian casualties."

Hume and Adams met four times during 1989, but it wasn't just the SDLP who were talking to republicans. The IRA and the British had kept a line of contact in place throughout the Troubles and, in October 1990, Sinn Féin's Martin McGuinness and Gerry Kelly began meeting with British government official Michael Oatley, who was known to be a senior figure within the MI6 intelligence agency. Those discussions were to continue until November 1993.

It is understood that the British had held talks with the Sinn Féin leaders on May 1, the day that Alan Lundy was shot dead at Alex Maskey's house. Maskey believes it is inconceivable that the British did not know there was active targeting of his house while they were preparing to meet the delegation from his party.

Christmas 1990 saw the IRA announce a three-day ceasefire, its first for 15 years. While all sides were talking behind the scenes, the IRA's campaign resumed in the New Year, most notably with a mortar attack on 10 Downing Street in February 1991 as Prime Minister John Major and his Cabinet were meeting inside the building.

In August that year, Gerry Adams wrote to the British and Irish governments and the North's religious and political leaders, offering to take part in open-ended discussions aimed at developing a peace process. Private talks aimed at finding a permanent peace continued throughout 1992. For republicans, the efforts suffered a setback when

Adams lost his West Belfast seat to the SDLP's Joe Hendron, largely due to tactical voting by the unionist minority in the constituency.

While the SDLP repeatedly accused Sinn Féin of stealing votes through rampant impersonation, the SDLP itself also came in for scrutiny over its electoral practices. The Election Court found Dr Hendron and his agent guilty on a number of counts of illegal practices, but the election result was allowed to stand on the grounds of "inadvertence".

Despite the continuous battle for the "hearts and minds" of nationalist voters, the two parties continued their dialogue. Both appeared to be developing a new understanding within nationalism, but loyalist paramilitaries seemed determined to scupper the talks by exerting pressure on the moderate nationalist party to abandon its contact with republicans. In February 1993 the UFF left bombs outside the homes of two SDLP councillors.

By April, Hume and Adams were again in discussions, publishing a joint statement reaffirming the right of the Irish people to national self-determination. In September the UFF bombed the homes of four more SDLP councillors. Later that month, the leaders claimed that they had made considerable progress during talks. In October, Ulster Unionists on Belfast City Council announced they were cutting off all contact with the SDLP until the Hume-Adams talks were abandoned. At the end of that month the UFF shot dead 54-year-old James Cameron and 28-year-old father-of-two Mark Rodgers at the council's Kennedy Way cleansing depot in West Belfast. The Catholic employees were killed when two gunmen, dressed as road sweepers, tricked their way into the depot shortly after 7.30am as the 25 workers prepared for that day's work. Maskey remembers the Kennedy Way killings as a seminal moment in his determination that the peace process would become a reality.

"I remember the thousands of people who turned up to a peace vigil after the deaths of Jim Cameron and Mark Rodgers. That was a particularly bad period of the Troubles, with people literally being killed every day. I remember speaking to Gerry Adams at the time and saying that we were in very real danger of slipping into a civil war situation. We had to make sure that the peace process worked. The divisions between the two communities were very deep at that point in time."

In the autumn of 1993 Hume and Adams delivered a document to the Irish government aimed at moving the peace process forward. In December of the same year, John Major and Taoiseach Albert Reynolds produced the Downing Street Declaration which set out both governments' proposals for the way forward. In early 1994 it appeared that hopes for peace could become a reality when the IRA released a statement, claiming: "We are prepared to be flexible in exploring the potential for peace. All concerned should leave no stone unturned."

A three-day IRA ceasefire followed in March. Then, on August 31 1994, the controversial ten-year talks between Hume and Adams appeared to bear fruit when the IRA announced "a complete cessation of military operations".

"We believe that an opportunity to create a just and lasting settlement has been created," read their statement. "We are therefore entering into a new situation in a spirit of determination and confidence, determined that the injustices which created the conflict will be removed and confident in the strength and justice of our struggle to achieve this."

In the weeks preceding this announcement, Maskey and other leading Sinn Féin figures were tasked with briefing the republican grassroots. As a key figure, Maskey was crucial to the Adams leaderships' ability to bring rank-and-file members along the road to peace. He recalls speaking at a large number of internal republican briefings in the run-up to the ceasefire and afterwards. Some meetings, Maskey said, were held in huge halls while others took place in people's kitchens.

"A lot of these meetings were tense occasions. I remember one on the New Lodge Road (in North Belfast). The hall was packed. People wanted to know what was going to happen. I had to explain the context for the ceasefire and the hopes for peace and political progress. It is fair to say that people were anxious at the move. I remember one former prisoner asking, 'Is that it. Is this what the whole war was for?' I looked at the crowd and I said that I would make no apology for trying to bring about a situation which would mean that no one else had to die.

"I told them that, if the ceasefire broke down, my conscience and the consciences of everyone else who had put so much time into creating this opportunity would be clear because at least we'd tried. The ceasefire was a risk worth taking if it meant no one else had to die or go to prison."

On October 13, loyalists followed the IRA lead when veteran Gusty Spence declared that the UVF and UFF were calling their own ceasefires. The decision had been taken on the understanding that union with Britain was safe. While they offered "abject and true remorse" to the "innocent" victims of their violence, it also warned that their ceasefire was dependent on the continued cessation of "nationalist and republican" violence.

The process appeared to be moving forward at pace when, in April 1995, Sinn Féin councillor Tom Hartley joined Taoiseach John Bruton, Secretary of State Patrick Mayhew and senior Ulster Unionist Ken Maginnis at a commemoration in Dublin to remember Irish people who had died during the Second World War and the Holocaust. Hartley's participation in the event led to him being severely criticised by the republican grassroots, despite the fact that he was the party's representative at the ceremony.

However, by the end of 1995 initial hopes of a lasting peace appeared to be slipping away. In November Gerry Adams announced that talks between Sinn Féin and the British government had ended in failure. The writing appeared to be on the wall when four days later he accused the British of having "subverted the peace process" to the point where it "no longer existed".

In January 1996 former US senator George Mitchell, who had been brought in to facilitate talks between the North's political parties, warned that the IRA was in danger of splitting if all-party interaction did not begin immediately. Mitchell's warning was not without foundation. On February 9, the IRA ended its ceasefire with a huge explosion in the heart of London's financial headquarters in Canary Wharf. Two men were killed. Republicans blamed the collapse of the IRA ceasefire on the British government's refusal to fulfil its obligations in the peace process.

Maskey admits that he had resigned himself to the end of the ceasefire by the end of 1995.

"The breakdown in the ceasefire had been well signposted. The total inaction of John Major and John Bruton (Fine Gael Taoiseach) meant that it was inevitable that the ceasefire would come to an end sooner rather than later. I remember being in a social club in West Belfast on the night it broke down and at first people were shocked. But then there was a sense of anger at Major and Bruton for wasting such a valuable opportunity."

Almost immediately, efforts got underway to try to salvage what was left of the process. On February 21 Hume and Adams met the IRA's Army Council in Dublin in an effort to have the ceasefire restored. Despite the breakdown in the process, political life in Northern Ireland went on. In May 1996 elections to the new Northern Ireland Forum took place. In West Belfast, Maskey was elected alongside Gerry Adams, Dodie McGuinness and Annie Armstrong, with Sinn Féin winning four out of the constituency's five seats.

While Sinn Féin received 15.5 per cent of the overall vote in the Forum elections, the party was excluded from taking part in talks at Stormont in June, due to the breakdown in the IRA's ceasefire. Neither Sinn Féin nor the SDLP were ever to take part in the Forum talks.

Events appeared to be moving forward in May 1997 when Labour's Tony Blair replaced John Major as British Prime Minister. One month later, Sinn Féin's Caoimhghín Ó Caoláin became the party's first member to be elected to the Dail since Maskey's friend Kieran Doherty in 1981.

On July 17 1997, the IRA reinstated its ceasefire and two months later Sinn Féin entered the talks process chaired by George Mitchell at Stormont. Maskey was chosen to be part of Sinn Féin's team.

"One of my roles was to organise bi-lateral talks with the other parties and to help make sure that all of our people were kept aware of everything that was going on," he says. "I regularly arranged for groups of party members to visit the talks venue at Castle Buildings to see for themselves what we were doing. It was an intensive period of negotiations and it was important that everyone was kept onboard."

In December Gerry Adams travelled to London to meet with Tony Blair coincidentally creating a little piece of history. It was the first time a Sinn Féin leader had met a British Prime Minister in Downing Street since Arthur Griffith and Michael Collins met Lloyd George in 1921. Maskey made a statement in January which appeared to signal a growing willingness on the part of republicans to compromise with unionists. "We have said from the outset," he said, "that there will be very difficult decisions which will have to be taken by republicans. After all, republicans have paid a very heavy price for our involvement in this struggle and we have no intention of going back on that."

The talks went on through the spring of 1998. In April an agreement seemed to have been reached. The deal, which would become known as the Good Friday Agreement, included the establishment of an Assembly at Stormont that would have a power-sharing Executive with ministerial powers. While the re-establishment of Stormont was seen as a concession to unionists, there was also a guarantee to establish a North-South Ministerial Council, which enshrined an input from the Irish government. Unionists argued that they had succeeded in bringing back powers to Stormont. Republicans insisted that the Good Friday Agreement and the Stormont Assembly were merely a "half-way house" towards the ultimate goal of a united Ireland.

In the days and weeks following the signing of the agreement, key Sinn Féin figures took on an exhaustive series of meetings with the republican grassroots across Ireland.

"The agreement was concluded on Good Friday after days and weeks of intense negotiations," Maskey now recalls. "On the Saturday morning I set off in a car bound for Cork to address an Easter Commemoration and to chair a series of meetings to tell people what was in the deal. I remember Gerry (Adams) insisting that those of us who were involved in addressing those first meetings across the country should not try to sell the agreement in any way. We were to explain to people what was involved in the agreement, but the people had to make up their own minds. We could give our analysis, but the issues were so critical that people had to make their own judgements."

Maskey found himself addressing a meeting of grassroots members in the heart of staunchly republican South Armagh.

"I remember one meeting in Cullyhanna, which went on for nearly five hours. People were anxious about what was going to happen next. One prominent republican, whom I regard as a friend, was very sceptical about us having to sign up to the Agreement. There were questions as to whether we had sold out the republican cause.

"I looked around and pointed out some of the people in the hall who were well respected in the republican family and who had signed the non-violence pledge as councillors. I asked if these were the kind of people who would allow the republican cause to be sold out. The following morning some of us had a meeting to discuss the mood of people in the various areas. I said I believed the people of South Armagh would support the deal. The night before had told me all I needed to know."

Around this period, Maskey and a number of key republicans, led by Gerry Kelly, were allowed into the H-Blocks to brief IRA prisoners on the Agreement. The delegation was joined by African National Congress (ANC) leaders, Cyril Ramaphosa and Nakedi Phosa, who were providing the party with their own experiences of conflict resolution. It was to be a key meeting with 120 IRA prisoners, men and women, being brought together for the first time in many years.

"There were republicans there who hadn't seen each other for 20 years," says Maskey, "and it was a very emotional meeting with people hugging each other and catching up on old times. The meeting lasted about four hours and at the end I was confident that the prisoners were one hundred percent behind us. These were the people who fought the war and now they were giving their support to the peace."

In June 1998, Maskey appeared to show an acceptance that all sides had suffered when he acknowledged that members of the RUC had also been victims of the Troubles.

"The RUC have been in the front line of this conflict," he said. "As a result, they have, of course, suffered and we have no hesitation in acknowledging that reality. But also, and this is at the heart of the issue for nationalists, they have inflicted great hurt and suffering on the nationalist people."

Assembly elections were also held that month. Ulster Unionists won 28 seats, the SDLP 24 seats, the DUP 20 seats and Sinn Féin 18 seats. Maskey was elected in West Belfast where Sinn Féin picked up four of the available six seats.

The new Assembly convened for the first time at Stormont on July 1. Maskey was appointed Chief Whip for his party and as such was in charge of party discipline and ensuring that things ran smoothly for his Sinn Féin colleagues. It was to be a turbulent time for the ill-fated body.

Having turned 50 and now a grandfather, Maskey rejected suggestions that he should close the door on his City Hall career.

"With no certainty that the Assembly would last, I could not risk losing my electoral mandate. The Assembly was a challenge, but I remember thinking that I'd been in City Hall for 15 years and hadn't achieved everything I set out to change back in 1983."

Although republicans were still barred from the two most senior positions in City Hall, there did appear to be signs of hope. Sinn Féin lost a High Court legal challenge against being barred from council chairmanships in May, but a new pact between SDLP, Alliance and Sinn Féin paved the way for the sharing of committees along party strengths.

In June 1999, republicans had something to celebrate when veteran Sinn Féin councillor Marie Moore was elected Deputy Mayor while the Ulster Unionist's Bob Stoker took the office of First Citizen. However, within days, there was a political row when Stoker announced that he would not be inviting his deputy to his inaugural dinner. The UUP Mayor denied that he was discriminating against Sinn Féin.

"This is a personal invitation from myself. I don't believe that Sinn Féin warrant an invitation at this point in time," he said.However

Marie Moore was not impressed with Stoker's explanation and described the "snub" as an insult to the party's voters.

"This is an outrageous decision and a blatant act of discrimination against a significant proportion of the city's electorate," she said.

In June 1999, a 21-year period of anguish for the Maskey family circle came to an end when the bodies of John McClory and Brian McKinney were discovered at Iniskeen, County Monaghan. McClory was Maskey's cousin and had lived opposite him in Gartree Place. John and his friend, Brian, were killed by the IRA in May 1978. Maskey knew both young men very well.

It was speculated at the time that the pair had been abducted and questioned by the IRA about anti-social activity in West Belfast. McClory, aged 18 at the time, was said to have been shot while attempting to escape while McKinney, aged 22, was killed after he witnessed the shooting. The two young men became part of a group of people known as the "Disappeared" who had gone missing, believed dead, during the Troubles.

In June 1999 the IRA supplied information about a number of makeshift graves to a commission which had been set up to locate the bodies. After a 30-day search the remains of the two young men were finally uncovered. Alex Maskey, who has rarely spoken publicly about the death of his cousin, said: "I think what happened was one of the darker episodes of republican history. It is a very tragic part of our family history, which affected all of us enormously. I was very close to the McClorys while I was growing up and I visited their home an awful lot.

"John's parents Mary and John were always very kind to me. My Uncle John was a renowned boxer and was my idol when I was growing up. Everyone in the family was deeply affected by John's death and I don't think my Aunt Mary ever really got over it. It is a very difficult issue for the whole family to come to terms with.

"Given my position as a republican, and a relative, I accept that the family would have felt let down, but despite the tragedy of John and Brian's death, the McClorys and the McKinneys remained close to me."

Maskey may have thought the attempts to negotiate between nationalists and unionists in City Hall had been difficult, but in the summer of 1999 he was to learn that the negotiations surrounding the Good Friday Agreement were on another plane entirely. Attempts to establish an Executive had begun with all-party talks in April 1999. The talks broke up with all sides calling for the establishment of an Executive within three weeks.

Unionists insisted that the IRA would have to decommission their weapons before the establishment of any Executive. Conversely Sinn Féin argued that the Stormont institutions would have to be seen as working effectively before the IRA could consider any act of decommissioning. When the Assembly met on July 15 to nominate ministers to the new Executive, the Ulster Unionists refused to attend, citing the IRA's refusal to disarm.

With a deadlock in place, Senator George Mitchell returned to the North to begin a review of the talks. The deadlock appeared to have been broken when the IRA announced on November 17 that it would meet with the international decommissioning body chaired by retired Canadian General John de Chastelain. The group had been set up under the Agreement and was meant to oversee the decommissioning of loyalist and republican weapons

The Assembly re-convened twelve days later and duly elected ten ministers to the Executive, including Sinn Féin's Martin McGuinness and Bairbre de Brún as Education and Health Ministers respectively. The DUP's two new ministers, Peter Robinson and Nigel Dodds, announced they would not attend Executive meetings in protest at the presence of the two Sinn Féin ministers. The Executive, minus the DUP ministers, finally met on December 2, the same day the Irish government formally removed Articles 2 and 3 from its constitution.

However, despite initial hopes that the power-sharing Executive might succeed, Secretary of State Peter Mandelson officially suspended the Stormont Assembly in February 2000, blaming the IRA's failure to decommission. The process appeared to be back on track when on March 17, UUP leader David Trimble declared that he would be prepared to go back into the Assembly prior to republican decommissioning if there was a guarantee that the issue would be dealt with.

On May 6, the IRA announced that it would begin a process with General de Chastelain's decommissioning body to put weapons "completely and verifiably" beyond use. One-time ANC leader Cyril Ramaphosa and former president of Finland, Martti Ahtisaari, were appointed as the general's weapons inspectors. On May 29, the Assembly's powers were restored.

Two days after the Assembly was re-established, Alex Maskey finally looked to be on the verge of becoming Belfast's first republican Lord Mayor when the Alliance Party signalled that they would support him for the post in the June election. But within Alliance there was an element of grumbling over the issue of electing a Sinn Féin First Citizen. Days before the election was due to take place, East Belfast councillor Danny Dow resigned from Alliance in protest at the party's plan to support Maskey. Dow's resignation meant that the combined vote of Sinn Féin, SDLP and Alliance was one short of the overall majority needed for Maskey to become Mayor. Defending his decision to defy the party line and block Maskey's election, Dow said: "If I stood on an election platform and said Danny Dow was going to vote for a Sinn Féin lord mayor the first opportunity he gets, Danny Dow would not have been elected. I'm there to do what the people in the street tell me to do, the people that actually vote for me. That's what I'm there to represent, not to represent some high and mighty know-better-than-you attitude."

There was a palpable tension in the council chamber on the night Dow took his seat on the unionist benches. His defection allowed the combined UUP and DUP votes to elect Sammy Wilson as Lord Mayor.

Afterwards, Dow said of his former Alliance colleagues: "There was a terrible atmosphere, they didn't seem to want me."

The Alliance leader in the chamber, David Alderdice, was less than courteous about his former colleague, saying: "Danny finds it difficult to look me in the eye. He looks much more comfortable sitting over there in front of Hugh Smyth."

Despite Dow's defection, it was the decision of the pro-agreement UUP to vote against him that most annoyed Maskey. Ulster Unionists Reg Empey and Michael McGimpsey, who as ministers in the Stormont Executive sat alongside Martin McGuinness and Bairbre de Brún, had left Stormont that evening and rushed to City Hall to help elect Wilson, whose DUP party was avowedly anti-agreement."It is ironic," said Maskey, "that Reg Empey and Michael McGimpsey came from a meeting of the power-sharing Executive, which is boycotted by the DUP because of the presence of Sinn Féin ministers, and then voted for Sammy Wilson to ensure that I could not become Mayor. To me that is utter hypocrisy and sheer sectarianism."

McGimpsey denied the accusation that his party had voted along sectarian lines. "We had disagreements with the DUP over the Agreement and we made those disagreements voluble. We made those disagreements quite clear. But in local government, in the City Hall, this is a different situation and, as I said, we had an arrangement."

McGimpsey's colleague Fred Proctor also defended the party's decision to vote for an anti-agreement candidate, insisting that his party would have supported any DUP candidate "because it was their turn". Nationalists highlighted the fact that unionists had blocked Maskey's bid to become Mayor, but had elected as Deputy Mayor Frank McCoubrey whose Ulster Democratic Party (UDP) was closely linked to the UDA.

Speaking after his mayoral victory, Sammy Wilson said that it would have been "intolerable" to have a Sinn Féin lord mayor. The DUP man insisted that he would represent all the communities in Belfast "as fairly and faithfully as possible without compromising my traditional unionist beliefs and principles".

The SDLP's Catherine Molloy branded Wilson's election as a "night of shame". David Alderdice of Alliance accused unionists of having sent Belfast City Hall "back to the bad old days".

"They were not prepared to vote for Sinn Féin, but they were prepared to vote for a UDP candidate, a party that is associated with the UFF and UDA," said the Alliance man. "That is sheer hypocrisy."

Sinn Féin's hopes of having a republican mayor for Belfast had again been dashed, but events outside City Hall were moving onwards at pace. At the end of June the international decommissioning body announced they had inspected IRA arms dumps. Weapons inspectors again returned to the IRA caches in October to verify that they had not been opened. The apparent distance which mainstream republicans had been prepared to move was seen when, in March 2001, Maskey condemned a dissident republican bomb attack on BBC headquarters in London.

"I view this action last night as both wrong and irresponsible and indeed we have consistently called on this micro-group not only to stop their activities but indeed to disband," he said. A month later Maskey again condemned dissidents after a bomb attack on the RUC's training headquarters at Garnerville in East Belfast.

"I absolutely deplore their activity and we are totally opposed to them. These organisations, and there are loyalist organisations totally opposed to the Agreement ... have no role to play and have no vision for the future."

On June 7, Sinn Féin scored an important victory when it overcame the SDLP in the Westminster elections to become the largest nationalist party in the North. Gerry Adams, Martin McGuinness, Michelle Gildernew and Pat Doherty were returned to Westminster as MPs.

Republican morale was further boosted a week later when, after the local government elections, Sinn Féin became the single biggest party in City Hall. The party had captured 28.4 per cent of the overall vote with 14 councillors, ten percentage points more than the Ulster Unionists, who with 11 councillors, were the second largest party.

Maskey had moved from his West Belfast constituency to another in the south of the city. His old seat, however, stayed in the family after being won by his younger brother, Paul. While the unionist parties had a total of 25 councillors, the opposition once again held the majority by a single vote. A fortnight later, Maskey made a second bid to become the city's first Sinn Féin mayor. This time Alliance refused to support his bid, citing the arrest in Colombia of three republicans who were alleged to have been training left-wing guerrillas. Defending his party's decision, David Alderdice insisted that republicans had not done enough to persuade Alliance to help elect Maskey as mayor.

"Yes, there has been some co-operation in City Hall committees, yet there is much progress to be made," said Alderdice. Maskey branded the Alliance Party's refusal to support his candidature a "disgrace".

"It flies totally in the face of the democratic wishes of people in this city and ensures that the status quo of unionist domination at City Hall remains," he blasted. He pointed to the fact that Alliance had agreed to support UUP candidate Jim Rodgers, who was publicly opposed to the Good Friday Agreement.

"Alliance is totally contradicting itself by supporting the election of an anti-agreement unionist and is lining up with the UUP, the anti-agreement DUP and people who align themselves with the loyalist paramilitaries who have been causing the instability on the streets of this city in recent days." It would be a turbulent and violent year before Maskey made his third bid to become Belfast's First Citizen. In October, the international decommissioning body said it had witnessed the IRA putting a significant amount of its weaponry beyond use. The following day David Trimble re-nominated ministers to the Executive, preventing the threatened collapse of the institutions. The number of bombings and shootings in Belfast during 2001 had been the highest for two decades. The year 2002 started as the previous year had ended with serious rioting continuing along a number of Belfast interfaces throughout the spring.

In April the IRA announced that it had put a second tranche of weaponry beyond use in line with its discussions with the decommissioning body. At the beginning of May, a number of meetings took place between Sinn Féin and Alliance in the council to discuss support for a republican mayor. The initial talks did not involve Maskey, but were carried out by Sinn Féin's Tom Hartley and Chrissie McAuley and Alliance's David Alderdice and Tom Ekin. "On previous occasions when I ran for mayor, Alliance councillors actually said they would support any Sinn Féin candidate other than myself,"

Maskey recalls. "Rightly or wrongly, they looked upon me as being a hard-line republican who would be too extreme for unionists. They made it clear that they didn't want me and said on more than one occasion that they would support anyone Sinn Féin wanted to put forward, other than myself."

He says that Alliance was told in "polite but emphatic terms" that they were not going to pick Sinn Féin's mayoral candidate.

"To be fair, when I sat down with David Alderdice in the run-up to the 2002 mayoral vote, the discussions were good-natured. I outlined in general terms the way in which I would approach my year in office, particularly the way in which I wanted to reach out to unionists. I wanted to be sensitive to unionist thinking and was determined that I wasn't going to discriminate against the Protestant community in the same way that nationalists had been mistreated for so long."

Maskey believes that any serious concerns that the Alliance leader may have had were removed when he informed Alderdice that he did not intend to remove any of the unionist symbols that adorned City Hall.

"I had already decided that I wouldn't remove any of the vestiges of unionist history in the Mayor's parlour, even though I would have been justified in doing so."

He was well aware, though, of the popular presumption that if elected he would choose to neutralise the Mayor's parlour, as had happened in the case of Alban Maginness' year in office, or alternatively that he would replace all symbols of unionism with the trappings of his own republican history.

"I knew people were convinced I would try to remove the unionist symbols; that was one of Alliance's main concerns. I had decided to leave the unionist symbols in place but would seek to introduce symbols from the nationalist-republican tradition to go alongside them."

Ironically, Maskey believes that working relationships built up in the Assembly at Stormont played a crucial role in Alliance deciding to support his bid to become mayor. As Sinn Féin's Chief Whip there, Maskey had worked alongside all the senior Alliance members. These included David Alderdice's older brother and former party leader, John Alderdice, who was Speaker of the House, and David Ford, who acted as Alliance's Chief Whip before becoming party leader.

"I worked closely with John Alderdice and David Ford and we developed a good relationship. I believe those relationships helped convince Alliance that I was determined to use my year in office for the good of everyone in this city. It was ironic that we could work with the unionists and the other parties in the Assembly, but once the unionists crossed the door of the City Hall, they were immediately transported back to 1690 and the Battle of the Boyne."

The debate over support for Maskey's mayoral bid was conducted throughout the Alliance Party and the decision to back him was by no means unanimous. A number of prominent figures in the ranks had been vocal in their opposition to Maskey becoming mayor. Ultimately it was decided that the party's three Belfast councillors should make the decision.

The pressure on the Alliance councillors was tremendous, particularly from senior Ulster Unionists. One of the party's MEPs, Jim Nicholson, warned Alliance that Maskey's election as mayor could destabilise unionism and could even damage Belfast's bid to become European City of Culture.

"Even at this stage, have a long hard re-think," Nicholson urged the three Alliance councillors in the run-up to the mayoral vote.

On May 31, Alliance representatives held a press conference at Belfast's Europa Hotel to announce their decision. David Alderdice – seated alongside party leader David Ford and his two council colleagues, Tom Ekin and Naomi Long – admitted that his party experienced "great difficulty" in reaching a decision about supporting Maskey for mayor.

The IRA's two acts of decommissioning during the previous year, said Alderdice, had influenced members greatly and persuaded them to overturn their previous opposition to Sinn Féin. Referring to the decision not to endorse Maskey for mayor twelve months before, Alderdice said: "Primarily, we felt Sinn Féin had singularly failed to meet its main obligation under the Good Friday Agreement, it had failed to convince the IRA to begin the process of putting weapons beyond use. Since then, there had been two acts of decommissioning which had aided the peace process."

Insisting that Alliance was "acting for the greater good", Alderdice said the party expected unionist criticism. The matter, however, was by no means settled. The pressure on Alliance councillors intensified in the run-up to the mayoral election. Loyalists threatened to protest outside the homes of the councillors. Sectarian graffiti was painted on a wall opposite Tom Ekin's business premises in South Belfast. Maskey admits that it was still not certain that Alliance would stand by its public support for him, right up to the day of the election. The tension in City Hall on the evening of Wednesday June 5 was palpable. An army of cameramen and reporters packed the hallway leading to the council chamber as the usher rang the bell at 5.55pm to warn councillors that they had five minutes until the start of the monthly meeting.

Unionist councillors were huddled together in one corner of the ante-room leading to the chamber, desperately trying to come up with a last-minute deal that would bring Alliance back from the brink. Sinn Féin councillors were huddled in an opposite corner, anxiously carrying out a head count of everyone present to check that they had the numbers needed to carry the vote.

Alex Maskey did not appear in front of the waiting media scrum until a moment or two before the meeting was due to begin. Greeted by a barrage of light as the photographers' flash bulbs exploded into life, the veteran of 19 years of City Hall politics strode purposefully into the chamber.

When he became Sinn Féin's first Belfast councillor in 1983, Maskey had followed the same lonely steps to the chamber, his only comfort being the warm feeling of his bullet-proof vest. It had been judged too high a security risk for his wife or parents to accompany him to City Hall to watch him take his seat for the first time. Despite the warning Maskey's father unexpectedly turned up in the public gallery to survey events on the night. This time around, however, Maskey's parents, wife, two sons and grandchild were on hand to witness the event.

"I wasn't taking anything for granted," he admits. "I had been here before and been let down at the last minute. Until every vote was cast, nothing was guaranteed."

Sinn Féin head-counters became increasingly concerned when the Alliance members had still to appear. Earlier in the day loyalists had threatened to block the roads in an attempt to stop Alliance following through on their decision to elect a republican as the First Citizen of Belfast. At the last moment the group appeared in the hallway leading to the chamber. Refusing all requests from journalists for interviews, the stern-faced trio headed straight for the protection of the chamber where they could not be questioned.

As the city's 51 councillors filed into the chamber, one reporter remarked that some unionists looked as thought they were going to the gallows. The remark may have been made in jest, but the atmosphere in the ornate auditorium certainly did feel more like that of a courtroom.

Unionists stared sullenly across the floor of the chamber at the accused on the Alliance benches. From Sinn Féin benches the questioning glances towards Alliance reflected republican anxiety that the trio would recant at the eleventh hour and plead "not guilty" to the charge that they were handing the keys of unionism's citadel to the "Provo Pariah".

The public gallery, scene of hand-to-hand fighting between the RUC and nationalist protesters in June 1994, was equally divided. It was populated by Sinn Féin supporters there to witness an historic moment and a DUP contingent that had turned up in the hope that victory could be snatched from the jaws of defeat.

Ulster Unionist Lord Mayor Jim Rodgers called the meeting to order. Following tradition, the first item on the agenda was the election of the new mayor. The UUP's Chris McGimpsey's name was put forward; the DUP's Robin Newton was nominated by his party colleagues. Tom Hartley nominated Alex Maskey and the SDLP's Margaret Walsh seconded the Sinn Féin candidate.

Outgoing mayor Jim Rodgers called for a vote on the three nominations. Unionists called for a recorded vote, which ensured that each individual councillor would have to call out the name of their preferred candidate. It was a final effort to publicly pressurise the Alliance councillors into backing down at the last moment. When David Alderdice, whose name came alphabetically second on the list, called out "Maskey", there were bitter cries of "Judas" from the unionist benches.

When the votes were counted, Maskey had 26 ticks against his name compared to McGimpsey's 15 and Newton's 10. As Maskey stepped forward to accept the chain of office the unionist benches went into uproar. A new die had been cast; the 80-year mould of unionist domination had been broken.

Unionists immediately filed out of the chamber before the incoming Mayor's official acceptance speech. As they left the chamber, they vented their anger not on Maskey, but on the three Alliance councillors whom they accused of betrayal. Sammy Wilson shouted angrily at the Alliance benches: "Well done, Provo David."

Other unionists warned the Alliance trio: "Your days are numbered."

It was left to Maskey's one-time sparring partner Eric Smyth to land the first verbal blow on the new Mayor.

"Mr Maskey, you are not wanted on the Shankill Road. You are not wanted in this city," the DUP preacher shouted as he left the chamber.

With the unionist benches empty, a new sense of tension engulfed the chamber: no one knew if they had left for a few minutes, or for good. A solitary DUP councillor stared through the ornate porthole-shaped window in the door of the chamber, watching silently as the non-unionist bloc voted to defer the election of deputy mayor to await nominations from the unionist benches – if any were forthcoming.

Ten minutes after they had left en masse, the unionists returned to carry on normal council business. Only the DUP refused to re-enter the chamber. Ulster Unionist Davy Brown was one of the first to observe protocol and refer to Maskey as "Mr Mayor". The North Belfast man told the new First Citizen that, while he opposed everything Sinn Féin represented, he would nevertheless be prepared to work with him on any issue that benefited both sections of the community.

Outside the chamber, however, other unionists were not as gracious in "defeat". Former DUP mayor Nigel Dodds described Maskey's election as the "most divisive thing to have happened in Belfast for many a long year". Warning that Alliance would suffer for their "betrayal", Dodds added: "I have no doubt that the consequence of this disgraceful and despicable decision is that Alliance will incur the wrath of voters at the ballot box." David Alderdice said he stood over his party's decision to help elect the city's first republican Mayor but he warned that there was an obligation on Alex Maskey to "live up to his word to be inclusive".

Standing on the same imposing marble staircase he had bounded up 19 years earlier to confront Frank Millar Sr on his first day in City Hall, Maskey faced a melee of television cameras in his mayoral chains. While the Belfast docker had been willing to go "toe-to-toe" with Millar in 1983, he had a new message for unionism that night.

"I would ask the unionist community to look, listen and learn. Judge me on what they see me doing and saying."

Pledging that he would carry out his role in a way that would include every citizen and section of the city, Maskey said: "I am very conscious of the historic import of my election. I am also conscious of the concerns that have been expressed by some politicians. I would like to assure them, and the citizens of this city, that I have worked and will work with the political parties in a collective way to provide civic leadership for everyone in this city of ours."

It had taken Alex Maskey nearly 20 years to reach the office he now occupied. During the previous two decades, his public profile in City Hall had led to nine attempts on his life from loyalist paramilitaries. The state had been proven to have actively colluded in attempts to kill him. He had been shot and seriously wounded. His close friend Alan Lundy had been killed helping to protect Maskey's home from attack.

Few unionists, and fewer republicans, could have predicted what Belfast's first republican Lord Mayor had in store for the city.

Chapter Seven

REMEMBERING THE DEAD

SOME of the worst violence seen in the city for more than 20 years took place in the months preceding Alex Maskey's election as Mayor.

On January 4, William Campbell, a 19-year-old loyalist, was killed in Coleraine when a pipe bomb he was carrying exploded prematurely. Three days later, Colombian authorities investigating alleged republican links with left-wing Revolutionary Armed Forces of Colombia (or FARC) guerrillas claimed that as many as 25 IRA members could have visited the South American country in recent years.

The following week Holy Cross girls' primary school in Ardoyne, scene of a three-month loyalist protest in 2001, was forced to close for the day after serious sectarian clashes. Two days later the UFF shot dead 21-year-old Catholic postman Daniel McColgan as he arrived for work in the staunchly loyalist Rathcoole estate on the outskirts of North Belfast. Hours afterwards, the UFF issued a statement warning that it would attack Catholic schoolteachers and postmen working in Protestant areas. Later that same month thousands of people attended trade union rallies across the North, calling for an end to the killing and the withdrawal of the threat against Catholic workers. While the rallies were supported by all of the major political parties, the violence continued unabated.

On St Patrick's Day, Special Branch offices at Castlereagh in East Belfast were raided with dozens of sensitive documents said to have been stolen. In the immediate aftermath of the robbery, RUC Chief Constable Ronnie Flanagan said he did not believe that paramilitaries or criminals could have carried out the theft. The IRA denied involvement, but within weeks the police arrested a number of republicans in a series of high-profile raids on homes and offices belonging to Sinn Féin. On March 23, violence again flared in North Belfast with one woman being injured when a blast bomb was thrown at her car.

One man was shot and 28 others injured amid disturbances in North Belfast in May. PUP leader David Ervine warned that the peace process was in a "substantial and serious crisis" and said he believed the illegal loyalist UVF was re-arming. That same month, UFF leader Johnny Adair was released from Maghaberry prison. He had been returned to jail in August 2000 when his early release licence was suspended by then Secretary of State Peter Mandelson after being accused of starting a feud between the UFF and UVF.

At the beginning of June, eight people were treated for gunshot wounds after serious sectarian clashes erupted in East Belfast with up to 1,000 people involved in rioting. Fears that Belfast was sleepwalking into the abyss led to Gerry Adams and David Ervine holding face-to-face talks in a bid to bring the violence to an end. Adams and Ervine's meeting took place the day before Alex Maskey's expected election.

The decision to elect Belfast's first republican Mayor was not helped by the ongoing tensions on the streets. Following Maskey's donning of the chains of office, unionists threatened to mount protests outside the City Hall but, despite initial fears, the demonstrations failed to materialise. Organisers claimed that the rallies had been cancelled due to a "mix-up" in arrangements.

Maskey admits to having had initial concerns that any protest might have ignited opposition against him that could have easily spiralled out of control. In 2001 teenagers from a number of loyalist schools had protested against Sinn Féin's Martin McGuinness becoming Minister for Education in the Stormont Executive.

"If there had been protests it could have gathered momentum and caused serious damage to my year in office even before it had begun," Maskey recalls.

He says that when the demonstrations failed to materialise, it convinced him that it was his political opponents in the council, and not ordinary Protestants, who were trying to block his attempts to reach out to the unionist community. Although he enjoyed the odd pint of beer, Maskey had already decided that he would be entirely teetotal for the duration of his year in office. He had arranged with the party leadership to drop the rest of his portfolio for his twelve-month period in office, including his role as Chief Whip in the Assembly and his place on Sinn Féin's negotiating team.

"I had a serious job to do and I wanted to be properly focused throughout," he told colleagues.

Maskey insists that while he was determined to reach out to the unionist community, he did so as a republican and not as an individual.

"This was about healing relationships between nationalists and unionists, not Alex Maskey and unionists," he says.

The day following the election, Maskey travelled to County Donegal with Liz, his brother and sister-in-law to begin to formulate a strategy for his term in office. He was aware that he needed to escape from the intense media interest his new role had created in the city.

"I knew if I stayed in Belfast I would have been pacing the floor worrying about what I was going to do. I needed some time to think and work out in detail what needed to be done."

Almost immediately, he was faced with his first mayoral dilemma. Four days after his election, he was due to attend the official opening of the Presbyterian Church's General Assembly. While each newly elected mayor traditionally received an invitation to the General Assembly, the fact that Belfast's First Citizen was a republican created a potential problem. Maskey said there were "intensive discussions" between his office staff and Presbyterian Church leaders over the weekend as to whether the visit would go ahead as planned. In the days after his election, there had been serious rumblings within Presbyterian circles over the dilemma of inviting a republican as an honoured guest to the General Assembly opening. There were serious concerns that his presence would lead to demonstrations.

"To be fair I don't think they ever suggested that the invitation was going to be withdrawn," Maskey says. "The possibility of protests, if I attended, worried organisers that it might jeopardise the remainder of the Assembly. It was due to last for a week and had other important matters to discuss."

Throughout that weekend a series of telephone calls took place with the organisers in Belfast as Maskey, in Donegal, reflected on what to do. While the Sinn Féin Mayor did not want to imperil the smooth

153

running of the General Assembly, he was well aware of the effect the cancellation of his invitation would have had on his year in office.

"For me it would have been disastrous if the invitation had been withdrawn. It would have seriously upset the plans I had for the whole year and, in particular, what I wanted to do in relation to the Somme commemoration, which was just weeks away."

Confirmation of his intention to attend was received at the last moment. Maskey says that he was unsure about the form of protest he was going to face on the Monday night. He had already discussed possible objections to his presence with the organisers and told them he was prepared to accept any dissenting voices. However, when he arrived at the General Assembly, there was just one lone demonstrator to meet him. Maskey had overcome his first hurdle. Nevertheless, he admits to having had some anxiety about the possibility of being shunned by the Presbyterians gathered inside.

Outgoing Presbyterian Moderator Dr Alastair Dunlop defended the decision to invite Maskey. Dr Russell Birney, who was due to take over as the Church's new moderator, also welcomed the Mayor's presence, insisting that the visit showed the need for nationalist and unionist communities to enter into dialogue.

"He knows exactly what he's coming to," said Dr Birney, "and as the moderator has already said, we have been working consistently for the day when we can dialogue with each other, when we can talk with all people, and I think Alex Maskey is taking a risk as well."

Despite initial fears that his attendance would be controversial, Maskey insists that the event turned out to be a key factor in convincing him that he could achieve his stated goal of reaching out to unionists.

"I can honestly say it was one of the most exceptional events I took part in throughout my whole year in office."

Although the original intention was for Maskey to participate in an informal gathering for just 15 minutes after the Assembly, in the end he stayed for over an hour.

"People shook me by the hand and thanked me for coming. Some criticised me and others highlighted issues they wanted me to address. But every one of them thanked me for being there and told me I was in their prayers. It was a seminal moment which I knew could be built upon. I knew any unionist protest against me was almost certainly doomed to fail. I was convinced people were going to give me a chance."

Notwithstanding the personal boost the General Assembly visit had given him, Maskey admits that Sinn Féin had initially been caught off guard by his election. Republicans had earned a reputation for establishing internal committees to deal with controversial issues, but when Maskey was elected, no actual structure had been put in place to deal with his year in office. Just hours before going to the General Assembly, he met with Sinn Féin chairman Mitchel McLaughlin to discuss his concerns.

"Usually, as a party we observe that an issue or event is on the horizon and set up a working group to deal with it. But because it was not certain that I would be elected Mayor, we hadn't actually brought a group together when I was elected."

He quickly realised that he would not be able to cope with the issues ahead on his own and wanted movement quickly. McLaughlin readily agreed that a group should be established to surround Maskey during his mayoral year.

"I informed Mitchel at that meeting that the Somme commemoration was just weeks away and that I would be coming to the party with proposals for the way in which I wanted to tackle the issue."

He admits that the unexpected announcement caused some initial trepidation with the Sinn Féin chairman. McLaughlin had a vivid memory of the fall-out from a previous decision to send Tom Hartley to attend a similar event in Dublin and the repercussions that it had had with grassroots republicans.

The Mayor also met Gerry Adams that day to argue that the Somme commemoration provided an opportunity to show unionists that he would be prepared to act in an inclusive manner during his year in office. Maskey informed Adams that if he did something positive around the Somme event, it would stand him in good stead for the rest of his year in office. If, however, he failed to deal with the issue properly, he would fall at the first hurdle, as unionists had predicted.

"I pointed out that Belfast had a large Protestant population and the last thing I should do, just weeks into my year in office, was to ignore that. I can say now that both Gerry and Mitchel gave me total support and said they would give their backing to whatever feasible proposals I would come up with over the Somme commemoration and any effort to reach out to unionists."

Maskey says that, at the time, he did not know exactly what he intended to do. However Adams and McLaughlin moved quickly to surround the Mayor with some of the party's key strategists. The 'Mayor Maskey Think Tank' included some of the city's most senior republicans. Jackie McMullan had served 16 years in the H-Blocks and spent 47 days on hunger strike before it ended in October 1981. McMullan was already acting as Maskey's political aide on a day-to-day basis.

In 1975, Chrissie McAuley had been sentenced to four years in jail in the Republic for possession of explosives after she was arrested in County Cork. She had been a Sinn Féin councillor in Belfast for five years and was one of a number of women to hold senior positions within the party. Her portfolio included responsibility for the party's policy development as well as human rights and equality issues.

Tom Hartley, a key republican strategist from the early 1970s, had played a part in every significant political development involving Sinn Féin throughout the Troubles. He had been a councillor since 1993 and had taken over the City Hall leadership from Maskey in 1997. In April 1995, Hartley was chosen by the party to be the first republican to attend a ceremony in Islandbridge outside Dublin to commemorate those killed in the Second World War and the Holocaust. He had found himself in the unusual position of standing side by side with then Secretary of State Patrick Mayhew, Taoiseach John Bruton and senior Ulster Unionist Ken Maginnis. The widespread criticism from rank-and-file republicans at Hartley's participation gave the mayoral think tank much to ponder.

Jim Gibney had been interned in Long Kesh during the early 1970s. It was he who first suggested that Bobby Sands should be put forward for the Fermanagh-South Tyrone by-election in 1981. In the mid-1990s, Gibney and Hartley held a series of meetings with Protestant churchmen and community leaders in an effort to identify common ground with unionists on social and cultural issues. The discussions had a significant impact on the way in which republicans would view the cultural history and philosophy of unionism.

Paud Devenny was Sinn Féin's Belfast chairman and had spent eight years in the H-Blocks. Weeks before Maskey's election, Devenny had been left seriously injured after an incident involving police in his native Short Strand in East Belfast. The 40-year-old republican had his skull fractured in two places and underwent neurosurgery after he was beaten around the head, allegedly by members of the Police Service for Northern Ireland's (PSNI) riot squad.

Video footage of the incident showed Devenny urging nationalist residents to withdraw from police lines seconds before he was knocked unconscious and left seriously injured. An investigation carried out by Police Ombudsman, Nuala O'Loan, later cleared PSNI officers of any wrongdoing. Nationalists accused the ombudsman's office of a "whitewash".

Well-respected within the republican movement, Devenny was key to selling difficult decisions to the grassroots during Maskey's year in office. While others would be drafted onto the think tank to work on various issues, this was the nucleus surrounding Alex Maskey during his mayoral term.

Mitchel McLaughlin and Gerry Adams were both consulted on each major issue involving Maskey's year before any final decision was taken. Jim Gibney explains the significance that republicans placed on Maskey's position as Lord Mayor of Belfast.

"We knew that having Alex as Mayor was a perfect opportunity to show the unionist community and the outside world that, when republicans were in a position of responsibility, we were prepared to act for the greater good of the wider community. Alex's election as Mayor was never going to be used for party political gain for Sinn Féin. Neither was his year in office going to be used to celebrate nationalism in the city at the cost of unionists."

Gibney says republicans wanted to use Maskey's position to show the unionist community what they could expect in a united Ireland.

"It may sound strange to some people, but that is exactly what we set out to achieve."

The senior Sinn Féin strategist said republicans wanted to use Maskey's mayoral term as a continuation of a confidence-building process directed at unionism, a process that had begun when Martin McGuinness and Bairbre de Brún were appointed as Education and Health Ministers in the Stormont Executive.

While there had been initial fears within the unionist community when McGuinness and de Brún took their posts, the two ministers were largely accepted as having acted in a professional and non-partisan manner during their terms in office by the time the Assembly was collapsed in October 2002.

"We wanted to use Alex as a kind of ambassador, following on from the success of Martin and Bairbre," Gibney explains. "We wanted to prove to unionists that they would be under no threat whenever Sinn Féin was in a position of power, whether that was in Belfast or in a united Ireland. We were determined to show unionists during Alex's year as Mayor that this is what it will be like for them in a united Ireland; that when Sinn Féin was in power it would treat each community on an equal and fair basis."

Maskey's mayoral term was much too important to simply become one long photo opportunity and a series of obstacles had to be overcome if he was to succeed in his bid to build confidence and show to unionists that he was "a safe pair of hands".

No issue was more contentious or symbolic than the City Hall service commemorating those killed at the Battle of the Somme in France where, on July 1, 1916, the British army suffered its single biggest loss of life. More than 20,000 soldiers were killed with another 60,000 men wounded. Some 10,000 of the dead were from Ireland, north and south.

The carnage in the trenches knew no sectarian divide. Thousands of Irish Catholics had joined the British army's 10th and 16th Divisions at the outset of the First World War in 1914. Similarly, thousands of northern Protestants joined the 36th Ulster Division to fight the Germans. Around 5,500 soldiers from this Division were killed when they launched an offensive against German lines at the Somme. A third of the entire regiment was wiped out on the first morning of the battle.

The huge loss of life was catastrophic for the unionist and working class communities in the North, with almost every household having lost a loved one. July 12 celebrations were cancelled that year in memory of those who had died less than a fortnight before. Eight months later the 36th and 16th Divisions joined forces to fight and die together at the battle for Messines. Thousands more Irishmen, Catholic and Protestant, died side by side before the war ended in 1918. In total some 250,000 Irishmen fought in the conflict, with 50,000 losing their lives.

Some observers commented at the time on the fact that Catholics and Protestants, having fought together in France, might help end divisions in Ireland. Those hopes were not to become reality.

Separate events taking place in Ireland meant that the sacrifice of the nationalists and unionists, who died on the battlefield of the Somme, would be remembered in very different ways. Partition led to a rewriting of the history of Ireland's involvement in the First World War and the loyalty of those who died, on both sides of the border. The birth of the Irish republic and the anti-British ethos that emerged with it meant that the nationalists who died fighting for the British army between 1914 and 1918 were deliberately ignored by the new state.

Conversely, Northern Ireland Protestants chose to view those who died during the war as being exclusively loyal to the British Crown. As the two states developed, their respective versions of history became entrenched in the spirit of their separate institutions. In the North, commemorating the Somme became indelibly linked to the Orange Order and allegiance to the British Crown. For many northern nationalists, their loved ones who died during the Great War became a part of family history that was rarely, if ever, discussed.

The situation became even more ingrained with the onset of the

Troubles in 1969, with an even stronger affiliation between Somme commemorations and Ulster loyalism. At the site of the Somme itself, different sections of the battlefield were renamed after well-known loyalists or loyalist symbols of the state, such as Sandy Row and Paisley Avenue.

Although thousands of northern Catholics lost their lives in the battle, by the early 1970s, the nationalist community as a whole felt alienated from all state ceremonies held to remember the war dead. The Maskey family was no different from the hundreds of other Catholics who had relatives who had fought in the British army. Maskey's maternal grandfather had served as a soldier with a Scottish regiment in the First World War. Maskey says that, like hundreds of other nationalist families, his grandfather's career as a British soldier was rarely mentioned and neither did it impact on his thinking about the Remembrance ceremony. But while Alex Maskey the republican might have been reluctant to participate in an event designed to remember the fallen of the British military, Alex Maskey the Mayor was left with a predicament – how to fulfil his obligation to represent all of the traditions in Belfast?

Jim Gibney was in no doubt that the debate over what role, if any, Maskey should play during the city's Somme commemoration, was the single biggest issue the republican Mayor would face during his year in office. The fact that the event was at the start of July meant that Sinn Féin had only a matter of days to decide on what Maskey would do. There was added pressure on the mayoral team to come up with a solution that was equally acceptable to both unionists and republicans.

"We knew that whatever Alex chose to do, he would be criticised by someone," Gibney says. "If he were seen to have ignored or mishandled the situation, it would have dogged his whole term as Mayor in the eyes of unionists. Equally, Alex was the city's first republican Mayor and could not be seen to be abandoning that tradition either."

Maskey's eventual decision to play a part in the commemoration would later be criticised. The flak would come not only from unionists but also from some Sinn Féin voters who claimed that the grassroots had not been properly consulted prior to the announcement that he would be laying a wreath at the City Hall's Cenotaph.

Gibney defends the fact that discussions surrounding Maskey's participation were kept to a small number of key people within the leadership.

"There were republicans who were shocked at what Alex was going to do and that they had not been consulted about it beforehand. We understood those concerns, but the simple fact is that there are times when difficult decisions have to be taken by the republican leadership, which, because of the reality of this society, means the grassroots cannot become involved until a later stage. The peace process is full of examples when the republican leadership has had to make difficult choices which could only be discussed with the grassroots once the decision had been taken. Issues such as ceasefires, decommissioning and going into Stormont were discussed and debated with the grassroots, but the ultimate decision had to be taken by the leadership."

Gibney insists that Maskey's resolution to take part in the Somme commemoration was one of those cases. While it had been acknowledged that the break with republican tradition on this issue would occur, Maskey and his advisers were aware that his involvement in the remembrance ceremony could only go so far. Wide-ranging discussions were held on what part he should play in the commemoration, including the possibility that he would take part in the main council ceremony itself.

The mayoral think tank studied videotapes of previous ceremonies in a bid to find an acceptable compromise that would not upset unionists or alienate the republican support base. In an effort to find a way through the impasse, Maskey also met with unionist representatives, who warned that his participation in the commemoration would be perceived as offensive by some of their community. He was told that his presence at the Cenotaph would prompt others to walk away.

"I was left with the belief that the bolder the step I chose to take, the more damaging it could have been for everyone," Maskey recalls.

Finally a decision was taken that Maskey would indeed go to the Cenotaph, but not as part of the actual council-led ceremony. Just two weeks into office, the Sinn Féin Mayor announced that he would lay a wreath in memory of the war dead at 9.00am on July 1, two hours before the main commemoration.

But even the choice of wreath was to prove controversial. Maskey had decided that he would lay a laurel, rather than a poppy, wreath at the Cenotaph.

"The poppy wreath was judged to be too closely identified with the symbolism of British militarism," he says, "so instead I decided to lay a laurel wreath, which was viewed as an internationally accepted symbol of commemorating the dead."

Jim Gibney explains that Maskey could not have been seen to be take part in the main ceremony because of the overt military symbolism which surrounded it. While it was feared that loyalists would protest at his participation, there were also concerns that republicans would choose to demonstrate their objection to his presence at an event which was historically associated with the British and unionist establishment.

Inside Sinn Féin itself there were those who wondered what impact Maskey's attendance at the Cenotaph would have on other republican politicians across the North.

"The problem which we faced with the main Somme commemoration was the fact that it was so closely identified with the British army," Gibney says. "Large sections of the commemoration are surrounded by the military paraphernalia of the British establishment and for Alex to have been seen to be playing a role in that part of the event was just not possible."

When Maskey informed his party's grouping in City Hall that he had decided to lay a wreath, he insisted that he would do so alone.

"I told them that because of the understandable emotions that the issue had caused within the nationalist and republican community I did not expect anyone to accompany me. This was my decision and I had to see it through on my own."

Both mainstream unionist parties were informed of Maskey's plans. The DUP's Wallace Brown, who as High Sheriff of Belfast would take the Mayor's place at the main ceremony, was made aware of discussions in the run-up to the day itself.

While Maskey would not attend the main ceremony, he had offered to open up the Mayor's parlour to all who were due to take part in the commemoration, including the British army's GOC in Northern Ireland, Alasdair Irwin. He broke further with tradition by indicating that he would chair a special council meeting on the morning of July 1, attended by the unionist grouping, directly before the Somme commemoration. Even this move carried political implications.

"The special council meeting before the main commemoration is a very specific part of the event," Maskey explains, "and one which I, as a republican, did not agree with. As the Mayor, I was obliged to read out a motion paying tribute to the King of England, the British Commonwealth and the British soldiers who died at the Somme. The entire text, which is traditionally read by each Belfast Mayor completely ignores all of the Irish nationalists who died at the Somme and during World War I."

He says that, despite his own reservations, he decided to read the motion so as not to cause offence.

"If I had refused to read it, there would have been a huge controversy as to who would take my place. The unionists would have used it to accuse me of being disrespectful to the war dead. That was something which I could not allow to happen."

At 8.55am on July 1, a sombre Alex Maskey and a dozen Sinn Féin councillors, who had turned up unbidden to support him, emerged from the front entrance of Belfast City Hall and walked the short distance to the Cenotaph situated on the west side of the grounds. Just three weeks into his year in office, he was about to do something which no unionist or republican could have ever predicted.

Dressed in a knee-length black overcoat and carrying a laurel wreath, the Mayor was watched by an army of journalists, photographers and camera crews as he approached the Cenotaph flanked by colleagues. The Belfast republican, who had spent 20 years battling the British and unionist establishment in City Hall, walked purposefully towards the war memorial as the First Citizen of the city. As the Sinn Féin group came to a halt, Maskey stepped forward alone and carefully placed the laurel wreath on the granite plinth. On his election to the council in 1983, unionists had warned of the first step being taken in a republican strategy to smash City Hall. Now the man whom Margaret Thatcher had excluded from Britain in 1987 on the grounds that he was an "undesirable person" found himself in the position of representing the citizens of Belfast in a commemoration to the British war dead.

Maskey took three steps back and stood head bowed, observing a minute's silence. He then returned to the Sinn Féin group and left the Cenotaph. In those few short moments, he had rewritten one of the unspoken tenets of Irish republicanism. Speaking to the media after the ceremony, he called for unionists and republicans to accept the act of remembrance as genuine and an act of reconciliation.

"This is a major step for republicans and nationalists on this island. I hope that this initiative will be seen at face value and as a positive gesture," he said.

The decision to lay a wreath at the Cenotaph was broadly welcomed by his political opponents in following days. Ulster Unionist councillor Alan Crowe admitted that the republican Mayor's decision to mark the Somme anniversary was "significant".

"The fact that it was a laurel wreath did still cause offence in a lot of quarters," said the East Belfast unionist. "But I think, on balance, people felt that at least it was a gesture and showed that the grassroots unionist opinion, which was saying that we had to move forward, were right in their assumption that here was a guy who was prepared to … make those gestures to show that they (republicans) were starting down that road."

Crowe predicted that the Mayor's decision to break with republican tradition would mean that unionists and nationalists could now move into a new era where there was mutual respect for each community's respective dead.

The Secretary of State, John Reid, described Maskey's participation in the Somme commemoration as a sign of "encouragement and hope for the future". Dr Reid said the Sinn Féin Mayor's actions were an encouraging sign of "changing nationalist attitudes" to the war dead.

The DUP's Sammy Wilson appeared to be a lone voice, accusing Maskey of insulting the memory of the war dead and having turned the commemoration into a "political football" for his own ends.

"He refused to step back from the cul-de-sac which republicans have backed themselves into," said Wilson. "In doing so, he has insulted people and shown that he is not fit for office."

However, the decision to lay a wreath at the Cenotaph was not entirely welcomed within republican ranks either. At a meeting of Sinn Féin Cuige (northern body) the following week, all but one comhairle ceantair (local grouping) opposed the Cenotaph gesture.

Jim Gibney says: "People were very unhappy and we understood their concerns. But as a party we had to accept that, as Mayor of Belfast, Alex had to be seen to be giving civic leadership to a section wider than the republican base. Certainly Alex couldn't compromise on the fundamental beliefs of republicanism, but he had to be a Mayor for everyone in Belfast. The decision for Alex to lay the wreath at the Cenotaph was taken at leadership level and we stood by that decision."

At Sinn Féin's Ard Fheis (annual party conference) the following April, a motion was put forward by a South Armagh cumann criticising the laying of the wreath at the Cenotaph and calling for an end to such gestures towards the unionist community. The motion was defeated and Maskey was given a standing ovation for his efforts during his year in office.

Maskey knew that his actions would receive both criticism and praise, but his decision to attend the city Cenotaph also sparked off an unexpected reaction. Soon after the Somme event, he was inundated with letters and telephone calls from nationalist families who had lost loved ones in the First World War, but had never been able to publicly acknowledge their deaths. Ironically, it was public support for Maskey's stance from prominent republicans such as Martin Meehan, which appeared to pave the way for open debate within nationalism.

"Since the formation of the Northern state," says Maskey, "nationalists had felt unable to speak about their loved ones who had died with the British Army in World War I. Now people were openly talking about it for the first time and the stigma that had existed for so long seemed to disappear overnight."

Jim Gibney argues that Maskey's decision to attend the Cenotaph was part of a larger debate within the council about how nationalists and unionists should remember their dead.

"This was a debate which needs to take place and Belfast City Council, because of its position, needs to give leadership on how we commemorate the dead. If we cannot respect the dead, how do we respect the living? Alex going to the Cenotaph was a massive move away from tradition for republicans. It could only be equated with a unionist mayor of Belfast attending an Easter Sunday commemoration to remember those republicans who died fighting for Irish freedom. Could anyone honestly say they could see that happening in the near future? That is the size of the gesture which unionists would need to reciprocate."

Within weeks the IRA itself appeared to be reaching out to unionists. While their ceasefire announcement of August 1994 had been broadly welcomed they, unlike loyalist paramilitaries, had failed to address the issue of innocent civilians killed by republicans. On July 16, five days before the 30th anniversary of one of the worst atrocities of the Troubles, the IRA issued a public apology to the families of all the innocents it had killed.

The statement came as the anniversary of Bloody Friday approached. On July 21, 1972, the IRA had detonated 27 bombs across Belfast over a three-hour period. While huge economic damage had been caused, it was the killing of nine people, seven of whom were civilians, which caused widespread revulsion across the world. Television pictures showed firemen lifting pieces of human limbs out of the wreckage and placing them into plastic bags.

The IRA said that while it had not intended to kill civilians, it acknowledged the reality was "that on this and on a number of other occasions, that was the consequence of our actions". Offering its "sincere apologies" to the families of those killed and injured by republicans throughout the Troubles, the statement continued: "The process of conflict resolution requires the equal acknowledgement of the grief and loss of others. On this anniversary, we are endeavouring to fulfil this responsibility to those we have hurt."

Insisting that it was still committed to the peace process, the IRA declared: "This includes the acceptance of past mistakes and of the hurt and pain we have caused to others."

In a telling move, it was Alex Maskey who was the first Sinn Féin spokesman to publicly welcome the IRA apology, insisting that it was a "genuine effort" to address the pain and suffering of those who had lost loved ones.

"I think this apology and condolence is a very worthwhile step," he said. "I think it's a very considerable statement. The IRA, in its statement, does recognise the grief and suffering endured by all those killed as a result of this conflict. It has to help in the process of how we identify victims and commemorate them properly." But Belfast's first republican Lord Mayor was to go further than anyone could have predicted in his efforts to reach out to unionists. Undaunted by the controversy caused within his own constituency by his participation in the Somme commemoration, he travelled that September to Belgium and France to visit the war graves at Messines and the Somme where thousands of Irishmen had lost their lives fighting in the First World War. He took part in a special wreath-laying ceremony, organised by the Messines Fellowship, which included unionist politicians, leading loyalist John White and the Lord Mayor of Dublin, Dermot Lacey.

Defending the decision to take part in a second remembrance ceremony, Maskey said he had wanted to witness first-hand the "tragic site" where so many Irishmen had lost their lives. It was important, he said, that he was seen to act in an inclusive manner to remember all those who died.

"I have said to people in the city that I want to make all the genuine efforts that I can to show that I can give respect to other traditions and other cultures in the city of Belfast and I think this is another … important example of how I intend to do that."

Insisting that he had agreed to be present at the Messines commemoration because "it was the right thing to do", Maskey said he hoped unionists would accept his attempts to break new ground between the two communities.

"I hope people see it as a genuine initiative on my behalf to ensure that the unionist community in particular, who have held this up as an important issue for themselves, see that I am prepared to reach out to them and work with them, and I appeal to them to reach back to me in these circumstances."

On September 4, the Sinn Féin Mayor unfurled another initiative in his efforts to embrace all traditions in City Hall, but this move was not so popular with unionists. At a specially arranged press conference, former fellow internee Dickie Glenholmes presented him with an Irish tricolour. The Irish national colours were to join the more traditional Union Flag, a long-standing feature of the Mayor's parlour. The two flags would be draped on either side of the fireplace. Rejecting unionist criticism, Maskey said it was a "matter of equality and respect for both traditions in the city".

"I think I am entitled to, if not obliged, to now have a sense of equality in the Lord Mayor's parlour by putting up the Irish national flag," he said. "If anyone sees that as an insult, I am sorry, I cannot help them, but I am asking people to see it as one step that I am taking to balance up these offices."

Sammy Wilson however did not see the need for parity of esteem.

"This is a Lord Mayor who talks about doing away with sectarianism and tackling sectarianism," said the former unionist mayor. "We see that his actions are totally to the contrary. There is no doubt that the Irish tricolour is seen as a sectarian symbol. It is used as a sectarian symbol and the Lord Mayor is not content to just put it up in his room, he must fly it in the face of the unionist population."

Barely had Belfast ratepayers caught their breath at the audacity of their republican Mayor when he was again breaking new ground. In November, he held a reception in City Hall for members of the

FRANKIE QUINN

Left: Maskey and former Sinn Féin councillor and hunger striker Pat McGeown lead an Easter commemoration along the Falls Road

Below: Liz and Alex pictured with the Dalai Lama during his visit to Belfast in October 2000

MASKEY PRIVATE COLLECTION

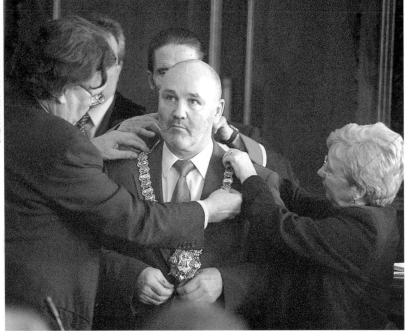

Above: Maskey receives the chains of office from Sinn Féin's Tom Hartley and SDLP councillor Margaret Walsh in June 2002
Left: Alex Maskey with his granddaughter Tierna on June 6, 2002, the night he was elected Belfast's first republican Lord Mayor

Top: Alex and Liz celebrate his election in the Felons Club in West Belfast. Also pictured are brother Liam (left) and veteran republican Martin Meehan (right)

Above: Maskey is accompanied by party colleagues on July 1, 2002 to the City Cenotaph as he becomes the first republican to lay a wreath in memory of those who died in the First World War

Right: Alex Maskey's maternal grandfather Patrick McClory who was a member of the British army in the First World War

Above: Maskey stands between the Union flag and the Irish tricolour, which he installed in the Mayor's parlour in September 2002
Below: Alex making sure he's been given the correct fare from Sinn Féin president, Gerry Adams, at the opening of the new black taxi rank in Belfast

Right: Maskey joins children from Bunscoil Feirste during a celebration of the diversity of culture in Belfast

Below: Liz and Alex visit the H Blocks in January 2003. In the background is H3

Above: Maskey is welcomed to London by Mayor Ken Livingstone for St Patrick's Day celebrations in March 2003.
Below: Relaxing in the Mayor's parlour during a meeting

Above: Mayor Maskey welcomes the St Gall's GAA Club squad to City Hall
Below: Liz and Alex with Special Olympians Rhoda Nesbitt and Conor Maguire taking a ride in a horse and carriage at the Lord Mayor's Show in May 2003

Above: Maskey welcomes Joe Cahill and singer Christy Moore into the Mayor's parlour.

Right: Alex and his mother Teresa in the council chamber in August 2002.

Below: "The darkest moment ... the death of Alan Lundy, there could be nothing to surpass that. I have great hopes for the future but at the same time I would have a dark anger because it has been paid for at such a high price." Alex Maskey speaks of the personal pain felt over the death of his friend Alan Lundy.

old soldiers' charity, the Royal British Legion – surprisingly, the first Mayor to do so.

The reception was held ahead of the city's Remembrance Day commemorations.

Although Maskey could not attend because he would be on council business in China, he refused to use the trip as an excuse. He said that as a republican, he would have felt obliged to decline an invitation to the ceremony even if he had been in Belfast.

Former soldiers from across the North attended the Mayor's City Hall reception which, ironically, was boycotted by unionists. British Legion president Brigadier David Strudley, who had served as a soldier on the streets of the North during the Troubles, praised the Mayor for his "brave and enormous contribution to crossing bridges". Strudley said he fully appreciated that Maskey was in "an extremely sensitive position and it would be foolish not to recognise this". The Legion, he said, was without political leanings and was certainly not sectarian. It had been "honoured" by its invitation to City Hall by Alex Maskey as it represented an acknowledgement of the work done by the ex-serviceman's organisation. Strudley said he would be willing to continue dialogue with Maskey about further ceremonies, which would be inclusive to all the people of Belfast.

"If there is common ground, let us discover it," he added.

In a telling insight into the relationships which the Mayor was now developing with unionism, Brigadier Strudley described the former republican prisoner thus: "He is a very straightforward, very open person with whom I have found it possible to do business with thus far. He states his opinions very directly, he brings to bear the facts of a given situation very straightforwardly and therefore I find it very straightforward in turn to do business with him."

Maskey, acknowledging that his participation in such ceremonies represented another break with republican tradition, said: "It is important that I reiterate that fact and I am gratified that others also accept that my presence at those events was in itself an act of reconciliation and a gesture of peace. The reality is that nationalists and unionists fought and died during the First World War. In life they fought side by side and that is how they should be remembered in death.

"There are a lot of people who believe I have perhaps been reaching out too far, but I believe it is important that I, as a republican, by what I am doing, am reaching out to people across different communities."

Maskey had indeed travelled a road that few people could ever have imagined him travelling. Belfast's First Citizen, however, was to go even further – he had now decided to speak face-to-face with the loyalist paramilitaries who had tried so many times to kill him.

Chapter Eight

TALKING TO THE ENEMY

DESPITE the ceasefires, there was no let up in the violence with sectarian attacks and murders taking place throughout the summer of 2002. Alex Maskey had been Mayor for less than a month when 27-year-old Protestant William Morgan was knocked down and seriously injured by a stolen car in North Queen Street in Belfast.

The father-of-one, whose wife was pregnant with the couple's second child, died in hospital from head injuries five days later. The car used in the attack was later found burned out in the nationalist New Lodge area.

Two weeks later, on the evening of Sunday, July 21, violence erupted once more in North Belfast. Stone throwing had continued throughout the day along the peaceline separating the nationalist Ardoyne area from the loyalist Glenbryn housing estate.

The INLA was blamed for shooting a teenage Protestant in Glenbryn. An hour later, two loyalist gunmen on a motorbike tried to shoot Catholic man Ryan Corbett as he stood outside a bar on the nearby Oldpark Road. The 19-year-old escaped with his life when the pillion passenger's weapon jammed.

Soon after, a second nationalist, Jason O'Halloran, was shot in the upper thigh as he walked along the Oldpark Road. The 29-year-old later told how his life had been saved when the gunman's weapon again appeared to jam.

Sectarian gun attacks were also reported that night on the Old Cavehill Road and Ligoniel Road. Shortly after midnight, UFF gunmen spotted teenager Gerard Lawlor as he walked towards his home on the Whitewell Road. The killers are believed to have identified the 19-year-old as a Catholic by his clothes. The father-of-one was wearing a Glasgow Celtic football shirt – enough evidence to condemn him to death. Like the attack on Corbett earlier in the evening, the killers are believed to have used a motorbike to escape.

Gerard Lawlor died at the scene. He was killed three days before he was due to move into a new home with his girlfriend and 18-month-old son.

Lawlor's parents pleaded that no one carry out retaliatory attacks, with his mother, Sharon, adding that she would pray for her son's killers. Ironically, one of the two Catholics who had escaped death hours before the killing had known Lawlor. Ryan Corbett said he and Gerard had played Gaelic football against each other for their local North Belfast clubs.

"We were good friends through Gaelic," the teenager revealed. Unconsciously referring to his friend in the present tense, he said: "We have been playing football together for years. There has been peace here for a couple of months. Now, we're going to have to look over our shoulders again. I feel like packing up and going."

Corbett's final comment was a poignant little footnote to a sordid and pointless killing. "If they had got me," he said, "they might not have killed Gerard."

Two days after Lawlor's murder, hundreds of people attended a vigil at the spot where he was killed. They heard parish priest Fr Dan Whyte question whether politicians were doing enough to safeguard the peace process. Fr Whyte said many people felt that hopes of peace engendered by the signing of the Good Friday Agreement now appeared to have been thrown away by the inability of politicians to work together. Ordinary people, he said, were demanding that every effort be made to ensure that opportunities for peace were not squandered.

"Nationalist people are now becoming convinced that their opposite numbers only want peace on their own terms and that they can't handle equality. All this pressure for expelling Sinn Féin from government is being seen as a determination to get back to the old days of one-party government when nationalist people were effectively disenfranchised."

Alex Maskey joined more than 1,000 mourners following Gerard Lawlor's coffin on the journey from the family home to St Gerard's Church on the Antrim Road. The cortege stopped for a moment in silence at the spot where he had been gunned down. The Sinn Féin Mayor admitted at the time that the anguish in the eyes of the young mourners at the loss of yet another of their friends left a deep impression on him. Afterwards, Maskey said Fr Whyte's speech had convinced him further that nationalist and unionist councillors in Belfast City Hall had an obligation to unite to attempt to bring the killing to an end.

Maskey had met with senior members of the northern branch of the Irish Congress of Trade Unions (ICTU) during his first weeks in office as part of his effort to establish an anti-sectarian working group within the council. Now, as he mingled with mourners at Lawlor's funeral, he was one of only a handful of people who were aware that trade union leaders, also present at the funeral, were due to meet UDA chiefs that evening.

The ICTU delegation did in fact meet UDA brigadiers Jackie McDonald, Mo Courtney, Andre Shoukri, John White and Johnny Adair in a secret location in North Belfast. Confirmation came from John White, who told the author: "The trade unions asked to meet us and we agreed. They wanted to know what could be done to bring an end to the violence and how they could help. We explained to them that the UDA had serious concerns at what was going on in interface areas and at republican violence."

Veteran trade union activist Brendan Mackin backed up White's revelation, insisting that "someone had to bring the violence to an end".

"If someone is murdered, it doesn't matter to us what religion they are or who killed them. The trade unions have always condemned sectarian killings regardless of who the person was," he said.

Maskey acknowledges now that he was aware of the behind-the-scenes efforts to bring an end to the bloodletting.

"I was aware of what the ICTU was doing and I fully supported what they were doing. Because of the sensitivities of what was going on, I was careful not to speak publicly about it."

The day after Gerard Lawlor's murder the Mayor met with Security Minister Jane Kennedy to discuss his concern at the ongoing violence.

At a press conference afterwards, he reiterated his view that City Hall politicians could do more to help bring the killing to an end. Maskey also travelled to Dublin to meet with Foreign Affairs Minister Brian Cowen in a bid to have the Irish government put pressure on their British counterparts to take decisive steps to stop the killing.

"I think the general public out there must rightly expect the local government here to take direct responsibility. We have six parties in the council and surely we can get together to come up with some kind of programme which will at least help to alleviate these depressing problems that are facing us as a community."

One of Maskey's main priorities when he was elected Mayor was to establish an anti-sectarian campaign group within City Hall. Amazingly, Belfast City Council had no strategy for the promotion of positive relations between Catholics and Protestants. The council had withdrawn from a statutory programme in the early 1990s and had never rejoined. Maskey was scathing in his condemnation of this lack of engagement to deal with such an important ongoing issue.

"I think it was criminal that, as a council, we had nobody working on bringing the two communities together. At the height of the Troubles people were getting killed in this city practically every day as a direct result of sectarianism and we … did not think we needed someone to work on this issue. What made matters worse was the fact that we had actually withdrawn from a government-funded community relations project in the 1990s. We should be ashamed of the fact that we had no strategy to bring people together and tackle the serious problem of sectarianism."

He revealed that £300,000 funding had been available for the implementation of a policy to improve relations but the council had decided not to use the money. Maskey said he was determined to ensure that a new committee was established and, more importantly, was seen to be working.

"If I achieved one thing during my year in office," he says, "it was the fact that a group was established which continued after I left office and remained accountable to public scrutiny. The committee is now pledged to holding public meetings in different parts of the city to show people exactly what City Hall is doing to improve community relations and to seek further opinions and support. We were the only council in the North not to have a community relations strategy. To me, that was an absolute disgrace."

But the public image which City Hall had engendered over the years, meant that not everyone believed councillors were capable of working together on this issue. Maskey said he was met with a lukewarm response when he initially invited trade union groups, church leaders and other civic and statutory bodies to become involved in the new group. Many felt that the political parties in City Hall would not be able to agree when it came to building bridges between the differing peoples of the city. Some argued that the council itself was sectarian.

"Some in the trade unions and other bodies more or less said to me they wouldn't touch City Hall with a barge-pole when it came to community relations because the parties would not agree with each other. Eventually I convinced people to work with me because this was too important to be allowed to fail. People were dying and we were arguing amongst each other in City Hall. It just wasn't acceptable."

Five days after Gerard Lawlor's murder, Maskey called a special council meeting to seek condemnation of the recent killings and to call for public support for a demonstration against the violence. Crucially, it was agreed that an anti-sectarian group would be established, comprising the parties within City Hall, church leaders, trade unions and other civic bodies.

All parties except the DUP supported a motion condemning the killings. Afterwards, Maskey said the fact that nationalist and unionist parties were seen as uniting against the violence sent out a strong message that the council was prepared to play its part in tackling sectarianism.

Ulster Unionist Chris McGimpsey said that all parties had an obligation to show that they were united behind the opposition to sectarian killing, adding: "We hoped we would have had all the parties behind us and we did, except the DUP."

Sammy Wilson defended his party's decision to vote against the cross-party motion condemning sectarianism.

"Whilst the other parties oppose sectarianism with their words, when it actually came to voting against the violence of the IRA, they refused to put their hands up," said the East Belfast councillor. "We actually come out of this with some integrity, the other parties came out of it stained with dishonour."

Ironically, it was the DUP's Nelson McCausland who eventually became vice-chairman of the anti-sectarian working group. However, despite five of the six parties calling for an end to the violence, there were serious disturbances in South Belfast that weekend when loyalists clashed with police in the Sandy Row area. Cars, shops and fire crews were attacked during two nights of violence.

On Wednesday July 31, the British government held talks with nationalists and unionists to discuss ways in which the killing could be stopped. All parties, except the DUP, attended.

At the beginning of August, 51-year-old Protestant civilian worker David Caldwell was killed when a booby trap device inside a lunchbox exploded at a Territorial Army base on the Limavady Road in Derry. The dead man left behind a wife and four children. The breakaway Real IRA claimed responsibility for the murder. The following day, Alex Maskey addressed thousands of people at an anti-sectarian rally outside City Hall. Also present were UUP minister Michael McGimpsey, SDLP leader Mark Durkan, Gerry Adams, the four main church leaders, trade unionists and business leaders. Once again all the main political parties, except the DUP, attended the rally.

"Homes are being wrecked and people are being killed," Maskey stated. "Stop now."

The Mayor told the rally that Belfast City councillors had decided that "to do nothing" was no longer an option.

"This is a day," he said, "when we say to those engaged in sectarianism, please, please, stop!"

Maskey had been in touch with the families of two of the latest victims, William Morgan and Gerard Lawlor to ask permission to read out the victims' names at the rally. None objected. Trade union leader

Bob Gourley told the crowd that David Caldwell had shouted to his co-workers to stay back seconds before the Real IRA bomb killed him. Gourley said that people should be able to work free from intimidation and fear.

What Alex Maskey did not reveal until later was that, on the morning of the rally, he had received a death threat from the loyalist extremist Orange Volunteers. For added emphasis, the group had included a 9mm bullet with the message. Explaining why he had decided not to publicise the threat that day, he said: "If I had said anything publicly about the threat before the rally, it would have taken away from everything the event was about and that was not something I was prepared to do. It was ironic, that on a day when we were trying to establish a campaign against sectarianism, I had become another one of the victims of sectarianism."

However, behind the scenes, Maskey had become involved in another initiative aimed at convincing loyalist paramilitaries to bring the killing to an end.

Liam Maskey was five years younger than his brother, the Mayor. The two men had been interned together in the cages of Long Kesh. Liam was just 17-years old in the summer of 1973 when he entered the prison compounds. He shared the Nissan hut in Cage Six with prominent republicans such as Gerry Adams, Ivor Bell and Brendan Hughes. It was, he said, a bittersweet experience to have his older brother join him in the cage. The older Maskey had been re-interned after serving his sentence for the attempted escape in Crumlin Road Prison.

"It was good to see Alex again and we were more or less together until we were both released in 1975," Liam says.

While his older brother would become a key political figure in the early 1980s, Liam married and set up home in North Belfast where he worked at a variety of jobs. In 1988, he was employed as a car salesman at a showroom on the mainly loyalist Shore Road when a stranger entered the premises and walked over to him. The man pulled out a gun, placed it against Liam's head and pulled the trigger several times. After failing to clear the jammed weapon, the would-be assassin ran off. Liam left the job that day and never returned.

Throughout the late 1980s and 1990s loyalists would try to kill him on four more occasions. Despite the attacks Liam began, through his new job as a community worker, to develop relationships with his loyalist counterparts whom he met at various conferences and public meetings in North Belfast.

"It didn't take long to work out that some of these people were just like ourselves and that there were common bread-and-butter issues which we could work on together to improve working class communities," he says.

One of those he forged a close alliance with was former UVF leader Billy Mitchell who had also become involved in community work after serving a life sentence for a double murder. In 1995 Liam and Billy made the unusual move of forming a cross-community development group. Known as Intercomm, it later employed former IRA, UVF and UDA prisoners to go into interface areas to help defuse tensions.

Intercomm inaugurated a scheme whereby former enemies travelled together to countries such as South Africa, Nicaragua and El Salvador, where they could observe other peoples divided by conflict and study the efforts to bring them together.

In late 1997, Liam and the trade unionist Brendan Mackin acted as conduits between the INLA and the British government during discussions that ended with the republican group announcing a ceasefire. Although Liam and Brendan were no longer involved in politics, they were well known and trusted by both the INLA and the government and were in a perfect position to act as honest brokers.

"Brendan and myself facilitated a process in which both sides could enter into dialogue, which was what they both wanted," Liam explains.

Throughout 1997 and the first eight months of 1998, the two men carried a succession of messages between the INLA and the British. Eventually, in the second week of August, the group was ready to announce a cessation.

"We had actually passed on the INLA ceasefire statement to the British," he says. "Each side was happy with what it contained and the announcement was to be made public the following Tuesday."

Liam travelled to Donegal with his wife for a weekend break, confident that everything had been set in place for the announcement the following week. However, the single worst atrocity of the Troubles was to unexpectedly jeopardise the republican group's intentions. On Saturday, 15 August, a Real IRA car bomb exploded in the middle of Omagh killing 29 people and two unborn babies.

The INLA contacted the conduits to say that it would find it impossible to make its statement calling a halt to activity in the climate immediately after the atrocity. Following a round of serious discussions, the group was persuaded to go ahead with the announcement. On August 22, the INLA announced a complete cessation of operations and offered a "sincere heartfelt and genuine apology" for the "faults and grievous errors in our prosecution of the war", including the killing and injuring of innocent people.

In 2002, however, nearly four years later, people were still being killed on the streets of Belfast and many were predicting that more would die during that summer. In mid-May that year, UFF leader Johnny Adair was released from Maghaberry prison. Adair had originally been sentenced to 16 years in jail in 1994 after pleading guilty to charges of directing terrorism but had been released early under the terms of the Good Friday Agreement. Adair ran the UFF from his power-base in the lower Shankill and had been responsible for the murders of dozens of nationalists in the late 1980s and early 1990s. Noted for his hatred of Catholics and willingness to travel into the heart of republican areas to carry out killings, he was suspected of being behind the majority of loyalist murders during that period, particularly the attacks on Sinn Féin councillors and their families. He had been arrested and charged with the June 1990 attack on the home of Sean Keenan, but the charges were dropped when a witness, who turned out to be Adair's girlfriend, withdrew her evidence.

Adair unwittingly contributed to his own downfall in 1994 when, during a series of casual conversations in the street with RUC officers, he admitted taking part in numerous gun attacks. The officers, part of an undercover unit carrying concealed microphones and recording equipment, taped the UFF leader's admissions. On September 6 1995, when Adair was jailed for 16 years for directing terrorism, the RUC held a special press conference to highlight the fact that they had taken one of the North's most dangerous killers off the streets. As Alex and Liz Maskey watched the press conference on television at home that evening, they were shocked when a police inspector produced an assault rifle and informed journalists that it was the weapon that Adair had used to shoot up the Maskey home. It was the first time the couple had learned that Adair had been involved in the January 1994 attack during which 30 shots had been fired at their house. More was to follow. During questioning in Castlereagh, Adair provided a detailed account of the 1993 attack in which Alan Lundy was killed.

Adair's release from prison in May 2002 came just five weeks before Alex Maskey was due to be elected Mayor. Nationalists feared that the Shankill loyalist would quickly return to killing Catholics, but behind-the-scenes efforts were already being made to engage Adair in talks to end interface violence.

As a community worker in North Belfast, Liam Maskey had built up contacts with various loyalist leaders since the ceasefires of 1994. One of the loyalists he had initiated talks with was Adair's close associate, John White. In 1977, White had been sentenced to life imprisonment for the particularly gruesome murders of nationalist politician Paddy Wilson and his companion Irene Andrews. White's credentials within hardline loyalism were second to none, having been a founder member of the UFF and Adair's closest confidant. By the late 1990s, however, White was privately indicating to journalists and nationalist politicians that he was fed up with the violence. Few believed the notorious killer.

Liam felt obliged to explore White's assertion that he wanted to bring an end to the carnage. For the first time, he feels free to talk publicly about the secret discussions with the UDA.

"I didn't know if John White was truthful or was just building a smokescreen for the killing of more Catholics, but if he was being truthful, someone had to test him and see if the killing could be stopped."

In the autumn of 2001, Liam says, he began to meet White in secret. When Liam privately consulted his older brother he was told to be careful.

"Alex warned me of the dangers that I would be putting myself in," Liam recalls. "He told me in no uncertain terms that I could be walking into a trap and that White could be using me for cover to carry on attacks on the nationalist community. He was also concerned that loyalists might wrongly see my personal efforts as me acting for republicans, when in reality I had not spoken to them about any of this. While he warned me of the dangers to myself and our family, he said he supported me and would do everything he could to help."

Ironically, in view of what would happen later, the first meeting between Liam and John White was in a café beside Belfast City Hall. The two held more talks in January and again in February 2002 when White warned that the main obstacles to peace were the hard-liners on the UFF's ruling Inner Council who were opposed to the Good Friday Agreement. Amongst these, White highlighted John Gregg as the most vociferous and dangerous opponent of the peace process.

John Gregg became a loyalist icon after shooting and seriously wounding Gerry Adams and Sean Keenan close to City Hall in 1985. Despite Gregg's notorious reputation for hating Catholics, Liam told White he wanted to meet the loyalist hard man for face-to-face talks. While White said the meeting might help, he refused to make the arrangements himself. Gregg detested both White and Adair and any hint that either was involved in secret talks with nationalists would be enough to spark a feud within the UDA. A different tactic was called for. Senior figures within the PUP were approached and they agreed to make contact with Gregg to arrange the meeting with Liam.

In utmost secrecy, the details of the rendezvous were arranged. It was eventually scheduled to take place on the last Sunday of February at a hotel on the outskirts of Larne. Less than 24 hours before the meeting was due to take place, Liam was contacted by a reliable figure within the establishment and warned not to travel to meet Gregg.

"Because of the obvious sensitivities of the situation, only a small number of people knew about the meeting," Liam explains. "A particular person telephoned me on the Saturday morning and said he knew who I was due to meet the next day. His exact words were 'Liam, don't go to the meeting, because if you do, you won't be coming back'. As I said, only a handful of people knew about the arrangements, so I can only assume that the British security services had received information from within the South-East Antrim UDA that I was to be killed at that meeting."

Liam heeded the warning and cancelled the appointment with Gregg. Two days later he was in contact again with White and informed him that he had been warned that Gregg had planned to kill him.

"I honestly don't believe White knew anything about it," he says. "He seemed as shocked as myself. White then said, 'Okay, then we'll just have to deal with Johnny Adair'."

Liam admits to having had serious reservations at the impromptu offer to come face to face with the man who had tried to kill his brother and had been responsible for the murder of a number of his friends.

"For me this was not about making friends with Johnny Adair, it was about stopping more people being killed. I knew it was a risk, but I decided it was a risk worth taking."

Again Alex Maskey warned his younger brother of the dangers inherent in his unorthodox efforts to stabilise the peace process. Within a fortnight of Adair's release from Maghaberry prison, a meeting was arranged between the nationalist community worker and the UFF killer. It had been agreed that the two sides would get together on a Monday morning at Liam's office on the Antrim Road.

The fact that Intercomm's premises were next to the largest police station in North Belfast helped in two very different ways. Maskey says the location was chosen both for safety and to show that the talks were all above board. However, an hour before the meeting was due to take place Liam received a telephone call from John White to say that Adair was unable to travel along the mainly nationalist Antrim Road "for security reasons".

White asked if Liam would be prepared to meet Adair in his lower Shankill stronghold. Reluctantly, he agreed to the new arrangements.

He telephoned his brother and asked for advice.

"Alex told me straight that I could be walking into a trap and that these were very dangerous people who could not be trusted. Alex told me not to take any chances."

Liam and a close aide drove into the lower Shankill, unaware that police already knew of the meeting with Adair and had undercover units in the area in case it transpired that the two were driving to their deaths. At a pre-arranged spot, John White met them and walked the nationalists to a house in the heart of the loyalist estate. The encounter took place that afternoon in an upstairs room of a disused house in Boundary Way that Adair used as his base to run the UFF.

As the two Catholics sat down at the table, they couldn't fail to notice that the walls of the room were covered in UFF paraphernalia. Johnny Adair made his entrance unannounced and, without preamble, immediately planted himself down opposite the pair. White and Adair both carried electronic "buzzing" devices used to detect surveillance recording.

Liam Maskey spoke first, telling the UFF leader that his brother had sent a message to say he hoped that something useful could come out of the talks.

"Adair looked at me and said, 'I respect that bastard, he has balls to burn. I have always said that about him. Tell Alex I hope that some day we can sit down face-to-face across a table to talk about peace for everyone'."

The first meeting with Adair lasted for more than an hour and included discussions about establishing a telephone network between nationalist and loyalist community leaders to be used to defuse tensions along the interfaces.

A few days later, a follow-up meeting took place, again in the lower Shankill, with further discussions about tensions between the two sides. While relationships were strengthening, Liam was aware that he, as a community worker, could not bring the killing to an end.

"I knew that if these people were serious about stopping the violence, they needed to be talking to Sinn Féin face-to-face. The one person they could meet without losing face was Alex, because he was Mayor and because he had publicly stated that he was working on an anti-sectarian policy."

Liam approached his brother to determine if he would be prepared to meet representatives of the UDA. Maskey did not hesitate. He said he would meet anyone if it helped stop the killing. But he made it clear that he would have to consult the party. Initially, however, Adair and White argued that a meeting with a senior republican such as Maskey would cause serious problems for them within their own organisation. The loyalists said they would have to hold discussions before they could agree to meet him. They promised to get back in contact with Liam once a decision was made.

On the morning of the anti-sectarian rally on August 2, Liam received a telephone call from a senior UDA man close to Adair and White to say that he had a message that needed to be delivered in person. Liam agreed to meet at a pre-arranged spot in the centre of Belfast shortly before the rally was due to commence.

Conscious that he had been within hours of being murdered at the Gregg appointment, Liam asked a Belfast-based official from a foreign government to accompany him to receive the message. He knew that the UDA man would immediately recognise the foreigner accompanying him as an influential figure.

"The other person was there because I wanted the UDA to know that we were serious about this whole thing and that this chance could not be wasted needlessly."

At the allotted time, the UDA man met Liam Maskey and his "friend".

"We exchanged pleasantries for a few minutes and then he just said, 'Liam, that's okay for the meeting', and he walked away."

With those simple words, preparations were made for Alex Maskey to meet representatives of the organisation whose members had been trying to kill him for the past 15 years. Although the UDA men had agreed to talk to Maskey, they still harboured fears that hard-liners within their ranks would exploit the meeting to further fracture loyalism.

The loyalists Adair sent to meet Maskey were John White, Davy

Mahood and Shankill councillor Frank McCoubrey. Jim Gibney admits there were also discussions within Sinn Féin to decide if the talks should go ahead.

"Alex deciding to meet the UDA could have been misunderstood within the nationalist community," says Gibney. "The UDA was still killing Catholics and it was important that we were not legitimising these people, or allowing them to escape responsibility for their actions."

Gibney says it was concluded that as Mayor, Maskey had an obligation to do anything that could help end violence.

"It would be wrong to say that we did not have misgivings about this meeting, but it was decided that if it helped to ease tensions on the interfaces, then it was worth the risk."

Maskey recalls the lengths to which he had to go to meet the loyalists in City Hall in August.

"They didn't want to be seen to be meeting me on their own, so I had to invite a number of other groups and arrange it so that I spent ten minutes with each group. In reality the whole thing was arranged to meet them. They were paranoid that the meeting would be used against them by their own side."

While Maskey was prepared to meet the loyalists, he left them in no doubt that he would hold them accountable for the continuing violence.

"I told them that if they were serious about bringing peace to the interfaces, then I would do everything I could to help that. But I also told them that if the UDA were behind continued interface violence, I would publicly condemn them each and every time. They argued that they wanted an end to interface violence and, to be fair, they seemed to be looking for help in finding ways to improve their community infrastructure and I committed my office to supporting them."

He agreed there was no reason why Frank McCoubrey, as a city councillor, could not be a member of the anti-sectarian group. After the meeting, John White insisted that loyalists were prepared to play their part in any initiative aimed at defeating sectarianism.

"We are eight years into a peace process and sectarianism is as bad as ever," he said.

While White accused mainstream politicians of snubbing the UDA's political representatives, he praised Maskey's efforts, saying: "We are encouraged that this initiative has been established and although we are political opponents, it appeared to us that Alex Maskey is working hard to make it a success. It is a cross-party initiative and it is up to all those parties and groups in our society who want to see an end to sectarianism to support it and ensure that it succeeds."

But hopes were cut short by tensions within the UDA. White and Adair appeared willing to engage in discussions with Sinn Féin in the guise of the Lord Mayor, but as feared, anti-agreement hard-liners within the UDA used the meeting to attack the White-Adair faction.

The brigadiers who formed the UDA's Inner Council met two days later amid bitter recriminations over White's discussions with Maskey. An added complication was that beneath the opposition to the talks lay a power struggle for overall control of the UDA. Just weeks after the Maskey meeting, White and Adair were expelled from the organisation. Any hopes of further talks appeared to have gone. In November, Davy Mahood was shot in both legs by the UDA in North Belfast after he was judged to be too close to the Adair camp. In January 2003, a bloody feud erupted within the UDA. Adair was deemed by authorities to be a leading protagonist. Secretary of State Paul Murphy revoked his early release licence and he was returned to Maghaberry Prison to serve out the remainder of his sentence.

In February, John Gregg was ambushed and killed by Adair's men as he drove in a taxi through Belfast's docks. Within weeks, John White and the Adair supporters fled Northern Ireland for Scotland after the mainstream UDA attacked houses in Adair's lower Shankill power-base.

Liam Maskey said it was impossible to know if White and Adair were serious about stopping the violence.

"One conclusion was that they were genuine about bringing the killing to an end. The other conclusion was that they wanted to stop the violence along the interfaces so that they could continue with their criminal activities. Whatever ulterior motives they had, all I know is that their faction of the UDA was prepared to talk to nationalists and the others weren't."

By August 2003, the UDA and its political representatives in the Ulster Political Research Group (UPRG) were still refusing to take part in face-to-face talks with Sinn Féin.

In an ironic twist, Liam Maskey was awarded an international peace prize while he was secretly meeting Adair in the heart of the lower Shankill. In June 2002, he was the joint recipient of the US President's Prize, which recognises people for their contribution to promoting peace and fostering cross-community links. While Alex Maskey celebrated St Patrick's Day in Belfast, his younger brother was given a private meeting with US president George W Bush Jr in the White House.

"In 1973 Alex and myself were sharing a hut in the Cages not knowing if we were ever going to be released," jokes Liam. "But 20 years later Alex was celebrating St Patrick's Day as the First Citizen of Belfast and I was sitting in the White House chatting to the President of the United States. It was a long way from Long Kesh."

By one of the vagaries of northern politics, Alex Maskey found that he could, with relative ease, hold peace talks with loyalists who had repeatedly tried to kill him, yet he could not find a unionist councillor who would agree to work alongside him as deputy mayor. At his election in June, unionists had refused to nominate anyone from their benches to take the position.

The decision to snub Maskey's year in office appeared to have been taken at leadership level in the Ulster Unionist Party as at least one councillor had previously stated publicly that he would be prepared to fill the position. Two days before the mayoral election, East Belfast unionist Alan Crowe, aware that Maskey was almost certain to be elected, said he would be willing to put his name forward as his deputy.

"I am willing, if selected, to go forward," said Crowe. "But whether or not the unionist family would be prepared to allow that hasn't been decided yet. I am quite prepared to take on the role, partly because we need a counter-balance at the top of the council. There are a number of areas of responsibilities and functions which Sinn Féin will not be prepared to carry out. Whoever is deputy lord mayor will have a fairly crucial role to play in those circumstances."

Despite Crowe's courageous offer, when the city's first republican Mayor was elected, unionists refused point blank to nominate a deputy from their benches. With the council due to break for the summer after election night, the decision on the post was deferred until the next meeting in September. Maskey hoped that unionists would use this period to reflect on their decision, especially after his Somme initiative. The Mayor's groundbreaking efforts at the Cenotaph were, apparently, not enough to sway the hard-liners. When the council reconvened after the break, the party still refused to appoint a deputy to sit alongside the Sinn Féin Mayor.

UUP councillor Chris McGimpsey said his party was refusing to nominate a deputy mayor because Maskey "was not representing all the people in the city".

"We took a decision at the beginning of Alex Maskey's year that, because of his refusal to represent the city at certain events and when certain people are present, we felt that the time was not right. None of us wished to serve as his deputy and as such we have not nominated anybody."

Unionists insisted their decision not to share the top office with a republican was based on a reluctance to sit alongside a politician whose party was linked to a paramilitary group. Nationalists accused unionists of hypocrisy and pointed to the fact that both the DUP and UUP had previously been willing to work in City Hall with political representatives of paramilitaries – as long as they were loyalist.

The criticism did not appear to be without foundation. Unionists had previously elected politicians with links to the UVF and UDA to the positions of lord mayor and deputy mayor. In the late 1980s, they elected the PUP's Hugh Smyth as Deputy Mayor, even though the UVF were still active. Then, in June 1994, Smyth was elected as Belfast's First Citizen – four months before the UVF announced its ceasefire. In December 2000, mainstream unionists elected Frank McCoubrey, who was at the time a member of the UDA-linked Ulster Democratic Party, to the post of Deputy Mayor. During his term in office, McCoubrey acted as character witness for a leading loyalist who had appeared in court facing attempted murder charges relating to the UDA-UVF feud.

While unionist politicians had repeatedly condemned loyalist violence, contacts between the DUP, the UUP and loyalist paramilitaries had been something of a regular occurrence. In 1986, DUP leader Ian Paisley defended his decision to attend the wake of murdered UVF leader John Bingham. A number of other high-ranking unionist councillors attended the funeral. Those present when the loyalist's coffin – draped in a paramilitary flag and bearing his beret and gloves – was carried from the church, included the then North Belfast MP Cecil Walker, former DUP councillor George Seawright, former UUP Mayor John Carson and councillors Joe Coggle, Frank Millar Sr and Hugh Smyth.

Seven years later, a DUP councillor was jailed for his part in a UVF extortion racket. In 1993 Billy Baxter was convicted on charges of demanding money on behalf of the UVF. The North Down councillor was jailed for three and a half years for soliciting money from a Dublin businessman for the paramilitary grouping.

In September 1996, leading DUP figure William McCrea sparked controversy when he joined dissident Loyalist Volunteer Force (LVF) leader Billy Wright on a public platform in Portadown.

In 2001, DUP councillor John Smyth was elected to Antrim Borough Council. Smyth had previously served a five-year sentence in the 1970s for UVF activities. In the same year senior UUP figures Fred Cobain and David Burnside both admitted holding separate, private talks with the UDA leadership. During the negotiations that led to the Good Friday Agreement, UUP representatives made a public demonstration of "unionist unity" by walking into the talks shoulder-to-shoulder with loyalists linked to Protestant paramilitaries.

While unionists in Belfast refused to work with a Sinn Féin Lord Mayor, outside the city leading unionists appeared to have no difficulty doing just that. In 2002, William McCrea held the chairmanship of

Magherafelt District Council with Sinn Féin's John Kelly as his deputy.

In 2001, Strabane DUP councillor Tommy Kerrigan took the position of Deputy Mayor alongside Sinn Féin Mayor Ivan Barr. Kerrigan went so far as to shake hands and pose for photographs with Barr and said he was prepared to work with his counterpart. Within 24 hours, Kerrigan was forced to issue a retraction of his statement after reportedly being contacted by the party leadership.

Belfast's first nationalist Mayor Alban Maginness, accusing unionists of living in the "twilight zone", said: "The covert association which unionist politicians have had with loyalist paramilitaries has given these people a legitimacy and status which they do not deserve."

Warning that refusal to take the deputy mayor's position was ultimately failing their own constituents, Maginness went on: "There is serious work to be done and they are just not doing it. What the people of Belfast and Northern Ireland want to see is their politicians sharing power. What better symbol to promote around the world than a unionist and nationalist acting as mayor and deputy mayor? In my opinion, nationalism has shown it is prepared to compromise and share power.

"When I was the first nationalist mayor of Belfast, I received huge positive feedback from ordinary Protestants but absolutely nothing from the unionist politicians. Alex Maskey compromised with the British Legion event this week but there wasn't one unionist councillor there to see it. You are left asking yourself if unionist politicians actually want reconciliation."

Maginness said the unionist parties' relationship with loyalist paramilitaries was inconsistent with their refusal to appoint a deputy mayor alongside Maskey.

Former UUP mayor Jim Rodgers, defending his party's position, said: "The big problem for unionists is that the Lord Mayor represents a political party closely aligned to PIRA which has never said that it regrets its deeds of the past. If that happened it would be a small step."

Challenged on the issue of his party's support for mayoral candidates aligned to the UVF and UDA, Rodgers said: "The UUP supported Frank McCoubrey and Hugh Smyth because they have no criminal record and have condemned all paramilitary violence."

Insisting that he had no personal antipathy towards Maskey, the East Belfast unionist said: "Sinn Féin and the SDLP are trying to score cheap political points here, but it won't work. I don't hate anyone. I chat to Alex Maskey any time I see him, as an individual. It is what he stands for which causes great problems for unionists. Our record speaks for itself. We are not linked to any paramilitary organisation and have consistently condemned all paramilitary violence. We have nothing to be ashamed of."

The attitude of unionist councillors came in for criticism from the city's leading newspapers. The *Belfast News Letter*, with its almost exclusively unionist and Protestant readership, accused the UUP of having responded "churlishly" with regard both to Maskey's decision to lay a wreath at the Cenotaph in July and his decision to hold a reception for the Royal British Legion in City Hall.

Its editorial of November 5 read: "Simply put, Mr Maskey was doing the right thing, though he is well aware that, in Northern Ireland, doing the right thing is not necessarily enough to satisfy the critics."

The newspaper congratulated the Sinn Féin Mayor for what it described as his decision to set aside his republican principles in favour of taking on a mayoral role that was seen as being even-handed. The editorial went further, insisting that he deserved credit for "restoring an element of dignity to an important office" which had too often been occupied by people "who lacked the courage or inclination to live up to their wider responsibilities". Continuing the attack on the city's previous unionist first citizens, the *News Letter* editorial recalled that not every mayor in the past had lived up to the standards that the role required. The office of mayor had in the past been used to "cement divisions" rather than to reconcile the two communities.

Throwing down the gauntlet, the newspaper added: "The challenge now is for unionists to show that they are tuned into a new way of behaving and the most obvious starting point would be to appoint a unionist Deputy to Mr Maskey at the City Hall."

A day later, the nationalist *Irish News* described the decision not to nominate a deputy mayor as "a sad state of affairs". The empty chair in the chamber sent out a "particularly unfortunate symbolic" message on behalf of Belfast.

While accepting that unionists still had a right to oppose their republican counterparts, the newspaper's editorial said: "However, it is disappointing that some unionists still refuse to recognise the significant contribution Mr Maskey has been making towards the cause of reconciliation in Belfast. His decision to lay a wreath at the city's Cenotaph and to hold a reception in honour of the Royal British Legion deserves to be regarded as a sincere attempt to extend the hand of friendship beyond the sectarian divide."

Accusing unionist politicians in City Hall of having short memories, the newspaper continued: "In the recent past, non-unionists had to accept individuals with strong loyalist paramilitary connections in the top posts on the council. It would appear that these double standards are doing very little to enhance Belfast's wider image."

Maskey had to face the political reality that unionists would not appoint a deputy for the duration of his year in office, but he insists that they squandered a valuable opportunity to rebuild relationships between the two communities. Weeks before he was elected Mayor, he said, he had taken part in a council trip to the United States alongside unionist councillors, including Jim Rodgers.

"We were in America trying to encourage US firms to invest in Belfast and the core argument we made to potential investors was that we were there together, representing Belfast. However, as soon as I was elected Mayor, the unionists said they wouldn't work with me. In America we spoke with one voice, but when we came home it was the same old story."

Maskey describes the absence of a deputy mayor as his single biggest regret during his year in office.

"Just think of what could have been achieved if people saw a republican and a unionist working side by side for the benefit of Belfast. Other councils across the North were able to do it, but in Belfast we seemed to have been stuck in 1690. I think it was a travesty because so much more could have been achieved for the city during my year in office if I had been seen to be working alongside a unionist.

"One senior unionist councillor told me that my asking for a partner, as opposed to a deputy, was too big a challenge for the UUP. I honestly believe that the unionists did a disservice to their own community in their decision not to nominate a deputy mayor. It was a golden opportunity that was lost because of bigotry and outright self-interest."

CHAPTER NINE

MEETING THE ROYALS

A S 2002 drew to a close and Alex Maskey reflected on his first six months in office, he found he had been congratulated and castigated in equal measure. He had received public support for his decisions to lay a wreath in memory of those who died at the Somme and to hold a City Hall reception for the British Legion, although unionists and some sections of grassroots republicanism remained deeply unhappy with the actions of the Mayor.

Only a handful of key people were aware of just how far Maskey, the personification of republican local politics for more than 20 years, was prepared to move beyond the accepted boundaries of militant Irish nationalism in his efforts to reach out to unionists.

Nationalists and Ulster Protestants had traditionally held very different viewpoints when it came to the British monarchy. The monarchy, and the family that epitomised it, had been an anathema to republicans for generations. The philosophy of republicanism, steeped in anti-imperialist politics, found itself at the opposite end of the political spectrum to a British establishment system that was content to have a king or queen as its titular head of state.

The fact that Ulster Protestants regularly reiterated that their ultimate loyalty was to the British monarchy, rather than the democratically-elected Westminster government of the day, only confirmed republican antipathy towards the Royal Family and all it stood for. Veteran republican Martin Meehan explains the traditional nationalist attitude towards the British Crown, an attitude which was reinforced by the onset of the Troubles in 1969.

"These people were the very epitome of everything which we as Irish republicans were opposed to. They headed the British forces which illegally occupied the North of Ireland. You had British soldiers and the RUC shooting unarmed nationalists dead in the streets, but these people didn't go to jail like we did. More often than not, some prince or duchess, dressed in a British army uniform, would arrive over in the North for a day and pin a medal on their chests."

The Windsors, as republicans liked to refer to the royals, were viewed as the embodiment of the British establishment in Ireland. Republicans argued that the British nation appeared content to allow the Royal Family to live like "kings" while the working classes could not find jobs or proper housing – proof that the state was morally corrupt.

Republicans not only refused to recognise the monarchy, but had also tried to kill various members of the British aristocracy throughout the Troubles. Some members of the Royal Family were regarded as "legitimate targets" not simply because of their status as monarchs, but because of the fact that they were commanders-in-chief of the various regiments of the British army. Prince Charles, for example, was Commander-in-Chief of the Parachute Regiment, which was responsible for shooting 14 people in Derry on Bloody Sunday in January 1972. The Queen's other two sons, Andrew and Edward, had both been members of the Royal Marines regiment that was involved in some of the most controversial killings of the Troubles.

Martin Meehan explains the IRA's thinking on targeting members of the Royal Family during the conflict.

"If these people were happy to be a general in this regiment or a colonel in that regiment, then they had to take the same risk as the British soldiers who had terrorised the nationalist community in the North. Republicans believed that, as the heads of the British state, the Royal Family had to accept responsibility for what happened in Ireland."

The monarchy continued to be regarded as "legitimate targets" by the IRA until the ceasefire announced in 1994.

In July 1977, the IRA had threatened to disrupt Queen Elizabeth II's visit to Northern Ireland to mark jubilee celebrations the following month. Dozens of republicans were arrested and held in police stations across the North for the duration of the royal trip. Alex Maskey was working as a painter and decorator that year and was driving along Stockman's Lane on the edge of West Belfast when he was stopped at a UDR checkpoint. He was amongst a group of men taken to Fort Mona British army base where, he says, he was beaten and held for several hours before being released.

The IRA warning turned out to be no idle threat. On the second day of the royal visit a bomb they had planted exploded at the University of Ulster campus at Jordanstown, which the Queen was due to visit.

In August 1979, the IRA killed the Queen's cousin and Prince Charles' favourite uncle, Lord Louis Mountbatten. The former Viceroy of India died instantly when a 50lb bomb blew up his sailing boat *Shadow V* as it sailed off the coast of Mullaghmore in County Sligo. Three other people died in the explosion: Mountbatten's 14-year-old grandson Nicholas Knatchbull, Lady Patricia Brabourne, who was his daughter's mother-in-law, and 15-year-old Paul Maxwell from Enniskillen, who was working as a deck-hand for the summer.

On May 9, 1981 one day after Bobby Sands' funeral, the IRA said it had left a bomb at Sullom Voe oil terminal on the Shetland Islands. The device was meant to explode during the Queen's visit to the Scottish isles.

The threat to the British monarchy remained a constant throughout the Troubles with republicans protesting each time a member of the Royal Family visited the North. The relationship between the Crown and Irish nationalism as a whole had remained distant since partition. It was not until 1993 that Mary Robinson became the first Irish president to meet the British head of state in 70 years.

As the Irish peace process developed, a number of members of the Royal Family visited the Republic during the 1990s. The Queen, however, has never visited the South. A regular visitor to Northern Ireland, she received heavy nationalist criticism in 2000 when she flew in to award the George Cross to the RUC.

In May 2002, Mark Durkan became the first SDLP leader to meet the Queen when she visited Stormont for the first time in 50 years. Sinn Féin did not attend the event and, although they had been informed that the Queen was due, decided not to mount a protest.

In the late summer of that same year, Maskey met with the Lord Lieutenant of Belfast, Lady Romaine Carswell, the Queen's official representative in the city. The Mayor and Lady Carswell had met at various functions but now Maskey had decided to meet her on a formal basis.

"I had asked for the formal meeting so that I could inform Lady Carswell in person that the political realities meant it would be almost impossible for me to meet any member of the British Royal Family who visited the North."

Crucially, he advised her that he would consider each proposed royal visit on its merits and would consider attending a royal event. He assured her that his deliberations would not in any way disrupt the royal itinerary.

Maskey says that Lady Carswell accepted the situation. He describes the meetings as having been "good-natured". The dialogue with Lady Carswell on the issue of visits by any member of the monarchy was a clear sign of the lengths republicans were prepared to go to ensure that his year in office would not be embroiled in controversy.

In the first week of March, however, the Mayor initiated discussions that had the potential to stretch republican grassroots support to the limit. Prince Andrew, Duke of York and brother of the heir to the British throne, was due to make a trip to the North the following week. His itinerary included a visit to a rugby match, the final of the Schools Cup, which is traditionally played on St Patrick's Day at the Ravenhill sports grounds.

Protocol indicated that the Mayor of Belfast, the city's leading civic dignitary, should be invited to meet the Prince. No one really expected that Maskey would even consider becoming the first ever Sinn Féin politician to meet a member of Britain's Royal Family. His wreath-laying ceremony at the Cenotaph had brought him serious criticism from within the party. The level of dissatisfaction which surfaced in March had found its way on to the floor of the party's annual Ard Fheis which was being broadcast live on television for the first time. Even bigger trouble was likely for the Mayor if the rank-and-file members suspected he was looking at the possibility of accepting the invitation to meet Prince Andrew.

Maskey had managed to overcome criticism of his actions at the Cenotaph by holding a series of meetings with party activists to explain his position. However, he was aware that if he went further and met with any representative of the Crown, the repercussions within the republican movement could have caused serious discontent, not only for himself but for the whole party which was preparing for Assembly elections in May.

In the second week of March, an official from the Mayor's office was in contact with the Northern Ireland Office to discuss the possibility of Maskey meeting Prince Andrew. It had been suggested that the Prince would hold an informal gathering inside the main building of the rugby grounds, during which the Mayor could be present with other dignitaries.

Key to an acceptance from Maskey to be present at the event, however, was the proviso that there would be no British military symbolism at the gathering. That the encounter should take place in a civic, rather than a military format, was crucial to the possibility that the two would meet.

Prior to the Ravenhill engagement the Prince was due to travel to St Patrick's Barracks in Ballymena to meet soldiers from the Royal Irish Regiment (RIR) of which he was Colonel-in-Chief. The relationship between nationalists and the home-based regiments of the British army had traditionally been fraught. There were repeated allegations that members of the UDR and its successor, the RIR, not only colluded with loyalist paramilitaries by passing on official information, but also were actively involved in the murder of Catholics. The RIR had officially replaced the UDR in July 1992 in the hope that it would be more acceptable to the Catholic population in the North.

Nationalists and the Irish government had been critical of the regiment since it was formed in 1970 and had repeatedly called for it to be disbanded. Many felt they had good reason to be suspicious of a group they perceived as a unionist militia. In 1975 two UDR men were convicted of the murder of three Catholics who were part of the

Miami Showband. The musicians were killed when loyalists stopped their van at a bogus checkpoint. The "soldiers" had attempted to hide a bomb inside the vehicle while their colleagues searched the men, but the device exploded prematurely, killing two of the loyalist gang as well as the band members.

In the early 1990s an investigation by Sir John Stevens into security force collusion with loyalist paramilitaries led to ten members of the UDR being charged with possession of information likely to be useful to terrorists. In April 2003, Stevens stated publicly for the first time that army and police personnel had actively colluded with loyalists in the murder of nationalists.

UDR soldiers were prime targets for the IRA, with 197 serving soldiers and 47 former members being killed during the Troubles. Prior to its disbandment, Catholics made up just three percent of the UDR. British government hopes that the change of name from UDR to RIR would encourage acceptance from nationalists ended in disappointment. The RIR continued to be dogged with allegations that its members were involved in collusion.

In 1996, RIR man Mark Black was given a twelve-month suspended sentence after the personal details of nationalists were found at his home in Cookstown. The soldier claimed the information was for his personal use.

RIR soldier David Keys was charged in 1998 with his taking part in an LVF gun attack on a bar in Poyntzpass in which Catholic man Damien Trainor and his Protestant friend Philip Allen were shot dead. Keys was later found dead in his cell in the H-Blocks while awaiting trial. It was initially thought that he had committed suicide but was later discovered that he had been tortured and killed by fellow LVF prisoners.

In 2000, former RIR soldier William Thompson was charged with possessing an Uzi submachine-gun, a sawn-off shotgun, 30 shotgun cartridges and an explosive substance. It later emerged that Thompson had been questioned in connection with the 1999 murder of Catholic human rights lawyer Rosemary Nelson.

In October 2002, part-time RIR serviceman Glen Strong was

charged with the murder of 27-year-old Catholic man Colin Foy after the soldier walked into a bar in Fivemiletown and opened fire.

While grassroots members would have baulked at Alex Maskey meeting a representative of the British monarchy, the circumstances under which he would have come face to face with the Duke of York – after the royal had taken part in an RIR ceremony – would have been judged unacceptable by even the most broad-minded republican. Accepting that the potential encounter had serious implications, Maskey believed that another Rubicon could be crossed and a positive message could be sent to unionists if he managed to successfully negotiate his way around the obstacles of a Sinn Féin leader meeting a British royal.

"If I was to pull this thing off, I needed guarantees that there would be no British military symbolism at the event. As Mayor of Belfast I had to be seen to be representing everyone in this city. But at the same time I was not prepared to discard the fact that I was an Irish republican and socialist who had opposed everything that the British monarchy stood for all my life. I also had to represent all those who were totally opposed to the monarchy. If this meeting was to take place, there had to be compromise on both sides."

Maskey admits he had no personal aspirations to be the first republican in history to converse with a royal.

"Certainly I had no interest in the British Royal Family. But I wanted to show the nay-sayers within unionism once and for all that we were prepared to be proactive and … do things alien to our philosophy if it helped build a relationship between republicans and the unionist community."

Meeting Prince Andrew, Maskey believes, could have been the clearest sign to unionists that nothing was "beyond the bounds" and that everything was possible if the two traditions were prepared to work together.

While the Mayor's office negotiated with representatives from the Northern Ireland Office, Maskey kept his own party leaders aware of what was going on. He had agreed that he would not go to the party with any proposal to meet the Prince until he had received specific guarantees from the British that the event would have no military trappings.

"I had sounded out various people within the party to see what they thought the political fall-out would be. There was no use me meeting a member of the British Royal Family to show unionists we were prepared to work with them, while at the same time causing irreparable damage to the republican grassroots."

Maskey said that while he was aware of the anger he had caused by laying a wreath at the Cenotaph, he was still convinced that his new endeavour was a risk worth taking. He insisted that while he was shaking republican ideology to its core, the potential benefits were worth the gamble.

"I knew that what I was doing was causing republican grassroots to ask if I had lost my mind, but I argued that this was our chance to silence our critics once and for all. In political life you meet parties and dignitaries who you are ideologically and morally opposed to. You do not personally have to agree with these people, but as First Citizen of a city you have an obligation to represent the traditions of everyone who lives in that city. It was a question of balancing civic leadership with the political and ideological beliefs that you have lived with all your life."

He was prepared to argue that, as Mayor of Belfast he should meet a member of British monarchy, but he could not meet someone dressed in British military uniform. Discussions continued between the NIO and City Hall in the days before the visit with various proposals put forward as to how the Irish republican and British prince could meet. The discussions, he said, continued right up until 24 hours before the reception was due to take place.

"St Patrick's Day was on Monday, but on the Sunday the British came back and said the plans had been changed and that now there was to be a line-up at the entrance to the ground where the various dignitaries would meet the Prince."

Looking back on the situation, Maskey says he still does not know if the last minute change was created to jeopardise the possibility of a historic meeting or was designed to push republicans into a publicity stunt.

"I don't know why they decided to change it from a private, civic reception to a public event with military overtones. Was it that someone wanted to undermine my efforts to reach out to unionists by attempting to scupper the possibility that I would meet a member of the British Royal Family? I simply don't know."

Whatever the reason for the eleventh hour shift in plan, he knew the revised arrangements made it impossible for him to obtain permission from the Sinn Féin leadership to meet the Prince. He insists that it would have been unacceptable for him to have taken part in a public line-up to meet the man who was commander-in-chief of the RIR. He remains convinced, however, that because of the late change of plans, an opportunity was lost to break new ground between the two traditions.

"In the end, I dropped my proposal to the party, because I knew that it would be rejected. At the end of the day, if you are serious about reconciliation, you take initiatives which are risky. Sometimes they work out, sometimes they don't. But it shouldn't stop you trying to break new ground. I was aware of the problems which this meeting would have caused within my own community. I was aware of the historical barriers which I was crossing. But I felt that I had an obligation to show that we were serious about reaching out to unionists. If meeting a member of their Royal Family built confidence between the two communities then I was prepared to take that risk, but it didn't happen and you have to accept such things in political life."

It often seemed to Maskey that his year in office was taken up with efforts to reach out to unionists, but there were also occasions when he was able to revisit his past as a republican prisoner. In January, he and Liz were offered the chance to visit the now disused and semi-derelict Long Kesh prison camp. Maskey had been held in the internees' "Cages" and not the newer H-Blocks. He did, however, go into the H-Blocks in 1998 in his role to explain the implications of the Good Friday Agreement to republican prisoners.

He found his visit back to the compound where he was twice interned was not only a walk back in time, but an emotional experience also.

"Myself and Liz stood on waste ground where my old Cage 22 once was and I showed her where myself, George Burt and Billy Kelly had tried to escape from. It was amazing to go back to the Cages and see the conditions we were forced to live in, not knowing if or when we would be released."

The couple then visited the H-Blocks and prison hospital where the ten republican prisoners, including their friends Kieran Doherty and Joe McDonnell, had died on hunger strike.

"It was a very emotional experience because Jackie McMullan, who had been on hunger strike for 42 days in 1981, was with us, and it brought the whole tragedy and suffering back to all of us as if it was only yesterday. It reminded me of what the blanket men and the women in Armagh had fought for and what the hunger strikers had given their lives for."

Earlier that month, Maskey had been part of a Sinn Féin delegation that travelled to 10 Downing Street to hold talks with British Prime Minister Tony Blair on the stalled peace process. As Mayor of Belfast, he highlighted the need for government co-operation in tackling sectarianism and warned that the North's largest city was in danger of sliding into chaos unless the process was put firmly back on track.

"I told Tony Blair that all parties needed to show a commitment to peace and the best way to do that was for his government to re-establish the institutions."

When Maskey challenged Blair that his government had a direct responsibility to tackle sectarianism, the Prime Minister instructed Secretary of State Paul Murphy to meet with the Mayor separately on the issue. Maskey's call for the re-establishment of the power-sharing Executive fell on deaf ears, however, with the Stormont elections in May being initially postponed for one month and later cancelled indefinitely. By August 2003, no date had been set for elections to the Assembly.

Maskey's "think tank" had worked hard on planning his mayoral year down to the most minute detail, but in January a relatively minor slip-up allowed unionists to pounce. In a bid to derail his term in office, he says that a row was created over a photograph of him and his granddaughter Tierna which appeared in a republican calendar.

The Alliance Party and the SDLP called for an explanation from the Mayor, but the DUP and Ulster Unionists demanded that the council censure Maskey. He later released a statement effectively disassociating himself from the calendar explaining that no request had been made for the use of his photograph and that he had not given consent for its use. The Mayor insisted that, since his election, he had "studiously avoided" any possible misuse of his office and accused unionists of clutching at straws to wreck his mayoral term. The DUP motion of censure was defeated at a meeting of the full council where it failed to obtain the backing of Alliance, SDLP and Sinn Féin. Defending the Mayor's position, Alliance councillor Tom Ekin said Maskey had made clear, as asked, that he had no association with the calendar. The matter, therefore, should be dropped.

"The DUP will probably have a motion condemning Alex Maskey every month until the (mayoral) election," said Ekin. "But we believe that, on the whole, he is doing a reasonably good job."

In March, Maskey earned himself another footnote in history when he became the first Mayor of Belfast to take part in the annual republican commemoration at Milltown cemetery to mark the 1916 Easter Rising. As one of the most important events in the republican calendar, the selection of the Mayor as keynote speaker was seen as a public sign of support from the leadership for his year in office. But to show the grassroots that he had not "gone soft", he also publicly praised the IRA which, he claimed, had been responsible for creating the opportunity for the peace process.

Maskey applauded the IRA for its "continuing, unprecedented efforts to advance this process despite the many obstacles put in the way". Insisting that the republican goal of a united Ireland was now more achievable than ever before, he told his audience: "Today I stand before you as Mayor of this city. I am extremely proud and honoured to do so. The struggle for Irish independence has grown from strength to strength – in this city we have proved that. My election as Mayor is yet further proof of that."

Contrary to claims by his political opponents, Maskey's Easter address in no way signalled an end to his efforts to reach out to the unionist community. He was, he says, determined to push back the boundaries even further. Since his first week in the office, he had been developing a relationship with non-political unionists, in particular the British Legion, as evidenced by his reception for the association in November 2002.

While he had refused to attend the Legion's Remembrance Day ceremony, he had continued discussions with the association's president, Brigadier David Strudley. Although Strudley and Maskey came from very different backgrounds, they developed a working relationship that was to bear fruit. Through his discussions with Strudley and the positive feedback he had received from nationalists after laying the wreath at the Cenotaph, Maskey had indicated that, as an act of reconciliation, he wanted to organise a civic ceremony in which nationalists and unionists could collectively remember those who died in the First World War.

Initially, he said, he had hoped to arrange a series of public seminars to discuss the way in which the dead from both traditions might be remembered.

"The issue of how this society remembers its dead, republican and unionist, is something which people have never sat down and discussed. For 30 years, this society has not been able to properly discuss how to commemorate the dead, whether it's a British soldier, an IRA volunteer, a member of the UVF or UDA or someone completely uninvolved. I had hoped that we could begin a debate on the issue, which to me is long overdue, so that at the very least, people could agree that we would respect each other's right to remember our loved ones."

As it was, the combination of a lack of time and the political situation that existed in spring of 2003 meant he was not able to garner enough support to have the matter discussed on a public platform.

"I honestly feel that it is an issue which cannot be ignored and that, sooner or later, people will have to sit down and discuss a way forward which is acceptable to everyone in this city."

While Maskey felt that, yet again, a valuable opportunity had been lost, he did manage to mark another significant milestone in the relationships between nationalists and the British establishment. At the end of April, republicans and senior members of the British army found themselves sitting side by side in Belfast's St Anne's Church of Ireland Cathedral at a civic ceremony to commemorate the dead of the First World War. The ecumenical church service, entitled *Shared Sacrifice*, had been organised at the request of the Mayor by Monsignor Tom Toner of St Peter's Catholic Cathedral on Belfast's Falls Road and Dean Houston McKelvey of St Anne's.

Once again, the ceremony became the focus of controversy when unionists called for it to be boycotted because those attending had been asked not to wear war medals or military regalia. Ulster Unionist Jim Rodgers publicly stated that he would shun the ceremony because of the ban. He said that he had been contacted by a number of branches of the British Legion who had also vowed to boycott the event.

Describing the attempts to politicise the event as "regrettable", Maskey said: "I think it's unfortunate that this issue of the medals has been used by some people to mar an event which is inter-denominational and non-political. This is a church service dedicated to remembering those who lost their lives and those who suffered in the First World War and for their families and their friends and their loved ones."

However, the Mayor's idea for the civic ceremony did win praise from the two organisers. Monsignor Toner, whose grandfather was killed in the First World War, said he had no doubt that Maskey's decision to lay wreaths at the cenotaphs in Belfast and Messines was crucial to paving the way for the service which could allow republicans and British soldiers to sit side by side.

"I think he certainly was the catalyst that made it happen," he said. "I hope he is happy with the result, because I think it was a very memorable and moving and significant evening."

Dean Houston McKelvey expressed a hope that the series of initiatives carried out by the city's first republican Mayor could lead to more significant gestures of reconciliation. He added: "I found in Alex Maskey, as the Lord Mayor, a person who tried to set aside his own personal background, his own luggage, when he was fulfilling the role as the First Citizen of this city. I think he has behaved with integrity in doing so and I hope that, as a result of him being the First Citizen of this city, other people who would be close to him politically would have a sense of ownership that maybe they haven't had before."

After the April 30 service, Maskey admits to having had a sense of relief that the last major hurdle of his mayoral year had been overcome with very little genuine controversy. His final month in office would be taken up by a hectic series of invitations to City Hall from schools and community groups who wanted to visit the Mayor before his term ended at the beginning of June. He accepts that being the city's first republican Mayor meant that there was more public attention on him than on previous first citizens. He is, however, adamant that bringing ordinary people into City Hall gave him most satisfaction during his mayoral term.

"Obviously, there was a lot of attention given to the controversial decisions which I undertook and I accept that as a political reality. But what genuinely pleased me most was the fact that I was able to open up City Hall to communities which previously had little or no relationship with the council."

He said it was the regular visits by schoolchildren, Catholic and Protestant, that he enjoyed most about his year in office.

"For a lot of these children, it was the first time that they had set foot inside City Hall. To see them in the Mayor's parlour and the council chamber and getting the chance to try on the Mayor's chain was what it was all about for me. If I remember one thing about my year in office, it was the sound of the schoolchildren chattering and laughing inside the Mayor's parlour. To me that was one of the few times in 20 years that I can recall City Hall coming alive."

Ironically, few people were aware that Maskey cancelled the Mayor's annual Christmas dinner and used the £7,000 budget for the traditionally lavish event to help fund a public awareness campaign for the homeless. During his year in office, he had three nominated

207

charities: Action Cancer, which was celebrating its thirtieth anniversary, Friends of the Mater Hospital and the Autism charity. The Lord Mayor's Annual Charity Ball was in aid of the Friends of the Royal Victoria Hospital. As Mayoress, Liz also chose health charities including Multiple Sclerosis. Each of the charities was able to benefit from fundraising dinners and other events in City Hall.

During his term in office, Maskey also hammered home the fact that Belfast had more than just two communities. The outside world could be forgiven for thinking the entire population of the city could be separated neatly into nationalists and unionists, but the fact that Belfast had become a melting pot of multi-culturalism by 2003 was not lost on him. He welcomed into City Hall, among others, people from the city's Jewish, Hindu, Muslim, Sikh, African, Chinese and travelling communities.

"From the beginning, I was determined that my year in office was not just going to be about nationalists and unionists. The other communities that make up this city deserve to have as much of a sense of ownership of City Hall as anyone else. In the past, it was as if these communities were second-class citizens and I was determined to change that."

That determination for change led him to hold a special reception for the smaller communities where he made sure that artefacts from the various cultures that made up the city were permanently on show in the Mayor's parlour for visitors to see. He insists that the efforts to reach out to the various peoples who populate Belfast were much more than mere window-dressing.

"There were practical issues which these communities needed help with. Muslims highlighted the fact that they couldn't find land to build a mosque. There are little or no provisions for Muslim women to go swimming. They only managed to find swimming facilities one night every month. Every group had a particular issue which needed addressing. Belfast cannot and should not just be about nationalists and unionists. The ethnic communities helped to build this city and make it what it is and I feel that Belfast would benefit if we had more representation from these communities within the council."

Despite unionist accusations that he had abdicated his mayoral obligations by refusing to hold talks with the PSNI, Maskey found himself, not for the first time, in the company of Chief Constable Hugh Orde during a visit to the city's Chinese community. Admitting that he had been given prior knowledge that the Chief Constable would be attending the same event, Maskey says: "It was one of those occasions when you try to show political and civic maturity. I knew Hugh Orde was going to be there and he knew I would be there, but neither of us wanted to cause a fuss which would take away from the event."

Although the republican Mayor and the Chief Constable ended up in the same room, they diplomatically kept contact to a minimum.

Ironically, on another occasion, the Mayor was surprised that a visit to one of Belfast's ethnic groups had landed him in the midst of celebrations for Queen Elizabeth's jubilee.

"I had a long-standing invitation to meet members of the Indian community and, before I arrived at their centre, I was told that they were in the middle of celebrations for the Queen's jubilee. I never imagined that I would be taking part in celebrations for the Queen of England, especially in an Indian centre. But as a civic leader, you try to represent everyone in the community and when you take up an invitation to visit them, you can't turn around and walk away just because they are celebrating the head of another state or something you personally don't agree with."

Throughout his term in office, Maskey says, he always attempted to meet key international figures in a bid to bring external investment into Belfast. After his election, he took a conscious decision to travel abroad only on trips that could be justified as potentially bringing in investment or developing other meaningful civic links. Indeed, he declined invitations to travel to Moscow and Athens and turned down a chance to meet Pope John Paul II because he chose to stay in Belfast.

"I wanted to spend as much time in Belfast as I could and only travelled to China, America and England on foreign investment delegations during my term. My visits to the war graves in France and Belgium were part of my efforts to promote reconciliation."

Explaining why he chose to miss out on a meeting with the Pope, Maskey says that during his last two weeks in office, he had been invited to take part in a conference of world mayors. It was to be held in Rome and he had been asked to chair a number of seminars.

"There was an audience with the Pope but unfortunately, it was during the last fortnight of my term and I wanted to bring as many groups as possible to City Hall during those last few days. So, regrettably, I had to decline the invitation."

One of the offers that he did take up was an invitation from the Mayor of London, Ken Livingstone, to visit the English capital during their St Patrick's week celebrations. Livingstone and Maskey had known each other for 20 years. Both earned reputations for creating controversy during their respective political careers. Maskey recalled that if he had received the invitation ten years earlier, he would have been unable to attend, due to the fact that he was banned from entering Britain.

"I first met Alex in the days when he and I were a bit more controversial," Livingstone joked during a reception in his new city hall offices. "We met during my first visit to Belfast 20 years ago and I don't think either of us imagined then that we would be Mayors of our respective cities 20 years on. Nor did we imagine that either of us would be following the inclusive politics that we now are."

One of the engagements Maskey was determined not to miss was an invitation to officially open a play-park in Lancaster Street in North Belfast where he was born.

"I always remember, when we were in negotiations with the British and Irish governments in Lancaster House in London, my father saying it was a long way from Lancaster Street where I was born. When the local community asked me to open the park, I was proud as punch. It was a long way from the wee lad who played in Lancaster Street in the 1950s to the Mayor's parlour in City Hall, but I did it, and I wanted the people to know that I did it with them."

In May, he realised a personal dream when he brought Olympic gold medallist and former heavyweight world boxing champion Joe Frazier to Belfast to host a special awards ceremony for the unsung sportsmen and women of the city. The former Ulster amateur champion had met his idol during a visit to Philadelphia and the two had immediately struck up a friendship.

"As soon as I was elected Mayor, I was determined to do something for the sports clubs in this city because of the work they have done for the young people down through the years," explains Maskey.

Although boxing had been his first love, as part of his mayoral duties, Maskey had tried his hand at practically every sport available in the city, ranging from cricket, rugby, Gaelic football, martial arts and gymnastics to a stint with the world famous Harlem Globe Trotters basketball team.

"From my experience as a youngster with the Holy Family boxing club, I knew the positive effect that sport had on my life as I grew up. I was more convinced of the terrific work which the various sports clubs did as I met the different organisations during my year as Mayor. To have someone of the stature of Joe Frazier to present the awards was tremendous and I hope that the ceremony will continue when my year in office is long over."

As he prepared to hand over his chains of office in June 2003 and, determined to leave his mark on the role, Maskey called for a pledge of office for all future holders of the post.

"I would dearly like to see every future mayor in this city signing a pledge compelling them to represent all the people of Belfast," he said. "There needs to be an obligation on every mayor to really reach out to other communities. This is a deeply divided society. How are people expected to make the effort to know their neighbours if the lord mayors won't even make the effort themselves? The city council and the lord mayor should be an example of all that is good in this city, not an embarrassment on the international stage as has often been the case in the past."

On June 2, Alex Maskey's twelve months in office were over. As he passed the baton to the SDLP's Martin Morgan, the outgoing Mayor said: "The City Hall didn't burn down as some unionists had predicted and, hopefully, the efforts I made to reach out to unionists can be built upon and strengthened by myself and others in the years ahead."

There was no praise, however, from Sammy Wilson, who branded the republican's year as Mayor as an "annus horibilus".

"I believe," said Wilson, "he has brought along with him all his republican baggage. He hasn't been willing to shed one ounce of it."

Insisting that the city's first republican Mayor had escaped proper public scrutiny during his year in office, the East Belfast councillor accused the media of having given Maskey as "easy ride". He claimed that not enough had been done "to highlight the controversial aspects" of his term.

The West Belfast grandfather, however, did win plaudits from other parties within City Hall. Former Ulster Unionist Mayor Bob Stoker defended his party's refusal to nominate a Deputy Mayor to sit alongside Maskey, but he conceded that he had made some effort to reach out to unionists.

"I think he has been progressive for a nationalist lord mayor and certainly we welcome the fact that he took some of the steps that he did take. But obviously, as unionists we don't believe that he went far enough. He still didn't meet members of the security forces, police service or members of the Royal Family and, to us, that is something which is natural and normal and he should have done those things."

In his typical blunt fashion, Progressive Unionist Billy Hutchinson pointed out that Maskey was unlikely to be praised by grassroots loyalists, although he personally accepted that the republican had made strong efforts to reach out to unionists.

"I think the difficulty with my constituents and others is that they didn't see the work that he did," said the former UVF prisoner. "They only saw the reports that highlighted the controversy and negativity surrounding Alex Maskey's year in office.

"There is no point in me believing one thing and saying another. I think Alex Maskey did a reasonable job during his year in office. The best way I could describe it is that, if I was lord mayor, I would like to have done as well as he has."

Belfast's first nationalist Mayor and SDLP councillor Alban Maginness admitted he had been surprised at Maskey's efforts to travel beyond the traditional limits of republicanism.

"He has come a good distance from the orthodox traditional position of Sinn Féin and I think he has assisted in making this city a better place," he said.

An *Irish News* editorial on Maskey's final day in office proclaimed that "only the most churlish" of observers would dispute the impact made by the city's first Sinn Féin Lord Mayor.

"Apart from Mr Maskey's personal efforts on a range of fronts, there is a wider political significance to his deeds over the last twelve months. The Lord Mayor has demonstrated that Sinn Féin elected representatives are fully capable of working positively on behalf of people from all sections of the community." Applauding the outgoing First Citizen for approaching his mayoral obligations with "imagination, dignity and considerable determination", the editorial continued: "His decision to lay a wreath at the Belfast Cenotaph was the most publicised event of his period as Lord Mayor and forced many to review their opinions of him. It was one of the most significant gestures of reconciliation witnessed in Northern Ireland over recent years, and in many ways epitomised the spirit of the Good Friday Agreement."

Pointing out that the Mayor during his term in office had surprised even the most cynical, the newspaper concluded: "Mr Maskey may have had to face a challenging period, but his performance has altered many perceptions of both the Lord Mayor and his party."

Perhaps one of the most unexpected and telling tributes to Maskey came from a former British army officer and senior UUP politician. Sir John Gorman and Maskey had worked closely in the Stormont Assembly where the Ulster Unionist had been Deputy Speaker and Maskey was the Sinn Féin Chief Whip.

Gorman was one of those Maskey sought out when he needed advice about how he could reach out to unionists. As the Sinn Féin Mayor left office, Sir John broke unionist ranks to pay a personal tribute.

"I look back on his year in office with positive memories and I wish him well for the future," said the Second World War veteran. "I always found him friendly and co-operative and he was very helpful when we discussed matters to do with ex-servicemen. It was also an unusual situation to have a republican Lord Mayor produce a wreath on Remembrance Day. While we would have liked the ceremony to have been more traditional, it was progress, and this should be acknowledged."

He concluded: "Progress is not something to be sneered at."

CHAPTER TEN
BREAKING NEW GROUND

Alex Maskey's home stands out from the other two-up, two-down dwellings in Gartree Place in the heart of West Belfast. Callers are faced with the wrought-iron security gate, brick wall and steel railings that separate the front garden of the house from the rest of the street.

Mail is delivered to a steel letterbox attached to the inside of the gate. Parcels are screened by the Post Office for explosive devices before delivery.

An intercom is the only means of communication with the house itself. Once callers are identified, a buzzer signals that the iron gate is unlocked. Visitors are then able to enter the garden and walk up the same path that a loyalist gunman used in 1987 when the UDA came close to killing Maskey in front of his wife and children.

Standing at the concrete security porch waiting for the weighty lead-lined front door to be opened, visitors are reminded that Alan Lundy was shot and killed on the same spot in May 1993. Bullet marks are still visible on the first floor wall, the remnants of another UDA attack in January 1994 when the house was raked with automatic gunfire.

A guest sitting in the Maskeys' living room is protected, to an extent, by the bullet-proof windows that have been installed there and indeed throughout the house. Closed-circuit television cameras screen the front of the premises and the adjoining street, while a black and white television monitor sits neatly on the fifth shelf of a huge bookcase that fills the entire wall on the left of the room. A high pitched buzzing noise announces a caller at the outer gate and leads to the close scrutiny of the figure on the monitor.

The routine is not aimed at impressing guests. Maskey still carries fragments of lead in his groin from the shotgun blast that very nearly ended his life in 1987. He undergoes regular hospital check-ups due to the injuries caused to his kidneys, bowel and stomach in the murder bid.

He and his family have lived with the threat of violence for more than 17 years. In January 2002, British army bomb experts were called to examine a device that had been thrown into his garden. It was later described as an "elaborate" hoax.

Before leaving the protection of the extensive security measures covering the front of his home, Maskey automatically checks the street for unfamiliar figures, or anything untoward. He follows the daily routine of dropping down onto the tarmac to check the underside of his car for booby-traps.

Throughout his year as Mayor, Sinn Féin security personnel accompanied him to many of his engagements with community groups across Belfast. Despite the fact that he has now hung up his mayoral chains, the minders are still at his side for the greater part of his weekly routine.

While Maskey himself plays down the constant threat to his life, in 2003 the Northern Ireland Office judged the threat to his life at "the highest possible risk rating". He remains on the government Key Persons Protection Scheme, traditionally reserved for judges, MPs and NIO ministers. However, despite the danger, he is still refused permission to carry a weapon for personal protection.

Maskey insists he is lucky – more than a dozen other Sinn Féin members and their relatives were killed in the six years before the 1994 ceasefires. The precise details of just how many attempts were made on Maskey's life are still coming to light. During research for this book, Brian Nelson's involvement in a third plot on his life was uncovered. Maskey's lawyers had been attempting to re-interview Nelson as part of a civil action still being pursued against the British army when it was announced in April 2003 that the FRU agent had died.

The involvement of a senior UDA man in the 1993 attack on the Maskey household, which resulted in the murder of Alan Lundy, may now also be revisited.

Maskey prefers to play down the important role that he played within Sinn Féin in the last 20 years. Arguably, he has personified more than any other the evolution of modern-day Irish republicanism, from outright "armed struggle", through the "Armalite and Ballot Box" phase, to a position where an IRA statement in January 2003 insisted that it remained committed to a "just and lasting peace".

He has left a remarkable footprint in his personal journey along the republican movement's path to politics and peace. He has always acknowledged that he was ideologically opposed to any republican involvement in electoral politics up to the hunger strike elections of 1981. Two short years later he was to find himself the first Sinn Féin councillor to enter the "bastion of loyalism" that was Belfast City Hall. Twenty years later, he is still there.

In a telling insight into the republican psyche that led to the transition from "armed struggle" to democratic politics, he explains: "In 1969, I was like a lot of other young nationalists who decided that this state was fatally flawed and had no right to exist. The injustice in this state was not going to go away on its own; the state had to be removed."

He insists that nationalists had no viable alternative but to take up arms against the authorities, arguing that political leaders in the North and in the southern establishment were incapable of forcing the British government into change.

"The nationalist establishment has historically failed to exert any form of meaningful pressure on the British establishment to consider any withdrawal from Ireland. They couldn't even convince the British to right the wrongs that were being carried out by the unionist establishment in the North.

"Irish nationalism was fractured to such an extent that it allowed successive British governments to deny us our rights with impunity. In the circumstances that existed with the British army on our streets, I think that it was inevitable that the nationalist people took up arms. There was no viable democratic alternative at that period."

But while arguing that "armed struggle" was an inevitability, Maskey insists it was also certain that it would eventually come to an end once the political support base for republicans was seen as being capable of forcing real change.

"Before the 1980s it was impossible to effect change from within the state. What the 1981 hunger strike elections proved was that there was a substantial support base among nationalists, North and South, who supported the republican ideal of a united Ireland. The new strategy of fighting elections encouraged more people to join the republican struggle. The electoral victories at that time proved that there was another radical way to exert pressure, not only on the British government, but also on the nationalist establishment, North and South."

In a rare insight into the long-term strategy adopted in the early 1980s, Maskey draws comparisons between the IRA's 25-year campaign from 1969 to 1994 and other previous periods of armed resistance.

"No campaign in modern Irish history lasted anywhere near as long as the IRA's campaign from 1969. Between 1916 and 1922 there was an uprising, the War of Independence, British withdrawal and a civil war, and that all took place in just six years. No phase of struggle lasted as long as this one and I have no doubt that the IRA could have gone on for another 30 years if it had wished to do so.

"But armed struggle – indeed, any kind of struggle – is designed to achieve a stated goal. In this instance, it was to force the British into a situation where they had no option but to negotiate a settlement and, ultimately, the stated goal of a united Ireland with British withdrawal. Our entry into electoral politics showed that we could put added pressure on the British establishment with a strong and powerful mandate which could not be ignored.

"Look at us now. We are the largest party in City Hall, we are the largest nationalist party in the North and we have five TDs in Leinster House, which I am confident we can build upon. At the centre of this strategy is our ability to help people solve problems in the here-and-now while pursuing our primary goal of independence."

But with the power-sharing Executive collapsed, Assembly elections cancelled and the political divide in the summer of 2003 wider than ever, Maskey warns that the British government ignores at their peril the democratic right to free elections.

"The British government profess to be the guardians of democracy, but anyone who looks at the cancellation of the Assembly elections in May (2003) would have to question that commitment to democracy. What I will say is that Sinn Féin have successfully convinced republicans that the politics of the peace process is an effective road to take in achieving our stated goal of a united Ireland.

"When the British government cancels elections, simply because it doesn't like the potential results, it does not help our argument in any way. If the British are committed to democracy then they should let the people speak."

Despite the praise he won for his efforts to reach out to unionists during his year in office, Maskey insists that he retains the same ideals that he held in 1969. Few could have predicted that the man who epitomised the hard-line face of republican politics would have become the figure who broke new ground with the unionist community.

Every inch the image of a Belfast docker, the diminutive Maskey has always been careful to maintain his working-class roots. The former boxer bore all the traditional hallmarks of an uncompromising republican when he first appeared in City Hall with his trademark beard and tweed jacket which, he says, had been hand-picked from a local second-hand charity shop the day before.

While other politicians have adapted their personal image to the demands of the television screen, Maskey retains his working-class appearance. He did not possess the law degree that many of his counterparts in City Hall had obtained when he entered politics in 1983. Although an avid reader, he jokingly insists that he got his education at the "university of life". He learned his political trade in the late 1970s and 1980s in the cages of Long Kesh and during the heady days of street protests which so often ended in confrontation with the RUC. He freely admits that he has lost count of the fines he has incurred for public order offences.

There is little doubt that he was carefully handpicked as a representative of Sinn Féin's first steps into the uncharted waters of electoral politics. He was one of only a handful of candidates within militant republicanism who possessed the necessary credentials, the intellect and mental steel needed to cope with the antagonism that was sure to be directed at him from the unionist benches.

If republicans were to succeed in plotting a course through the precarious waters of local government politics, it would be up to Maskey to sink or swim. While the Sinn Féin leadership could direct their movement's overall political strategy, it was Maskey and those who followed him into the council chambers who laid the foundations for the party's political growth throughout the following two decades.

His new political role and the public profile that accompanied it came at a price. It is arguable that no other local politician has endured so many attempts on their life in recent years. At the last count there have been nine specific attempts to kill Alex Maskey.

As one of the most prominent faces of republicanism during the 1980s and early 1990s, the Sinn Féin councillor became, for the unionist-loyalist community, one of the most hated men in Northern Ireland. His image was not helped when he was regularly called on to face the media to defend IRA killings and bombings over the last 20 years. Enemies argued that the dangers came with the territory and were a result of IRA violence.

Maskey's political opponents pointed to the IRA's record of violence – republicans were responsible for over 50 per cent of all deaths during the conflict and had killed a number of unionist politicians in the 1980s and early 1990s. In November 1981, the IRA shot dead Ulster Unionist MP Robert Bradford, accusing the Protestant minister of "stoking-up" anti-Catholic hatred among loyalist paramilitaries. In December 1983, they killed Ulster Unionist Assemblyman Edgar Graham as he arrived at Queen's University, where he was a law lecturer. In July 1994, UDP leader Ray Smallwoods was shot dead by the IRA at his home in Lisburn just weeks before they announced a ceasefire. Such killings did nothing to improve relations between Sinn Féin and the unionist parties in City Hall.

Attempts to kill Maskey, however, appeared to be almost personal and certainly much more significant than the clichéd and often inaccurately described "tit-for-tat" murder bids.

While it was predictable that loyalist paramilitaries would view

Maskey as a "legitimate target", the fact that British "securocrats", in the form of Brian Nelson and the shadowy FRU, actively colluded to have him killed is perhaps one of the key indications of just how sordid the so-called "dirty war" became. In an interview for this book, a senior loyalist who was a key figure in the UDA, explains the "military" and "political" motives behind the repeated attempts to kill Maskey.

"Maskey was one of their key people. He was one of their public faces. You would see him on television every night defending the IRA and repeating this mantra that nationalists were suffering all of this discrimination. He was an obvious target. We never took him off our books. Every opportunity we had to kill Alex Maskey, we took.

"If we managed to get Maskey, it would be a real feather in our cap. It would make the rest of them (Sinn Féin councillors) think twice before they raised their heads above the parapet and would be a boost for our people. They killed (UDA Leader) John McMichael and Ray Smallwood. We tried to get Adams, McGuinness and Maskey. The thinking was if we got a hard man like Maskey, the doves wouldn't be so keen to take his place."

Expressing a complete indifference to the fact that the majority of personal intelligence on Maskey had been provided by the British security services, the senior loyalist insists: "We had our own reasons for getting Maskey. We weren't aware that the army was passing information to us through Brian Nelson.

"To be honest we didn't care where the information came from. As far as we were concerned, Maskey was a legitimate target. The fact that the security forces wanted him dead as well wasn't our concern. If you're asking me if the army were using us to kill Alex Maskey, then yes, I suppose they were. But to be honest, we would have tried to kill him any chance we got anyway."

Former Sinn Féin councillor Máirtín Ó Muilleoir highlights the fact that nearly two dozen republican councillors have passed through City Hall since 1983, but Maskey remained at the "coal-face" of confrontational council politics throughout.

"There is a saying that the bough that doesn't bend will break. Alex has shown the intellect and political maturity to adapt and accept change over the last 20 years while refusing to dilute his republican politics."

Arguably, Maskey's most important contribution to republican politics was the dogged determination he showed in wearing down unionists with a succession of court cases and public campaigns highlighting what he believes was the policy of discrimination being operated in Belfast City Council.

While it was predictable that nationalist parties would be reproachful towards unionists in the council, the fact that Belfast's two leading newspapers were also openly critical of unionist rule in City Hall would appear to confirm that inequality was indeed being pursued as a policy.

In an attack on unionist parties' rule in City Hall, the *Irish News* branded the council "a gentleman's club for bigots".

"Their past record speaks for itself, it is one of dismal, abject failure and quite open discrimination against Catholics," said an editorial in the early 1990s. "So unjust and so divisive was their rule in Northern Ireland that the British had to intervene to dissolve Stormont."

In 1991, the *Belfast Telegraph*, castigating the unionist parties for their attempts to gag their republican opponents, said: "The issue is one of freedom of speech, enshrined in every democratic forum in the world, but apparently unavailable in Belfast City Council."

While unionists may have been justified in condemning IRA violence, their actions in City Hall did little to convince the nationalist-republican community that they were willing or capable of sharing power with their political opponents. Whatever their true intentions, they arguably did more to help Maskey and Sinn Féin highlight injustice by pursuing a policy of banning republican representatives from council committees, outside bodies, the City Hall car park, and even denying them the right to speak.

With some level of justification, Maskey felt able to accuse unionists of being political dinosaurs who were incapable of change.

Ironically, Máirtín Ó Muilleoir argues that the IRA's 1994 ceasefire allowed Maskey and his party to mature politically.

"Nine years ago you couldn't hear Alex Maskey's voice on television because of the broadcasting ban. Everything in City Hall was confrontational and parties even refused to work together on bread-and-butter issues. The ceasefire allowed Alex the space to become the gifted politician that he has become and to develop the radical politics which was seen with his efforts at reaching out to unionists while remaining committed to the principles of republicanism.

"Pre-1994 there was no opportunity to make real politics, because no one could suggest any kind of radical change, because you were in a war. I think it is a tremendous credit to Alex that he has gone through so much over the last 30 years and is still there making a difference."

By 2001, Sinn Féin was the single largest party in City Hall with 14 councillors sitting on, and chairing, the various committees. The one remaining status, which continued to escape them, was the mayoral chair. As his party's longest-serving councillor, Maskey was an obvious choice to become the city's first republican mayor. Ironically, the hard-line image that he had projected during his 20 years in local government was used by the Alliance Party to argue that he could not be chosen for the role. Despite being a small party, Alliance held the balance of power in the chamber.

"They more or less told us they would support anyone but me," Maskey recalls. "I didn't know whether to take it as a compliment or a criticism."

Alliance's reluctance to back him is perhaps understandable given that their councillors vividly remembered the split in the party caused by Danny Dow's resignation over support for Maskey in 2000.

When he was eventually elected Mayor few, if any, observers would have predicted that his year in office would mark a significant shift in the future relationship between republicans and unionists. His decision to lay a wreath at the Cenotaph and his civic reception for the British Legion caused many to re-evaluate their opinion that he would gear his mayoral attentions to one side of the community.

While his efforts may have caused surprise among unionists, they also startled some republicans. Jim Gibney defends the moves that were made to go beyond the traditional bounds of Irish republicanism.

"Alex made those gestures and I think that we, as a republican party, proved our political maturity," he says. "We broke new ground that no one believed we would ever be capable of doing and I think that we are stronger for it."

It was an irony that mainstream unionists remained unmoved by Maskey's efforts to reach out to them and their constituencies, while politicians such as Billy Hutchinson, David Ervine and John White accepted his gestures. These men, all one-time loyalist paramilitaries who had been engaged in a 30-year war against the likes of Maskey and his colleagues, accepted that he had attempted to break new ground between the two communities.

A sign that he may indeed have succeeded, in no small measure, in his efforts can be seen in the praise he won from a number of Protestant community workers, most notably Craig Seawright, the son of former DUP firebrand councillor George Seawright.

Craig had been only a child when his father was shot and fatally wounded by the IPLO as he sat in a taxi on the Shankill Road in 1987. George was expelled from the DUP after he claimed that Catholics and priests should be publicly incinerated, and received widespread criticism for calling for loyalist revenge attacks on the IRA after his election agent, UVF commander John Bingham, was shot dead in September 1986. Ironically, Maskey recalls George as being one of the few unionists who would speak to him and his colleagues during his time in City Hall.

In an unusual move, George's son praises Maskey and his attempts to bridge the gap with unionists.

"I think Alex Maskey took brave and bold steps with his efforts as mayor," says Craig, a committed Christian. "Unionists would have liked to see him lay a poppy wreath at the Somme commemoration but, by and large, what he did was very encouraging and he should be applauded for his efforts."

Arguing that republicans should not allow these positive efforts to be lost with the end of Maskey's mayoral year, Craig Seawright insists: "The bolder the steps republicans choose to take, the less reasons unionists will have to ignore those gestures. What is needed on both sides is for working class communities to be brought together so that people can start to understand each other."

The respected veteran Shankill community worker, Baroness May Blood, accepted that Maskey's actions as Mayor had caused her to change her perceptions of him. Describing his decision to lay a wreath at the Cenotaph as a "brave gesture", she rejected criticism aimed at his not taking part in the main ceremony.

"If he had went to the Cenotaph, all of the other councillors would have stayed away. I think he made a very good decision to lay a wreath at a quiet time and then let unionist councillors get on with their own service. I mean, he was laying a wreath to the British army. In that sense, I believe that would have been a big tablet for him to swallow.

"Having seen him going to the Cenotaph; having seen him read the lesson at St Anne's Cathedral; having seen him doing a number of things and gestures towards both sides of the community, I have to say I changed my opinion."

As Maskey's term of office came to a close, observers were keen to see if his conciliatory moves would be left behind in the Lord Mayor's parlour.

Sinn Féin's ruling Ard Comhairle, however, moved quickly in a bid to keep the momentum going and appointed Maskey as their first out-reach worker to the Protestant community. He has now been tasked with drawing up a policy for the party to address its relationship with the unionist populace. He insists that his new duty will not be "mere window-dressing".

"My role is to establish and develop a strategy for the way in which the whole party deals with the unionist community," he explains. "It is a serious initiative that will involve all sections of the party and will try to develop a proper understanding between ourselves and the unionist community. It would be nonsense for me as a republican to think that the efforts to build a relationship with the Protestant community ended as soon as I took off the mayoral chains. That would be a waste of everything we set out to achieve and I do not intend to allow that to happen."

Maskey insists that it is not only republicans who have an obligation to bridge the gap between the community divide. In a stinging criticism, he accuses Belfast City Council of having abdicated its civic leadership to the people of the city.

"This council has had to be dragged, kicking and screaming, into the 21st century. While some people have tried, I think that we have abjectly failed to actively promote any kind of good relationships between the two communities. The council should be an example to the city as to how different traditions can dialogue and work together for the benefit of everyone who lives in Belfast.

"Instead it has often acted in a selfish and sectarian fashion that has led to the people of this city actually being ashamed of City Hall. In other cities across the world, councils are instruments to promote positive change. For 20 years, in Belfast City Hall, we have failed to tackle sectarianism and I think that is an absolute disgrace.

"In this council, almost every issue comes down to a sectarian head-count, regardless of social need. I think that some councillors need to take a long, hard look at themselves and work out if this is what proper civic leadership is meant to be about."

While Maskey admits to being frustrated at the slow pace of change, he is insistent that things will improve.

"I came into this council 20 years ago on my own and now we are the biggest party in City Hall. We cannot change things on our own, but we can push hard for those changes and work with those parties and communities who want to make a difference."

While, for practical reasons, many decisions taken during his year in office may not have been discussed with the republican rank-and-file, Maskey's actions were publicly and privately supported by the leadership.

Belfast's Brian Keenan is judged by many to be one of the founding fathers of modern day Irish republicanism. In 1980, he was sentenced to 20 years imprisonment in Britain for conspiracy to cause explosions. Over the next 14 years, he watched intently from various high-security prisons as the republican movement developed politically.

Released in 1994, he was perceived to be a key mover in pushing for an IRA cessation. Regarded by the British as an important figure within the republican family, Keenan's political acumen and support for the peace process has largely been overlooked. Speaking publicly for the first time on Maskey's role over the past 25 years, Keenan gives a telling insight into the impact of politics on the republican struggle.

"The lessons of history are only fully understood in evolving time," said the 61-year-old grandfather in August 2003. "Alex Maskey has learned the lessons well. At every step he attempted to democratise the situations confronting him and did so with solid ethics, so typical of the class he represented – the working class.

"During my years in prison, I was able to watch closely how the struggle for freedom and national democracy was evolving in a positive way. Nowhere within that struggle was the evolution more marked than in Belfast City Hall where Alex was, for a time, the sole vanguard of the struggle, finally culminating in his wonderful year of office as Lord Mayor.

"I felt very proud of Alex and all that he achieved during his tenure. Certainly he taught us all a very new lesson as he created his own history. I am proud to count Alex Maskey as a friend."

American Special Ambassador Richard Haass also praised Alex Maskey for his efforts during his time as Mayor. During a visit to Belfast in May 2003 to support the Special Olympics being held in Dublin the following month, Haass said: "While I understand a new mayor will be in place soon, I want to commend Mayor Maskey on his term in office and his support for the Special Olympics. I have been impressed with your determination to reach out to all your constituents in face of some challenging circumstances. Your willingness to fully represent the whole of Belfast is a welcome model of statesmanship, it has been a model of grace."

Reflecting on a political career in which he has been shot and seriously wounded and had close friends killed by loyalists and the security services, Maskey insists that it was that sacrifice and loss of life which pushed him forward.

227

"I am humbled when I look back on the sacrifice of all those who stood as Sinn Féin councillors throughout these last 22 years – people who lost their lives; others, including close friends, whose homes and families were targeted and yet remained committed to ensuring that the republican voice in City Hall was not silenced.

"As a party, we have achieved a lot in the last 20 years. I am proud to have played a small part in those achievements. But a lot of people lost their lives for those achievements – people like Alan Lundy – and it is their memories that drive me to continue fighting for a united Ireland. I want to see a time when we can all respect each other's traditions and cultures without causing offence.

"I want to see a time in my life when I can have Protestant neighbours again. As an Irish republican, I want that to be in a united Ireland."

ACKNOWLEDGEMENTS

This book would have been impossible to research and write without the help and support of countless friends and colleagues.

I am indebted to Jim Gibney, who gave up countless hours of his time to provide an invaluable insight into the republican psyche and the efforts made to try to make Alex Maskey's year in office a success. The help of Tom Hartley, Chrissie and Richard McAuley and Brian Keenan is also greatly appreciated. Máirtín Ó Muilleoir's ability to see the 'bigger picture' from Teach Basil was an inspiration. Thanks also to Ken Livingstone, Billy Hutchinson, Alban Maginness, Martin and Breidge Meehan, Gerard Brophy, Sean Keenan, Brian Feeney, Liam Maskey and Craig Seawright for their co-operation.

I wish to extend my gratitude to those unnamed unionist councillors and senior loyalists who co-operated with me on a work that they may not necessarily have agreed with.

At the *Irish News*, editor Noel Doran, Steven McCaffery, Billy Foley, Fiona McGarry and everyone in the newsroom helped me to find the time away from work to write this book. Thanks to the following photographers who allowed me to include their fine work: Ann McManus, Mal McCann, Brendan Murphy, Hugh Russell, Paul Murphy, Oistín Mac Bride and Frankie Quinn. Thanks also to *Irish News* librarian Kathleen Bell.

Invaluable support was provided by John Ferris, Maria McCourt, Sean MagUidhir, Thomas McMullan, Stephen Breen, Allison Morris, Kevin Magee, Anne Cadwallader, Thomas Hawkins, Martin Spain, John Martin, Jake Jackson, Joe Baker, Mickey Liggett, Denise O'Connor, Kelvin Boyes, Redmond O'Neill, Emer and Burt McWilliams, Kevin Winters, Arter Fegan, Conor Carolan, Deirbhile Clenaghan, Alva Kvalvaag, Katei Zagirre, Violet Anderson and Liz Maskey. Special thanks to Nuala Keenan for her "constructive" criticism.

I am indebted to publishers Brendan Anderson and Damian Keenan, who endured countless walks around the Giant's Ring to ensure that the wheels did not come off the wagon.

Finally I would like to thank Alex Maskey for the endless hours and support he afforded to me, as well as the often-painful memories which he agreed to share.

Any inaccuracies that remain in the book are mine alone.

LIST OF SOURCES

Andersonstown News archive

An Phoblacht/Republican News archive

BBC Radio Ulster archive

BBC Northern Ireland Television website archive

Belfast Central Library archive

Belfast City Council website

Belfast Newsletter archive

Belfast Telegraph archive

CAIN website

Irish News archive

Linen Hall Library archive

RTÉ website archive

Sunday Life archive

Sunday World archive

Ulster Television Insight programme

Ulster Television website archive

BIBLIOGRAPHY

Bew, Paul and Gillespie, Gordon *Northern Ireland: A Chronology of the Troubles 1968-1993*, Dublin, Gill and Macmillan, 1993.

Cochrane, Feargal, *Unionist Politics: the politics of unionism since the Anglo-Irish Agreement*, Cork, Cork University Press, 1997.

Davies, Nicholas, *Ten-Thirty Three: The inside story of Britain's secret killing machine in Northern Ireland*, Edinburgh and London, Mainstream Publishing, 1999.

Elliott, Sydney and Flackes, WD, *Northern Ireland: A Political Directory*, Belfast, Blackstaff Press, 1999.

English, Richard, *Armed Struggle: A History of the IRA*, London, Macmillan, 2003.

Farrell, Michael, *Northern Ireland: The Orange State*, London, Pluto Press, 1976.

Farrell, Michael, *Arming the Protestants: The formation of the Ulster Special Constabulary and the Royal Ulster Constabulary 1920/1927*, Pluto Press, London and Sydney, 1983

Feeney, Brian, Sinn Féin: *A Hundred Turbulent Years*, Dublin, O'Brien Press, 2002.

Lyons, F.S.L, *Ireland Since the Famine*, Edinburgh, Fontana and Collins, 1978.

Murray, Raymond, *The SAS in Ireland*, Dublin, Mercier Press, 1993.

Murray, Raymond, *State Violence: Northern Ireland 1969/1997,* Dublin, Mercier Press, 1998.

MacBride, Oistin, *Family, Friends and Neighbours: An Irish Photobiography*, Belfast, Beyond the Pale Publications, 2001.

McKittrick, David, Seamus Kelters, Brian Feeney, Chris Thornton, *Lost Lives*, Edinburgh-London, Mainstream Publishing, 1999.

MacUileagoid, Michael, *From Fetters to Freedom: The inside story of Irish jailbreaks*, Belfast, Sasta, 1996.

O'Brien, Brendan, *The Long War: The IRA & Sinn Féin from Armed Struggle to Peace Talks*, Dublin, O'Brien Press, 1993.

Ó Muilleoir, Máirtín, *Belfast's Dome of Delight: City Hall Politics 1981/2000,* Belfast, Beyond the Pale Publications, 1999.

Moloney, Ed, *A Secret History of the IRA,* London, Penguin Press, 2002.

Phoenix, Eamon, *Northern Nationalism,* Belfast, Ulster Historical Foundation, 1994.

Porter, Norman, *Rethinking Unionism,* Belfast, Blackstaff Press, 1996.

Taylor, Peter, *Provos: The IRA and Sinn Féin,* London, Bloomsbury, 1997.

Whyte, John, *Interpreting Northern Ireland,* Oxford, Clarendon Press, 1990.